Firearms Control

Firearms Control

A Study of Armed Crime and Firearms Control in England and Wales

Colin Greenwood

Chief Inspector   West Yorkshire Constabulary

Routledge & Kegan Paul   London

First published 1972
by Routledge & Kegan Paul Ltd
Broadway House, 68–74 Carter Lane,
London EC4V 5EL
Printed in Great Britain by
Unwin Brothers Limited
The Gresham Press, Old Woking, Surrey, England
A member of the Staples Printing Group

ISBN 0 7100 7435 2

Contents

Illustrations

Preface

This work is based on research done during my tenure as a Cropwood Short Term Fellow at the Institute of Criminology, University of Cambridge during the winter of 1970–71. I wish to record my special thanks to the anonymous benefactor of the Cropwood Fellowships and to Professor Sir Leon Radzinowicz, Director of the Institute, for the opportunity to undertake this work. I am also grateful to the Chief Constable and Police Authority of the West Yorkshire Constabulary who allowed me to take advantage of the Fellowship when it was offered.

A number of Chief Officers of Police have made information available to me, and I am grateful to them, and to their statistical and firearms officers. Previously unpublished data relating to 1969 has been made available by the Home Office and I am indebted to them for their assistance but the interpretation of the information they provided and the views I have expressed are my own. The Gun Trade Association and various shooting organisations offered every assistance and I was pleased to be able to take advantage of this.

The staff at the Institute of Criminology were consistently helpful. I am particularly grateful to Mr F. H. McClintock who acted as my adviser and to his Research Assistant, Mr Nicholas Miller. To list others who provided advice or assistance would be to provide a full list of the staff of the Institute, but special thanks are due to the then Librarian, Mr Martin Wright, for the unfailing way in which he produced or traced obscure works when requested. I am also particularly indebted to Mr D. G. T. Williams, Senior Tutor of Emmanuel College, Cambridge, who was extremely helpful with suggestions and discussions on the legal aspects of the work.

My wife has tolerated my interest in matters relating to firearms for many years and has greatly encouraged me in this project, despite the fact that it added considerably to her burdens during my absence from home. To her I am continually grateful.

Although the Institute and my Force facilitated this work, any views expressed or conclusions reached are my own and do not reflect the views or policies of the Institute of Criminology or of the police service.

It is usual, when entering a debate on a controversial subject, to give notice of any vested interest. On the subject of the private ownership of firearms, I must declare an interest in that, for many years, I have owned and used shotguns, pistols and rifles and have enjoyed many aspects of shooting sports. It could therefore be said that I have a bias towards firearms. If, however, I have that bias, it must be said that there is, in relation to the criminal use of firearms, a strong counterbalance. As a serving police officer I have a strong professional concern about the rise in the criminal use of firearms. Inspector Barry Taylor, West Yorkshire Constabulary, who was shot down whilst attending an alarm call in February 1970, was a personal friend. I have seen the concern of my fellow officers, and of their families, when they have been called on to deal with incidents involving armed men and, like many of my fellows, I am worried by the risks involved. If, therefore, I have these two interests, I feel confident that the latter weighs most heavily on my mind.

C. G.

Introduction

The use of firearms in connection with crime has been the subject of considerable public concern in recent years. That there has been a substantial increase in armed crime is beyond doubt, yet research into this subject has been noticeably sparse. Regularly, the national press carries reports of robberies or other incidents in which firearms have been used; indeed, these now seem to have become almost a daily occurrence. Such official figures as are available point to a rapid and worrying rise in the problem in recent years. Superficially, the problem appears to be new, at least in its scale. The impression gained is that, in the not too distant past, British criminals rarely used guns; yet now they do so with increasing frequency. But superficial assessments of such problems are rarely correct, and form no basis for effective action.

Many questions have been left unanswered, or have been inadequately answered. That there has been an increase in the use of guns in crime seems beyond dispute, but if the problem is to be gauged correctly, much more information is required. Precisely how great has this rise been? Is the rise connected with casual or professional criminals? What was the true position in the past? What steps have been taken in the past and how effective have they been? How many legitimately owned firearms are there in this country and how much of a problem do they present? How effective is the present, fairly comprehensive, system of firearms controls? From where and from whom do criminals obtain their guns? And, possibly the most difficult of questions, if there has been a rise in the criminal use of firearms, why? All these questions, and many more, are impossible to answer on the basis of a superficial examination.

This study has, therefore, been directed towards producing additional information on this problem and towards examining legislation, official attitudes, and policies, in an attempt to establish whether or not they are producing desirable effects. That the study is inadequate is accepted from the start. As far as can be ascertained, it is the first such study of this problem in Britain and as such it could not hope to supply all the answers. If, however, it

1

poses the correct questions and supplies some of the answers, a great deal will have been achieved.

There is clearly much which can be learned from a careful study of the history of the problem, and from the efforts made to tackle it in the past. If the mistakes of the past can be recognised, they can be avoided in the future. If certain measures were effective in the past, they may, with adaptation, be effective in the future. As part of this historical survey, an attempt has been made to produce statistics which might indicate the level of the criminal use of firearms at various times in recent history. Such statistics must be approached with caution, and with due regard for the elementary state of methods of recording crime at the time. Yet, if viewed correctly, the figures may help create a picture of the problem which faced legislators and police of previous generations. The development of firearms controls has been followed through to the present day and set against more recent events which may have been in the forefront of the minds of those responsible for the present legislation.

Superficial examination of press reports, or of statistics gathered on a broad basis, can rarely lead to a precise statement of the nature of any problem. The official figures for recent years have, therefore, been examined in considerable detail, and have been set against a detailed study of cases in what is considered to be a reasonable cross-section of the country. In this way it is hoped that the true nature and value of the official figures may be shown. Within the detailed study of sample cases, the incidents have been categorised in what is thought to be a meaningful way, and such relationships as may exist between crime and firearms controls are examined. The use of firearms in crime is the problem which receives the greatest attention, but the involvement of firearms in fatal accidents and suicides, though less publicised, is a matter which is examined over a number of years.

If these studies have set out the problem in something approaching its true perspective, it becomes necessary to examine in depth the present statutory controls on firearms and the manner in which these controls are applied by the police. It also becomes necessary to examine the cost to the police, not just in terms of cash, but in terms of time, for in these days of shortage of police and ever increasing burdens, it is the time of the regular officer which is important. Set against these costs in time must be an assessment of the effectiveness of the operations. Cost-effectiveness is becoming, perhaps, a rather over-used term, and yet it must be applied to the role of the police in firearms controls.

Finally, the study attempts to draw conclusions and make suggestions. It may be that readers will find some (or even all) of the conclusions controversial. It is hoped that the facts have been presented in such a way that any reader can draw from them his own independent conclusions and feel able to agree or disagree with those drawn in the study. Some will consider that the legislation needs a drastic overhaul in principle as well as in detail and suggestions for a change in the pattern of controls are included. Within the general framework of present legislation, suggestions are confined to ways of saving police time without loss of effect, and to a number of detailed amendments in areas where the law appears to be anomalous or can be shown to serve no useful purpose.

This study relates only to England and Wales, but it could, perhaps, be applied equally to Scotland where conditions may be somewhat similar. No attempt has been made to apply the results to other areas where conditions are frequently so different. Whenever firearms controls are discussed in this country, the situation in the United States of America, or in some other part of the world, is frequently raised. A detailed comparative study of conditions in various countries is far beyond the scope of this work, and superficial comparisons are almost certain to mislead. Those who wish to take the comparative approach are, however, invited to consider two points. Firstly, this study will show that firearms controls in this country are a relatively new innovation. Control by the police dates from late 1920. From 1903 an ineffective form of control on pistols was imposed by requiring a person purchasing from a dealer to buy a ten shilling gun licence from a Post Office before the transaction was completed (see Chapter 2). In the early part of the study, statistics are produced which allow of a relatively accurate assessment of the level of the criminal use of firearms during the early part of the twentieth century. Firearms controls of various types have existed in some parts of the United States for a considerable time. The oldest, and the most stringent, controls apply in the City of New York where the 'Sullivan Act' has made the ownership and carrying of pistols subject to a police permit since 1911. The Sullivan Act is considerably more restrictive than any controls imposed in England. Comparison is therefore invited between London and New York during the period following the passing of the Sullivan Act (say 1911 to 1920). Asbury's *The Gangs of New York*,[1] though flamboyantly and journalistically written, includes some evidence of the use of firearms at this time. *Violence in America—Historical and*

3

Comparative Perspectives[2] may help throw further light on the subject, particularly through its voluminous bibliography. What will be found, it is suggested, is that New York, with its strict controls on the private ownership of pistols, suffered infinitely more from the criminal use of firearms of all types than did London in a period when all firearms were freely available.

The second comparison invited relates to the hypothesis that the mere availability of firearms in the United States is a major factor in the rate of armed crime in that country. The situation in the United States could usefully be compared with that in Switzerland where, in fact, firearms are even more readily available. In Switzerland, shooting sports are rated highly and the incidence of private ownership of firearms is consequently high. The purchase of a firearm is subject to a police licence, but this is granted automatically to a person who is not prohibited (certain convicted criminals, the mentally ill, juveniles, etc.). Apart from this, virtually every male citizen is a member of the reserve forces and is required to keep his rifle, sub-machine gun or pistol at his home, together with a quantity of ammunition. Almost every household in the country, therefore, contains firearms and ammunition accessible to anyone who wishes to misuse them. And what is the rate of armed crime in Switzerland? An enquiry in 1969, confirmed as still valid in 1971, showed that the use of firearms in crime is so low that it is not recorded in any police statistics.

These comments are intended to do no more than to illustrate the dangers of a superficial examination of such problems. How well firearms controls work, or would work, in the U.S.A. or in Switzerland is a complicated question which is inextricably bound up with many factors peculiar to each country. The situation in these countries cannot be directly related to the situation in England and Wales, on the basis of the information currently available. It is hoped that, by dealing in detail with the situation in one country, this study will supply the sort of information which will enable useful comparative studies to be made in the future.

Part I A History of Firearms Controls

1 An Unrestricted Era

The possession of arms by civilians in England has been the subject of both Statute and Common Law for many centuries, although restrictions of the type now imposed on the possession of firearms are a development of the twentieth century. In Saxon times there was neither a standing army nor police force in this country. The defence of the country and the maintenance of law and order depended on a system under which individuals were encouraged to enrol in groups of about ten families known as tythings. The administrative divisions of 'Hundreds' consisted of about ten tythings and these, in turn, were part of the administrative counties or shires. The Shire-Reeve (sheriff) was at the head of each county and he was directly responsible to the king. The tythings were responsible for the conduct of each of their members and if any individual broke the law the group was required to produce him for trial or, if the offender escaped, they were liable to a collective fine. If any fugitive from justice was in the area, all the able-bodied freemen were required to take part in the 'Hue and Cry'. In addition to their responsibility for law enforcement, all male adults had a responsibility to serve in the army when called on. A limited number of professional soldiers were in the employ of the king and individual noblemen, but their duties were largely as commanders of an army drawn as required from the men of the shire. After the conquest the Normans retained this system with few changes.[1]

To discharge his duty under the system, every freeman had not just a right, but an absolute duty to keep arms. By 1181, this duty was clearly expressed in Henry II's Assize of Arms which detailed the type of weapons to be kept by persons of various ranks. The Statute of Winchester 1285 (13 Edw I c6) reinforced this requirement:

> and further, it is commanded that every man have in his house
> Harness for to keep the Peace after the antient Assize; that is
> to say every man between fifteen years of age and sixty years
> shall be assessed and sworn to armour according to the
> quality of their lands and goods.

7

The types of arms to be held varied according to the income of the holder, but even the poorest were included, 'and all other that may shall have bows and arrows'. To ensure compliance with the Statute there was to be a view of arms within each Hundred or Franchise twice in each year when the Constable was required to inspect all weapons.

The Statute of Northampton 1328 (2 Edw III c3) has been cited as an example of early legislation controlling the carrying of arms (see, for example, *Firearms and Violence in American Life*[2]). However, closer study of that Statute reveals that the offence was not simply, 'going or riding armed' as is frequently suggested. *Russell on Crime*[3] expresses the purport of the Act quite clearly, 'The wearing of arms was not punishable under this Statute unless it were accompanied by such circumstances as are apt to terrify the people'. Certainly, the Statute did not concern itself with the keeping of arms and the duty of citizens to arm themselves on the 'Hue and Cry' was specifically preserved.

As firearms developed, they intruded on to the scene and obviously caused concern. The use of firearms in crime is certainly nothing new, and the possibility that trained archers might lose their skills by meddling with these things was a cause of much concern and some legislation. The Tudors had accepted firearms, but apparently felt (and probably with justification) that they must not be permitted to replace the longbow. Guns were weapons for the gentry—of some value to mounted men in time of war, but in no way to be compared with the longbow as the principal military weapon. In 1541, Henry VIII expressed his concern about armed crime and the neglect of archery in his Statute (33 Hen VIII c6) when he reminded his subjects that he had legislated against 'handguns' (a term which appears to have included anything less than a cannon) and crossbows some eight years before, yet, he proclaimed:

> Diverse malicious and evil disposed persons, not only presuming wilfully and obstinately the violation and breach of the said Act, but also of their malicious and evil disposed minds and purposes have wilfully and shamefully committed, perpetrated and done diverse detestable and shameful murders, robberies, felonies, riots and routes with crossbows little short handguns and hagbutts, to the great peril and continual fear and danger of the Kings most loving subjects . . . and diverse Gentlemen, Yeomen and Servingmen now of late have laid apart the good

and laudable exercise of the longbow which always heretofore hath been the surety, safeguard and continual defence of this Realm of England.

To remedy these ills, Henry forbade the use or possession of 'crossbows, handguns, hagbutts and demy-Hakes'[4] by any person who did not have an income of one hundred pounds per year. Even this latter class were to have guns 'not less than one whole yard in length' in the case of handguns and 'not less than three quarters of one whole yard in length' in the case of hagbutts or demyhakes. However, this restriction on the right to keep arms was eased by exceptions which permitted the use of such weapons by the inhabitants of towns 'for shooting at butts or banks of earth' and by anyone for the defence of any house which lay outside the limits of a town. All this, of course, did not effect the duty of all men to keep arms both for the maintenance of order and for the defence of the realm. It merely restricted the then novel and relatively inefficient firearms largely to the wealthier classes whilst maintaining as the arms of the greater body of the people those weapons which were considered more suitable and efficient.

But firearms continued to be developed and, according to Cousins[5] in 1595, the bow lost its place as the chief weapon of war by order of the Privy Council. Greener reports[6] that, at this time, there were thirty-seven accredited gunsmiths in the Minories in London. The militia forces too had developed. The virtually untrained rabble which had formed the greater part of earlier armies was thought unsuitable for modern war and 1573 had seen the forming of the Trained Bands, men selected on a largely voluntary basis for drilling and training, and officered by volunteers. These Trained Bands consisted mainly of the freeman classes, the tradesmen, skilled workers and farmers, and the duty to provide their arms fell on the community.[1,5]

The system survived into Stuart times and, despite the growth of a standing army during Cromwell's Commonwealth, the part-time militia forces remained a most important part of the army. With the restoration of the monarchy, the Stuarts established the king's sole right of control over the militia. The duty to keep arms still existed, but the militia now required expensive firearms and other equipment and so the main burden was transferred from the individual to persons of wealth and to the communities. Anyone with capital exceeding £6,000 or an income from lands of £500 per year was required to provide and equip one horseman. A person with capital of £600 or an income of £50 was required to equip a foot soldier. Those whose incomes were less were required to contribute to a fund from which the local community equipped men according to its wealth.

The trained militia now required the fairly extensive use of firearms, pistols for the cavalryman and muskets for the foot soldier. In his Militia Act of 1662 (14 Chas II c3) Charles laid down the times of training and the types of arms to be provided for the militia. He continued the practice of holding periodic musters and Section 20 of the Act specifies the weapons to be brought to such musters.

> Every musqueteer shall bring with him half a pound of powder
> (at the charge of such person or persons as provide the said
> foot soldier) and a musket, the barrel whereof is not under
> three foot in length and the gauge of the bore to be for twelve
> bullets to the pound.

For the horseman, 'Defensive armour, back, breast and pott, the breast and pott to be pistol proof; a sword and a case of pistols, the barrels whereof are not under fourteen inches in length'. Such weapons were, of course, for the trained element of the militia. Pikes remained the weapons of the lower orders and thus, in 1671, for the purpose of reserving game to the wealthier classes, Charles could enact (22 & 23 Chas II c25) that any person who did not have an annual income of one hundred pounds or more (except persons of or above the rank of esquire and owners or keepers of forests) should not be allowed to keep, for themselves or for any other person, any gun, bow, greyhound, setting dog or long dog.

The duty to keep arms in connection with the militia had, as we have seen, gradually changed from being absolute upon every male adult, to being one falling largely upon the various communities. The duty to keep arms for the preservation of order—for the 'Hue and Cry'—remained, and alongside this duty there had existed a right to keep arms. In relation to guns this had been restricted on two occasions, once by Henry VIII and once by Charles II when, for widely differing motives, each had attempted to restrict the use of guns to the wealthier classes. With these minor exceptions, the right to keep arms seems not to have been questioned, and the importance of these exceptions has to be judged in the light of the conditions of the times, when the lower classes were generally considered to have few, if any, rights. The right and freedoms, of which Englishmen were so fond of boasting, belonged only to the upper and middle classes.

The Catholic king, James II, went far beyond anything done before in attempting to disarm those members of the community who were of importance. He raised the level of the standing army to a point unknown since the Restoration and, to preserve the loyalties of the militia, he dismissed many of the Protestants and disarmed them. The militia at this time consisted mainly of the descendants of the Trained Bands, the tradesmen, yeoman farmers and craftsmen. These were the emerging middle classes who were becoming dominant in parliament and impositions placed on them were not to be treated lightly. Many other impositions were forced on the Protestants until, finally, James was ousted and William of Orange, with his wife, Mary, was brought to the throne. On their accession parliament presented to them a Bill of Rights and this was accepted by the Sovereign and passed into law in 1688 (I Wm & M Sess 2 c2).

It is important to note that parliament considered that they were claiming no new rights, but merely reciting those rights which they understood to have existed at Common Law, and which had been trespassed upon. The object of the Bill was to enshrine these rights to ensure that they were not trespassed upon again. It was a statement of a part of the unwritten Constitution and has formed a basis of that Constitution since then. The Bill begins by setting out the various complaints against King James, that he did 'endeavour to subvert and extirpate the laws and liberties of the Kingdom'. There were thirteen specific complaints and the sixth of these, set well above such matters as free elections to parliament, corrupt juries and cruel punishments; was that King James had 'Caused several good subjects, being protestants, to be disarmed at the same time when papists were both armed and imployed, contrary to law'. For the purpose of asserting their ancient rights, parliament declared (*inter alia*) 'that the subjects which are protestants may have arms for their defence, suitable to their condition and as allowed by law'. The Bill did not seek to disarm Catholics, but merely to ensure that discrimination against Protestants in the matter of keeping arms for their defence should cease.

As with most of the great constitutional milestones, the Bill of Rights must be carefully considered against the conditions of the times. The Magna Carta is frequently quoted as the cornerstone of English liberty, yet there is little doubt that the noblemen who forced this document on King John would have repudiated any suggestion that the rights contained in the Charter applied to the common people. Magna Carta was, undoubtedly, intended by the nobles to serve their sectional interests and to grant them certain rights and privileges. It was not intended to ease the lot of the common people who suffered injustices forbidden by the Charter for many centuries until the Common Law and the Constitution developed to such a stage that all people were embraced by its provisions. So too with the Bill of Rights. Parliament was seeking to secure these rights, but the prime cause for concern were the freemen, and the lot of the lower classes was of little importance. The Bill of Rights set out many of the provisions of the Constitution which have survived intact and which are still jealously guarded. Unlike the written constitutions of many countries, the Bill of Rights does not set out fully the whole of the Constitution and, for a clear understanding of its importance and relevance, it must be considered along with the mass of Common Law which had developed. Rather than being a statement of the constitutional law of the time, it must be considered more in the nature of a signpost along the road on which the constitution developed. That previous legislation had conflicted with the constitution is certain; indeed, one of the aims of the Bill of Rights was to ensure that future Statutes conformed to its standards. However, an unwritten constitution is flexible and susceptible to change, either by Statutes passed with the consent of parliament or by the slow process of development, common usage and case law which produce the Common Law.

The Common Law rights and the Constitution which parliament was seeking to assert through the Bill of Rights were little understood until they were explored in depth by Sir William Blackstone (1723–80) in his *Commentaries*, first published in 1765.[7] Here, the Common Law rights, or liberties, were considered in depth, stage by stage and the following is quoted from the 17th edition of the work, published in 1830, fifty years after Blackstone's death, and edited by a notable lawyer of that period.

> The fifth and last auxiliary right of the subject, that I shall
> mention at present, is that of having arms for their defence,
> suitable to their condition and degree, and such as are allowed
> by law. Which is also declared by the same Statute 1 W & M St 2 c2
> and it is indeed a public allowance, under due restrictions, of
> the natural right of resistance and self presevation, when the

sanctions of society and laws are found insufficient to restrain the violence of oppression.

In these several articles consist the rights, or as they are frequently termed, the liberties of Englishmen; liberties that are more generally talked of than thoroughly understood; and yet highly necessary to be perfectly known and considered by every man of rank or property, lest his ignorance of the points whereon they are founded should hurry him into faction and licentiousness on the one hand, or a pusillanimous indifference and criminal submission on the other. And we have seen that these rights consist, primarily, in the free enjoyment of personal security, of personal liberty and of private property. So long as these remain inviolate, the subject is perfectly free; for every species of compulsive tyranny and oppression must act in opposition to one or other of these rights, having no other object upon which it can possibly be employed. To preserve these from violation, it is necessary that the constitution of Parliament should be supported in its full vigour; and limits, certainly known, be set to the royal prerogative. And, lastly, to vindicate these rights, when actually violated and attacked, the subjects of England are entitled, in the first place, to the regular administration and free course of justice in the courts of law; next to the right of petitioning the king and parliament for redress of grievances; and, lastly, to the right of having and using arms for self preservation and defence. And all these rights and liberties it is our birthright to enjoy entire; unless where the laws of our country have laid them under necessary restraints; restraints in themselves so gentle and moderate, as will appear upon further enquiry, that no man of sense or probity would wish to see them slackened. For all of us have it in our choice to do everything that a good man would desire to do; and are restrained from nothing, but what would be pernicious either to ourselves or to our fellow citizens.

Blackstone's *Commentaries* were then, and indeed still are, regarded as the definitive statement of the Common Law. In matters relating to Common Law they are still quoted with authority in the highest courts. His study of the Common Law and the Constitution as it relates to the right to have arms must, therefore, be accepted— as indeed it was by later English governments—as an accurate assessment of the state of the law at the time of writing. The right to keep arms appears to have persisted until the twentieth century and the effect of the Constitution on twentieth-century laws and practice is a matter for discussion under that heading. Certainly the right was jealously preserved by parliament during the nineteenth century.

The early eighteen hundreds saw the tremendous upheavals of the industrial revolution and the disorders of the era were of a type, scale and length not previously experienced. The Luddites of the industrial north required the deployment of no less than 12,000 troops to contain their machinery-wrecking, violence and, in a small number of cases, murders, during 1811 and 1812. Other, less destructive, industrial movements followed, culminating with the meeting in Manchester in August 1819 of some eighty thousand people bent, as far as can be established, on peaceful ends. However, the crowd was to be dispersed by the Yeomanry in such a way that history was to record the event as 'The Peterloo Massacre'. Eleven people were killed and hundreds injured. Amongst all the very real violence of the times there was talk of revolution, of secret stores of arms, and of men drilling with them. In retrospect, it is extremely doubtful if an armed uprising was ever seriously contemplated, but the contemporaneous observer must have feared the worst. It was against this background of a probably genuine fear of revolution that the government of the day rushed through legislation to ban drilling, seditious meetings, the publication of seditious libels, and other matters thought necessary to stop the move towards revolution.[1]

Among those Acts was the Seizure of Arms Act 1820 to authorise Justices of the Peace to issue warrants to seize and detain arms which might be used by revolutionaries. The preamble to the Act reads, 'Whereas arms and weapons of various sorts have in many parts of this Kingdom been collected and kept for purposes dangerous to the peace'. A Justice of the Peace was to be authorised, on the oath of one or more credible witnesses, to issue a warrant to enter any place by day or by night to search for 'Any pike, pike head or spear in the possession of any person or in any house or place; or any dirk, dagger, pistol or gun or other weapon which, for any purpose dangerous to the peace is in the possession of any person or in any house or place'. There is an important distinction here between pikes, pike heads and spears, and the dirk, dagger, pistol or gun. The former, were liable to seizure when found, but the latter were only liable to seizure if they were possessed for any purpose dangerous to the peace and this tends to support the view that the latter class of weapon might properly be kept for purpose not dangerous to the peace. Weapons which were seized were to be detained unless the owner satisfied a Justice that they were not kept for a purpose dangerous to the peace; and any person found carrying arms in suspicious circumstances was to be detained and taken before a Justice who could grant bail. The Act was to apply only to those industrial areas affected by the disturbances, Lancashire, the West Riding of Yorkshire, Warwickshire, Staffordshire, Nottinghamshire, Cumberland, Westmorland, Northumberland, Durham, Renfrewshire, and Lanarkshire; and to the Cities of Newcastle upon Tyne, Nottingham and Coventry, but could be extended to other areas by Proclamation. A further limitation on the Statute was that it was to remain in force for two years only.

The Act was the subject of a lengthy debate on 14 December 1819 when the question of the constitutional right of Englishmen to keep arms was brought to the fore. Mr T. W. Anson said:

> The principles on which it [the Bill] is founded and the temper
> in which it is framed appear to me to be so much at variance
> with the free spirit of our venerated constitution and so
> contrary to the undoubted right which the subjects of this
> country have ever possessed—the right of retaining arms for
> the defence of themselves, their families and properties that I
> cannot look upon it without loudly expressing my
> disapprobation and regret.

Mr George Bennet opposed the Bill on principle because he held that the distinctive difference between a free man and a slave was the right to possess arms, not so much, as had been stated, for the purpose of defending his property as his liberty. Neither could he do, if deprived of those arms, in the hour of danger.

There followed a lengthy debate on the constitutional aspects of the Bill. Finally, Mr George Canning, then a senior member of the Government and later to become Prime Minister, having apparently taken advice, said:

> I am perfectly willing to admit the right of the subject to hold
> arms according to the principles laid down by the Honourable
> and Learned Gentleman [Mr Anson], having stated it on the
> authority of Mr Justice Blackstone. The doctrine so laid down,
> I am willing to admit, is no other than the doctrine of the
> British Constitution. The Bill of Rights, correctly quoted and

properly construed, brings me to the construction of the Bill which, in fact, recognises the right of the subject to have arms, but qualifies that right in such a manner as the necessity of the case requires.

On the Third Reading of the Bill, Lord Castlereagh, then Foreign Secretary and later also to have oversight of the Home Office, confirmed this view of the constitution when, in discussing the areas to which the Bill should apply he said that he thought it was necessary to take districts which were, or had been disturbed, in a large and liberal sense. Though the Bill was an encroachment on constitutional rights, it was necessary for security's sake not only to cover the part where evil prevailed, but so much of the sound part as would prevent the disease from spreading.

It appears that the constitutional position, accepted by the government after full and careful consideration and taken into account in the drafting of the Bill, was that there existed a right for all people to keep arms, but that the unwritten constitution was sufficiently flexible to allow this right to be encroached upon only in limited areas and for a limited period of time, in other words, in accordance with Blackstone's formula of 'restraints in themselves so gentle and moderate that no man of sense or probity would wish to see them slackened'.

It could be said that, in pressing the Seizure of Arms Act, the government was acting on a very real fear of armed revolt, but that fear could have been dispelled to a considerable extent by proper enquiries into the manner in which the Luddites were in fact arming themselves. The absence of an efficient police force at that time had led to a reliance on paid informers and there can be little doubt that many of the reports supplied by these people were, from a variety of motives, exaggerated. When the Chartist troubles gave rise to similar misgivings, no attempt was made to get similar legislation through parliament. The Home Secretary caused enquiries to be made from the gun trade and was able to report to parliament on 15 May 1839 that 'There had been no very considerable quantity of arms made by the regular manufacturers, and the chief part of the sale which had taken place had been for exportation.' During the later disturbances of 1848, the then well established Metropolitan Police provided the Home Office with a return of arms sold in London in the first six months of the year. Table 1 shows the figures, as reported by F. C. Mather.[8]

TABLE 1   *Arms sold in London in the first six months of 1848*

	Guns	Pistols	Swords	Other weapons
To Gentlemen, Respectable Tradesmen, Gamekeepers, etc.	378	467	71	0
To Mechanics, Labourers, etc., who are believed to be, and others known to be Chartists	122	162	22	18

Metropolitan Police Memorandum, 3 July 1848. HO 45/2410.

These enquiries seem to have helped to dispel fears of a major armed uprising despite references, also quoted by Mather[8] in newspapers such as the *Stockport Advertiser*, which reported 'war like weapons' openly sold in the market place, and the activities of one man hawking pistols at three shillings per brace, during April 1839.

The Seizure of Arms was the only measure prior to the twentieth century which, in any real way, imposed on the right to keep arms, which by this time clearly included firearms; but the nineteenth century saw a number of attempts to introduce controls over weapons in some form or other. The possession of offensive weapons, including firearms, at the time of committing crime, or in circumstances which indicated that a crime was likely to be committed was penalised, for example, by Section 4 of the Vagrancy Act 1824 which provided a penalty for 'Every person being armed with any gun, pistol, hanger, cutlass, bludgeon or other offensive weapons with intent to commit any felony'. The Gun Licences Act of 1870 cannot be considered in any way as an attempt to control firearms. It was merely an Excise Act and required, with certain exceptions, that any person carrying or using a gun elsewhere than in or within the curtilege of a dwelling-house should pay a revenue fee of ten shillings. The licence was available, without question, at any Post Office. From the debates on the Bill it seems likely that one of the motives was the control of poaching and, in committee, one member (P. A. Taylor) condemned the measure as 'an attempt to bring our laws and customs into harmony with those of the most despotic Continental Governments—it is an attempt to disarm the people!' However, it is quite clear that the primary object of the Act was to raise revenue and it placed no restrictions on the keeping or owning of firearms. The Act remained in force until 1967.

The first real effort to control the carrying of arms was very short-lived. The Regulation of Carrying of Arms Bill 1881 had its First (and last) Reading in the Commons on 10 March 1881 and it was described as

A Bill to regulate and in some cases prohibit the carrying of arms in England and Scotland. The object of the Bill was, in the first place, to impose special licences for carrying arms, and to require any person possessing arms for the suspected purpose of committing an offence to obtain a licence from a magistrate of the district; and secondly, to render penal the carrying of arms by persons holding a ticket of leave, or by any person who has been convicted of any offence accompanied by violence against person or property.

The first object is rather difficult to understand and the Bill was never printed so that one is left to speculate about the chances of persuading a person who intended carrying arms for the purpose of committing an offence that he should first call on a local magistrate for a licence! It seems likely that the sponsor intended that the carrying of arms should require a licence issued by a magistrate, but that possession without a licence would only be an offence if the person was possessing arms for the 'suspected purpose of committing an offence'. Not surprisingly, the Bill was not proceeded with.

It is clear that the problem of armed crime was beginning to occupy the public mind. It seems doubtful that this was due to any sudden increase in the use of firearms in crime and it is more likely that improved communications, the growth of the newspaper industry, and the presence of a police force which was by then establishing itself as a reasonably effective and efficient body were all contributing to bringing 'newsworthy' crime to wider notice. Then, too, the breechloading repeating firearms, including a number of efficient revolvers, were well established, and the latter seem to have been one of the main causes for concern. In the absence of truly reliable evidence, one can but speculate on the cause of this sudden preoccupation with firearms controls, but there is certainly no real evidence of any sudden upsurge of criminal use.

1883 saw the presentation to parliament of the first Firearms Bill, a Private Member's Bill, which was concerned with the carrying of a loaded gun in public places, without reasonable excuse—a matter which finally reached the Statute Book in Section 2 of the Firearms Act 1965. This Bill sought to impose a penalty on:

> Every person who shall, after the passing of this Act carry a gun, revolver or other firearm loaded with gunpowder or other explosive substance, in any street or public place within the limits of any city, town or village. Provided always that if such person shall prove to the satisfaction of the Justices that he had reasonable grounds for believing that the carrying of a loaded firearm was, under the circumstances, necessary for self defence, it shall be lawful for the justices to dismiss the charge.

The Bill also sought to require any person carrying a gun to give the weapon up for inspection by a constable or inland revenue officer on demand (another provision which found its way into the 1965 Act). This Bill continued the respect for the constitutional provisions previously mentioned. It made no efforts to control the keeping of firearms and the carrying of firearms for self-defence was clearly considered to be acceptable. However, this Bill did not go beyond the First Reading and it was buried amongst the records without comment from the floor of the House.

The next attempt at legislation concerned itself only with the use of firearms by burglars and the Felonious Use of Firearms Bill 1887 reached the stage of being debated shortly on 1 February. The Bill sought to impose a minimum sentence of ten years' penal servitude on anyone who committed burglary whilst armed with any gun, rifle, revolver or pistol. Speaking at the Second Reading, its promoter, Howard Vincent, suggested that the use of firearms by burglars was on the increase (a questionable proposition for the reasons mentioned above) and quoted some statistics obtained, as far as one can gather, from the Commissioner of Police for the Metropolis. During the preceding nine years, 4 murders had been committed by burglars and during the same period, in London alone, 13 policemen and 5 private persons had been wounded by burglars' firearms. Eighteen burglars had escaped by using firearms; and firearms had been found on 14 others when arrested. Thus, over a nine-year period, in London alone, there had been 50 cases of burglary involving firearms. (This represents an average of 5·5 cases per year—hardly a crime wave by modern standards, even allowing for the poor reporting of serious crime.) Mr Vincent finally withdrew his Bill when the Home Secretary opposed it on the ground that simple burglary then carried life imprisonment and the imposition of mandatory minimum sentences was undesirable, particularly when a person armed with some offensive weapon other than a firearm would not be liable to such a minimum sentence.

Efforts to control the carrying of firearms were clearly still being given consideration in official circles, and in 1889, in accordance with an Address to the House of Lords, the Marquis of Salisbury sent a circular letter to each of Her Majesty's representatives in Europe seeking information about the laws of various countries with regard to 'the carrying of firearms by private persons in populous places'. The replies were presented to the Commons (Cmd 5819–1889) and revealed many differences in practice. In Montenegro, Norway and Sweden, Denmark, Serbia and Switzerland there were no restrictions on the carrying of arms and in Hungary restrictions were imposed only on convicted persons and the insane. Concealed firearms were prohibited in the Duchy of Coburg, Hesse, Saxony and Wertemberg as they were in France which also had complicated regulations about the manufacture and sale of many types of weapon. In the Duchy of Baden and in Germany the carrying of firearms at public meetings was prohibited and in the Netherlands the carrying of firearms on roads or in public places was forbidden with some exceptions. In Bulgaria, Belgium, Greece, Italy, Portugal and Spain a permit was required to carry any type of firearm whilst the same restrictions, with some exemptions applied to Austria, Romania, Russia and Turkey. It was clear from some of the reports that many of these laws were not well enforced. For instance, the Ambassador to Belgium reported, 'I am informed that the existing regulations, even about the carrying of pocket pistols, are rarely, if ever, enforced; and no serious effort has yet been made to check the growing use of cheap pocket pistols.' An interesting and informative note was struck by the Ambassador to Montenegro who reported:

The Montenegrin practice is very different from that in other countries, but then it must be borne in mind that every adult male is a soldier. Generally, we see some restrictions placed on the carrying of arms, but here, every man goes armed to the teeth. A revolver or pistol forms really part of a Montenegrin's dress and every man who can afford to buy one wears his weapon prominently in his belt . . . I cannot say that this indiscriminate display of arms really tends to increase crime. There is none of that carrying of concealed weapons which is so common in Greece and Italy (Both, it will be noted countries where the carrying of weapons without a permit was prohibited) and indeed in other countries. If a Montenegrin has a six barrelled revolver in his belt, he knows that his neighbour is similarly provided. Consequently, it may be said that all start fair.

The Montenegrin revolver was made in Belgium to the specifications of the Montenegrin government and was the largest revolver ever made on a commercial scale. It weighed no less than five pounds and fired a huge $11 \cdot 75$ mm cartridge much longer than most other large calibre cartridges. The picture conjured up, of a rough bewhiskered Montenegrin peasant, in breeches, colourful tunic and bolero, with a wide sash or belt supporting one of these huge pistols is something which must surely leave the cowboy of the 'wild west' very much in the shade!

It may be that the maze of different types of controls, together with the various reports of ineffective enforcement, dissuaded the government from whatever action they had contemplated, but in any event, no action was taken following the laying of the report before parliament. However, the problem of the armed burglar came once more to the fore when the Earl of Milltown sought to introduce a Bill (The Larceny Act 1861, Amendment (Use of Firearms) Bill 1889) to provide for flogging in the case of any burglary in which a firearm was carried. But he was behind the times; this was a period when flogging had been abolished in the armed services and when the number of criminal offences for which it could be imposed was being drastically reduced. Despite a good deal of support in the House of Lords, where the Bill received its Second Reading, it never became law.

The failure of previous legislation aimed at the carrying of all firearms seems to have persuaded the government and some other members of parliament, to concentrate their efforts on pistols which, because of the ease with which they could be carried and concealed, were a popular weapon amongst criminals. Pistol shooting as a sport was in its infancy and the only voice likely to be heard in defence of the pistol was that of the Constitution, or that of the gun trade. Certainly it appears from the debates that the only legitimate use for a pistol was considered to be self-defence. In 1893, the Home Office called for returns from hospitals and coroners of the number of woundings and deaths attributable to pistols or revolvers. They added to this details of persons sentenced to death for murders with pistols and presented their return to the House. The statistics merely showed incidents involving pistols and did not contrast such incidents with other causes of violent death. Homicides, suicide and accidental death appear in both the hospital returns and the coroners' returns and, as inquests would be held on violent deaths which occurred in hospital, this appears to be duplication. The coroners' returns showed that during the three years 1890 to 1892, there were 49 accidental deaths (about 16 per year), 443 suicides (148 per year), and 32 homicides (11 per year) attributable to pistols and revolvers. Non-fatal injuries attributable to these weapons totalled 226 for the three years (75 per year) and the numbers of persons sentenced to death for murders committed with pistols and revolvers were 3, 4, and 3 out of 24, 19 and 22 respectively. These figures were examined in 1907 in *The Causes of Decay in a British Industry*[9] where it was stated that in 1892 there was a total of 16,343 violent deaths of which those shown in the returns as attributable to pistols totalled 217 (1·32 per cent), and when they examined the number of accidental deaths due to pistols (16) they found that this was just three more than deaths due to perambulators! Poisons, which were then controlled by legislation, accounted for 400 deaths whilst vehicular accidents accounted for 2,500 (the majority caused by trains).

These comparative figures, which were presumably available to the Home Office, were not presented to parliament, but the Home Secretary did include a further return concerning the use of firearms by burglars, this time covering the whole of England and Wales. Although the figures may not be very reliable, the return for 1892 might usefully be compared with that for 1887; they were for continuous periods and both were gathered in similar ways (see Table 2). Although no firm conclusion could properly be drawn at this late stage, the comparison might well be valid, the more so in the case of reports of wounding of policemen. Figures relating to the activities of burglars might well not be accurate, but the figures relating to the wounding of policemen are pretty certain to be fully reported. The earlier figures concerned the Metropolitan Police District only and referred to a period of nine years, the latter concerned the whole of England and Wales and referred to a period of five years.

The Metropolitan Police District contained approximately one fifth of the population of England and Wales and, therefore, the yearly average for England and Wales might be expected to be much higher. Although these figures tend to show that, in fact, the use of firearms had decreased during the period, they are not sufficiently reliable for such a firm conclusion to be drawn. What is clear is that they do not show any marked increase in the use of firearms by burglars.

TABLE 2 *Use of firearms by burglars in London, 1878–86, and England and Wales, 1887–91*

| | 1887 return for 9 years MPD only | | 1892 return for 5 years England and Wales | |
	Total	Average p.a.	Total	Average p.a.
Police Officers wounded by burglars	13	1·4	3	0·6
Burglars who escaped by using firearms	18	2·0	18	3·6
Burglars found in possession of firearms on arrest	14	1·5	31	6·0

However, either not having made such a comparison, or being undeterred by the results, the government introduced its Pistols Bill on 24 July 1893. Controls were to be imposed only on pistols, defined as any firearm not exceeding 15 in. in length, and were to apply only on the sale of such weapons by way of trade or business and this, presumably, would have put private transactions between individuals outside the scope of the legislation. Provision was made for the licensing of persons to sell pistols by the County or Borough Councils and before such a person could legitimately sell a pistol, the purchaser had to produce either a gun or game licence (which, it will be recalled, was obtainable by anyone at a Post Office on payment of a fee), or one of a number of signed statements showing that the purchaser was an officer of the armed forces or merchant service, or that he was about to proceed abroad. Sellers of pistols were to be required to keep records of all sales, to retain such records for five years and to produce them on demand to a constable or revenue officer. The sale of pistols to persons under 18 was prohibited as was the carrying of pistols by such persons. Anyone who had been sentenced to penal servitude for any crime of violence was prohibited from carrying a pistol for a period of five years from the date of his release. The carrying, by anyone, of a loaded pistol in a highway or public place was to be subject to the grant of permission in writing by the Chief Officer of Police for the area, with an exemption in favour of the armed forces. The Bill also provided that every pistol sold should be marked with the maker's name or some distinctive trade mark. Wholesale trade was exempted from all the provisions of the Bill, as were dealings in antique pistols.

By comparison with today's legislative controls on firearms, this seems to have been a very mild measure and to be so full of loopholes that, in retrospect, one wonders how anyone could think it would have any effect. Nevertheless, when it was debated on 14 September 1893 it was subjected to strenuous attacks and received remarkably little support. The attack was led by the Member for South East Middleton, Mr C. H. Hopwood, who contended that the Bill was firstly unnecessary, it was not warranted by the returns submitted to the House, secondly, that it was ineffective and thirdly, that, 'It attacked the natural right of everyone who desired to arm himself for his own protection, and not harm anybody else'. This grandmotherly legislation was not, in his opinion, required and parliament should make a firm stand against it. 'Why should Englishmen not arm themselves? It was natural and parliament ought not to interfere with such a right.' Hopwood received a considerable body of support and the Bill was killed by the device of moving that it be adjourned.

The matter was not, however, to be allowed to rest for long. The Marquess of Carmarthen, who was a Member of the Commons for Lambeth and Brixton, was succesful in the ballot for Private Member's Bills in 1895 and he had the problem of firearms controls in his mind. When he introduced the Second Reading of his Pistols Bill 1895, he complained that he would have preferred a Bill which provided that no one but a soldier, sailor or policeman should have a pistol at all, because they were a source of danger to their possessors, but he had been obliged to fall back on the Bill of 1893 to which he had made one or two improvements. These improvements were small. For the requirement to mark each pistol with a trade mark, he had substituted a requirement for a consecutive number. He also sought to exempt toy pistols, defined as those which had no communication between the nipple (in the case of muzzle leaders) or the cartridge and the barrel; and to require an additional form of licence, similar to a gun licence and obtainable from a Post Office, for anyone possessing a pistol. The Bill was short-lived, for the redoubtable Mr Hopwood returned to the attack in a scathing manner to move 'that the Bill be read a second time this day six months'—which in effect was to defeat it. Mr Hopwood pointed out that the Bill was virtually identical to that rejected just two years before and his adjectives—grandmotherly, unnecessary and futile—were once more employed before he again protested that 'To say that because there were some persons who would make violent use of pistols, therefore the right of purchase or possession by every Englishman should be taken away, is monstrous'. Other Members rose to support Mr Hopwood; Sir A. K. Rollit was concerned about the restraint on trade, but he thought that even more objectionable was the restraint on personal liberty involved in the Bill. The Bill was not grandmotherly, but great-grandmotherly legislation and he was surprised that an advanced government like that in power should think it necessary to help people to take care of themselves instead of teaching them to do effectively what was their duty to themselves. It is clear that the Home Secretary had promised support for the Bill and, indeed, that the Home Office had assisted with the preparation, but when he came to speak on the matter, the Home Secretary said that although the government was exceedingly well disposed towards the Bill, he did not wish to make his statement any stronger than was absolutely necessary. Based on an extremely interesting collection of burglars' weapons at Scotland Yard (not, it will be noted, on comparative statistics) he thought the use of pistols by that class of criminal was increasing. There were, he said, grounds on which the government sympathised with the Bill, but they reserved the right to deal with details in committee. Support for the Bill was consistently lukewarm and attacks on the many loopholes and anomalies were substantial. The matter was forced to a division and the Bill was defeated by no less than 189 votes to 75.

The question of firearms controls was not before the House again until after the turn of the century and so England entered the twentieth century with no controls over the purchasing or keeping of any types of firearm and the only measure which related to the carrying of guns was the Gun Licence Act, requiring the purchase of a ten shilling gun licence from a Post Office. Anyone, be he convicted criminal, lunatic, drunkard or child, could legally acquire any type of firearm and the presence of pistols and revolvers in households all over the country was fairly widespread. Some indication of the practice of carrying loaded firearms might be gathered from a single incident when this writer, in the 1950s, acquired a muzzle-loading pocket pistol from a farmer, then in his sixties. The weapon was found still to contain a ball and the farmer recalled that, in his childhood, he had often accompanied his father to market and on each and every occasion that pistol, fully loaded, had been in his father's pocket; and this was in a quiet area of the Yorkshire countryside.

Some indication of the numbers of pistols in circulation can be gained from figures for proofs at the Birmingham Proof House (one of the two established in this country). Over four thousand foreign pistols and revolvers were submitted for proof after being imported in 1889 and whilst the figures for domestic production for that year are not readily available, over 37,000 British pistols were submitted for proof in 1902, although, of course, not all of these were for the home market.[9] England at that time was a country where guns of every type were familiar instruments and where anyone who felt the need or desire to own a gun could obtain one. The cheaper guns were very cheap and well within the reach of all but the very poor. The price mentioned by Mather[8] of one shilling and sixpence per pistol for those being hawked at Stockport, which presumably were second-hand and of poor quality, can be set against his earlier reference to four shillings and sixpence per week as 'a miserably low wage' suffered by some crafts which were in a chronic state of distress. Too much reliance should not be placed on such statistics as are available on the criminal use of firearms at this time, but the reports of injuries to the police by shooting must have been just as accurate then as they are now. Even allowing for the lower population (about 29 millions) and the lower police strength (about 44,000) the picture presented is not that of a serious wave of armed crime, indeed, if such figures could be claimed for this day and age, the results would be thought most satisfactory.

The right of the Englishman to keep arms for his own defence was still completely accepted and all attempts at placing this under restraint had failed. However, the prospect of effecting some controls, at least on pistols, was clearly in the public mind and had been taken up by various members of parliament and by the government. It was not to rest for long.

2 The First Steps

With the Pistols Act 1903, parliament took its first faltering step towards firearms controls. The Act was little more than a watered-down version of the Bills of 1893 and 1895, containing the same loop-holes and, when examined with the benefit of hindsight, was unlikely to produce any marked effects. From the debates it appears that the criminal use of firearms was not, in fact, the problem occupying the parliamentary mind; there is no mention of numbers of offences involving firearms and the most striking omission from earlier Bills is that the Act contains no provisions prohibiting the purchase or possession of pistols by convicted persons. The emphasis was placed on the dangers arising from the possession of pistols by children, or by drunken men. The Act made specific provisions about sales to these classes and it could perhaps be expected to have some effect, at least on the former.

The Act is short, containing only 9 Sections, and it applied only to pistols—'A firearm or other weapon from which any shot, bullet or other missile can be discharged, and of which the length of the barrel, not including any revolving detachable or magazine breech, does not exceed nine inches'. That part of the definition referring to a weapon of any description from which any shot, bullet or other missile can be discharged persists through all the legislation to the present day and, with improvements, still forms part of the basic definition of a firearm.

Section 3 made unlawful the sale by retail or by auction, or the letting on hire of a pistol to any person, unless at the time of the sale or hire the person:

1. Produced a current gun or game licence, or gave reasonable proof that he was exempt from the provisions of the Gun Licences Act OR
2. Gave reasonable proof that, being a householder, he proposed to use the pistol in, or within the curtilege of his own house OR
3. Produced a statement signed by himself and either by a police officer of or above the rank of Inspector, or by a Justice of the

Peace, to the effect that he was about to proceed abroad for not less than six months.

It is difficult to imagine, at this late date, how anyone could expect these provisions to have any effect. Private sales between individuals were completely outside the scope of the Act. It is now impossible to establish what proportion of pistols were acquired second-hand by private sales at that time, but as an indication in the broadest sense, a survey conducted in the U.S.A. and reported in *Firearms and Violence in American Life*[1] indicates that about thirty per cent of the pistols were acquired in this way. Certainly a person wishing to buy a pistol for illegal purposes was at least as likely to seek to acquire it from within his circle of acquaintances as he was to march into a gun dealer's shop and buy it over the counter, with the attendant risk of being remembered.

The requirement to produce a gun or game licence prior to a sale seems to be a wholly ineffective check on the bona fides of the purchaser. The licence was obtainable on demand and anyone who felt the need for a pistol could very simply call at a Post Office, spend ten shillings on a gun licence and then go to a gunsmith and buy his pistol. The provision probably reduced retail sales to some extent by placing an obstacle in the way of impulsive purchases, but it would certainly not have deterred anyone who had decided beforehand that he wished to buy a weapon. Just what was to be accepted as reasonable proof that a purchaser who was a householder intended using a pistol only at his own home is not clear, but this seems to have been a gap through which the proverbial coach and four could have been driven with ease. The final alternative authority for purchase seems to have been a little more strict, presuming that a police inspector or a magistrate would not lightly countersign a declaration that a person was proceeding abroad. Taken as a whole, the restrictions on purchase were such as would not have deterred anyone who felt the need for a pistol for either lawful or unlawful objects, and the failure to include private sales was virtually bound to render the Act wholly ineffective.

There were no provisions for licensing those persons who could sell pistols by retail, indeed, no restrictions or conditions of any type were imposed except to provide that a seller of pistols by retail should maintain full records of all pistols sold and produce these on demand to a constable or an officer of the inland revenue. The details which had to be recorded bore a marked similarity to those still required to be entered in the register maintained by a firearms dealer.

The restrictions on persons under eighteen were more specific and appear to have been capable of a reasonable degree of enforcement. With very limited exceptions, any person under eighteen was liable to a fine of forty shillings if he were to buy, hire, use or carry a pistol; and any person who sold or delivered a pistol to a person under eighteen was liable to a fine of five pounds. Anyone who knowingly sold a pistol to a person who was intoxicated or of unsound mind was liable to a fine of twenty-five pounds or to imprisonment with hard labour for three months. Whilst the penalty here was more severe, the effects of the provision were likely to be minimal—it was not an offence to give or lend a pistol to such a person. Possession of a loaded firearm in a public place by a person who was drunk was penalised separately under Section 12 of the Licensing Act 1872.

Section 8 of the Act exempted from its provisions antique pistols where they were sold as 'curiosities or ornaments' and an antique pistol was defined to exclude any pistol with which ammunition was sold, or which there was any reasonable ground for believing to be capable of being effectually used. This last part of the definition was ambigious, even an old flintlock pistol was capable of being effectually used by a person with a moderate knowledge, and such weapons were then (and indeed still are) currently in production, primarily for the African market.

The debates on the Bill provide an amazing contrast to the debates on previous Bills. No voice spoke in strenuous opposition, no mention was made of the right to keep arms, although this was not really called in question by the Bill and the provisions relating to householders purchasing without a gun licence may have been sufficient to still this argument from the start; there were no figures (reliable or otherwise) relating to burglaries or other crimes committed with pistols. It seems that the criminal aspect of the use of firearms was deliberately played down, being outside the scope of the Bill. The Bill's supporters relied on brief quotations from one or two specific cases of injury rather than on any comparative figures. The debate of the Second Reading was opened by the Bill's sponsor, Mr Hulme, who stated that his object was to prevent the sale of pistols to young persons and prevent the accidents that they heard of from time to time. He then went on to illustrate this by reference to one tragic incident in which a child had killed his brother with a pistol. The Honourable Member was then guilty of what Winston Churchill would have called a terminological inexactitude, when he informed the House that, 'In 1893 and 1895 the House gave Second Readings to Bills which were lost through accidents of procedure'. In fact, neither of the Bills was given a second reading and, far from being lost through accidents of procedure, both were literally flung from the House by overwhelming opposition. Yet the Pistols Act was virtually unopposed in both Houses and it ran an untroubled course to the Royal Assent.

Possibly the best explanation for this was given in the House of Lords by Earl Donoughmore who introduced the Bill there on 9 July 1903. 'Since 1888 this question has been before Parliament but the failure of previous Bills has been solely due to the fact that they were too extreme and have endeavoured to go too far. This was notably the case with the Bill of 1893.' Here, perhaps, is the key. The Pistols Act was weak and ineffective, so full of loopholes that it was unlikely to have any effect in controlling pistols and yet, in the prevailing climate of public and Parliamentary opinion, it was the best they could do. What effect did it have? In the absence of reliable records this is difficult to assess. Writing in 1907, two Birmingham gunmakers[2] indicated that sales of pistols were reduced:

A Birmingham wholesale dealer states that the number of English pistols sold by him for the home market has been upwards of 37 per cent less since the Act came into force. A London retailer states that there was a much increased demand for revolvers in 1903, due, he believes, to the publicity given to the matter by the Bill, and that since the Bill came into force the sales have declined.

The book gives figures to show that Proofs of revolvers in Birmingham declined from 37,010 in 1902 to 24,096 in 1904; however, this figure would include weapons for the export market and so cannot be related directly to the results of the Act. Allowing for the undoubted bias of the persons quoted, it seems clear that sales of new pistols did fall, due in all probability to the obstacle placed in the way of impulsive buying of these small, and frequently inexpensive weapons.

The book also shows figures for violent deaths in 1902 and 1904, to illustrate the view that the Act was 'remedially inoperative'. The source of the statistics is not given and there are slight variations from those given by the Registrar General's Returns (see Table 3).

scope of the Act, quickly appeared on the market. Not all of these were produced simply to defeat the Act. Target shooting with pistols was just beginning to gain in popularity and respectability, largely under the influence of an American, Walter Winans, who was an outstanding pistol shot and the author of several books on the subject. He was transforming the sport from its previous position—as a sideshow to competitive rifle shooting—to a sport in its own right; and long-barrelled pistols have always been popular as target weapons. It is clear, however, that many long-barrelled pistols were produced simply for the purpose of evading the restrictions of the Act and, for example, the matter was raised in the House of Commons on four occasions in 1912, when two incidents involving the possession of long-barrelled pistols by children, each of which resulted in a death, were mentioned. Prosecutions under the Act were infrequent. They were not given a heading in the return of criminal statistics, but a parliamentary answer in 1911 indicated that, in England and Wales, there were 26 prosecutions in 1908 and 16 in 1909. (Compare this with the 4,653 prosecutions under the Firearms Act during 1969.) There is no evidence to indicate whether the use of pistols by persons under eighteen, which was one of the problems to which the Act was particularly addressed, had decreased.

It would appear that the question of further controls on firearms was receiving constant attention at the Home Office, for by 1911 another Pistols Bill was almost ready for presentation to parliament. In the event, the Bill was not presented, but reference was made to it in the report of the Blackwell Committee[3] and from this it can be gathered that the proposed Bill still related to pistols only. The definition contained in another unsuccessful Bill (Aliens (Prevention of Crime) Bill 1911) suggests that the barrel length referred to in the definition has been extended to fifteen inches to bring within its ambit those long-barrelled pistols which evaded the 1903 Act. A certificate was to be required for the purchase or possession of a pistol, and this was to have been granted by the police, as a matter of course, on production of a statement from a reputable householder that the applicant was a person who could be permitted to have a pistol without danger to the public safety. This seems to have given the police little, if any, discretion on the issue of a certificate. A register of dealers in pistols was proposed, and this was to include manufacturers and wholesalers as well as retailers. All would have been required to keep records and would have been liable to removal from the register on conviction for an offence under the Act. It was also proposed that the police should have power to demand from anyone they believed to be carrying a pistol the production of a certificate; failure or refusal to produce the certificate was to confer a right to seize the weapon. Ammunition was to be included in the controls, but it is not clear how it was proposed to distinguish between ammunition for pistols and that for rifles since, in many cases (.22 in. weapons, some 'rook and rabbit' rifles and a number of carbines, particularly those imported from the U.S.A.) ammunition was interchangeable.

That some difficulty was being experienced in the various consultations which usually take place on proposed legislation is indicated by a comment in the Blackwell Committee report:[3]

> The Bill was the subject of protracted negotiations between the Home Office and the Gun Trade, and ultimately reached a shape when, subject to the settlement of some details, it appeared likely to receive the support of the Trade, or at any rate, no longer meet with their opposition.

The Bill was still not ready for presentation to parliament when there occurred in London two connected shooting incidents. A group of Russian anarchists were found breaking into a jeweller's shop in the City of London on 16 December 1910. Their motive appears to have been to finance their extremist activities and they were armed with automatic pistols. When the unarmed police arrived at the scene, the anarchists started shooting. Two police sergeants and one constable were killed, one sergeant and one constable were seriously injured. Two of the men escaped, leaving behind a third man who had been shot and killed by one of his comrades. The remainder were traced to number 100 Sidney Street and there, on 3 January 1911, was enacted the famous Sidney Street Siege. Another police officer was seriously injured and eventually the army was called upon to assist. It is believed that the wanted men themselves set fire to the house, but, in any event, it was burnt to the ground and both occupants were found dead inside.

Apart from demonstrating the unpreparedness of the British police to deal with incidents of this nature, the Sidney Street Siege once more drew attention to the state of firearms controls and, as a direct result, the Aliens (Prevention of Crime) Bill 1911 appeared before the Commons. The Bill merely provided that no alien was to have in his possession, use or carry a pistol unless he held written permission from the Chief Officer of Police of the area in which he resided. The definition, which in all probability was borrowed from the Home Office Bill, was:

> Any firearm, air gun, or other weapon of any description from which any shot, bullet or other missile (including noxious liquids) can be discharged and the barrel of which, not including any revolving detachable or magazine breach, does not exceed fifteen inches in length.

The Bill did not proceed beyond the First Reading and one can only speculate that it was withdrawn in favour of the Home Office measure which proposed wider controls applying both to aliens and to British citizens alike.

Considerable pressure was placed on the Home Secretary to bring his Bill before the House, but it seems that some opposition was expected. Four questions in 1912 merely drew replies that there was no possibility of introducing the Bill in the current session, but it was hoped to bring it before the House in the following year. In answer to questions in following years, it was merely said that there was no parliamentary time available, but in 1915 the Home Secretary said, 'The present time is not opportune for dealing with a matter which experience has shown to be very controversial'. In any event, the First World War intervened and more urgent matters must certainly have occupied everyone's attention.

During 1913, further information was sought about the use of firearms in attacks on the police and a return presented to parliament in that year showed full details of all incidents in which shots were fired at police officers, including cases where the trigger was pulled, but no discharge followed, for the years 1908 and 1912 inclusive. Of 47 cases reported, pistols were used in 35, shotguns in 9 (including one sawn-off shotgun) and rifles in two. In one case the weapon was an antique pistol which failed to fire although the offender tried to use it. The figures produced in 1887 to 1892 related to the use of firearms by burglars and so cannot be directly compared; although it might be possible to conclude that the Pistols Act produced little effect, no other conclusions can be drawn. The lengthy and detailed return which was presented to parliament produced no immediate effects, although it was much quoted in later debates (see Table 4 for a summary).

During the First World War, Regulations made under the Defence of the Realm Act imposed some restrictions on firearms. Manufacture and imports were regulated according to the needs of the

TABLE 4   *Summary of shots fired at police, 1908–12*

Year	Total no. of cases	Number and injuries of police concerned			
		Total no. shot at	Number killed	Number injured	Number not injured
1908	3	3	—	1	2
1909	8	29	2	4	23
1910	4	14	3	3	8
1911	14	21	—	10	11
1912	18	25	1	6	18
Totals	47	92	6	24	62

war and there were powers to restrict the sale, purchase, transfer or disposal of firearms, and to prohibit the carrying of firearms in certain areas. Regulations to control these activities were applied only to Ireland and certainly there was nothing in England and Wales to affect the large numbers of firearms already in circulation. Vast numbers of men were under arms throughout the war and all Commissioned Officers were required to purchase their own service pistols. The greater number of these were bought through service channels, but many were bought privately through normal trade outlets. These pistols were, of course, the private property of the officers and not government stores.

Statistics on the use of firearms were being assembled by the Commissioner of Police of the Metropolis and these were later supplied to the Blackwell Committee[3] (see Table 5) and indicate the relative use of firearms in crime for the periods 1911–13 and 1915–17. The Sidney Street Siege was still fresh in many minds, for the figures relating to aliens are shown separately. The term 'used' is not clarified, but the term 'possessed' refers to weapons found in the possession of persons 'when they came into the hands of the police' and not at the time when they were committing a crime.

The decrease in the latter period can be only partially explained by the internment of a number of aliens during the war and by the absence, in the trenches, of a substantial part of the age group most likely to use firearms in crime. The Blackwell Committee sought to add to these reasons the restrictions imposed by the Defence of the Realm Regulations, but this is, to say the least, questionable. Such Regulations would not have affected the large number of firearms in circulation before the war, and restrictions on purchase, carrying

TABLE 5 *Firearms used and possessed in crime in London, 1911–13 and 1915–17*

	1911 to 1913				1915 to 1917			
	Firearms used		Possessed		Firearms used		Possessed	
	Total Average p.a.		Total Average p.a.		Total Average p.a.		Total Average p.a.	
British	100	33·3	76	25·3	42	14	44	14·7
Alien	23	7·7	27	9·0	5	1·7	10	3·3
Totals	123	41·0	103	34·3	47	15·7	54	18·0

or possession of firearms were actually imposed only in Ireland. Any effect which the Regulations might have had in England and Wales would have been more than compensated for by the ownership of pistols by Commissioned Officers and the ease with which other ranks could have obtained firearms if they had wanted them.

The end of the war brought the firearms control question to the fore again. No progress had been made with the Bill prepared in 1911 and, rather than proceed with what must have seemed an out-dated measure, there was set up, on 27 February 1918, a committee under the chairmanship of Sir Ernley Blackwell, K.C.B., to

consider the question of the control which it is desirable to exercise over the possession, manufacture, sale, import and export of firearms and ammunition in the United Kingdom after the war, both from the point of internal policy and having regard to the Report of the Sub Committee on Arms Traffic of the Committee of Imperial Defence.

The committee met privately and reported in confidence.[3] It did not take evidence from outside individuals or bodies except by consulting with the Chief Constable of Birmingham on some problems which the police might have had in implementing their suggestions. The committee consisted largely of senior officials, and the 1918 edition of *Who's Who* gives their appointments, Sir Ernley Blackwell, K.C.B., Assistant Under Secretary of State for the Home Department; Edward Charles Cunningham, Secretary to the Board of Customs and Excise; Frederick John Dryhurst, a Principal Clerk at the Home Office; Leonard Dunning, one of H.M. Inspectors of Constabulary; Arthur Warren Samuels, Solicitor General for Ireland; plus J. E. Shuckburgh, Maurice Tomlin and B. M. Tomlinson, whose positions have not been traced.

The committee's deliberations covered the problem from three aspects; first, the internal situation in Britain, mainly a matter of the criminal use of firearms; second, they gave consideration to the special problems of Ireland; and third, they concerned themselves with the control of international trade in arms and munitions. After examining briefly the current state of the law, they detailed what they considered to be the grounds for strengthening the law relating to firearms under each heading. With regard to the use of firearms in crime, they examined the returns of police officers at whom shots had been fired, together with the returns of the number of persons using, or found with firearms in London, both of which have previously been referred to. They also quoted instances where, according to the Commissioner of Police for the Metropolis, officers dealing with disputes in a dock strike in 1912 had found seven men using firearms and five others had been found in possession. These figures were, of course, part of the totals in the return. After complaining that, 'The Courts appear to have taken an extremely lenient view of offences of using firearms', they concluded, 'there is good reason for so altering the law as to make it much more difficult to obtain firearms than it is at present'.

As to the special problems of Ireland, the committee made reference to the Peace Preservation (Ireland) Act 1881, under which the carrying of firearms could be (and had been) proscribed, and to those parts of the Defence of the Realm Regulations which had been applied to Ireland. The committee concluded that the control of firearms was essential in Ireland and quoted figures relating to incidents in which firearms had been used. The problems of Ireland obviously weighed heavily on the committee and, although they recommended that some of their final proposals should be applied differently in Ireland, they do not appear to have given consideration to the continuance of emergency, or separate, legislation for that part of the Kingdom.

International control on arms and munitions was also a matter of considerable concern. The report of the Sub-committee on Arms Traffic was quoted, with approval, as suggesting that the vast quantities of surplus weapons which might come on to the market after the war were a source of danger to the British Empire. The sub-committee had seen two main sources of danger—'Savage or semi-civilised tribesmen in outlying parts of the British Empire' and, it might be thought, prophetically, 'The anarchist or "intellectual" malcontent of the great cities, whose weapon is the bomb and the automatic pistol. There is some force in the view that the latter will in future prove the more dangerous of the two'. It was recommended that the government should take the initiative in raising this at the Peace Conference, and one result of the Blackwell Committee's deliberations was the government's participation in the Paris Arms Convention of 1919, at which they undertook to implement strict governmental control over exports of firearms to certain parts of the world.

Having regard to all three problems, the committee reported:

> There can surely be no question that the public interest demands that direct controls shall in future be exercised in the United Kingdom—whatever may be the policy of other powers—over the possession, manufacture, sale and import and export of firearms [they expressly construed this word in its widest sense] and ammunition, and the only practical question for consideration appears to be—how this control can be most efficiently established.

Their proposals in this direction were (summarised):

1. That the government should ensure that strict controls were established so that military weapons, including personal weapons, should not be thrown on to the markets.

2. That pistols and revolvers should be subjected to the most stringent controls.

3. That it would be unsafe to exclude sporting rifles from any controls.

4. That ammunition should be included in the controls and that the police should have authority to limit the quantity of ammunition purchasable by individuals and clubs. This was to be facilitated by requiring that all purchases of ammunition be entered in a firearm certificate.

5. That shotguns should be excluded from the controls except in Ireland. The committee thought that, 'The cases are rare in

which they are used for any criminal or illegal purpose in Great Britain'. They considered that it would be undesirable to interfere with any private industry except on good and sufficient grounds and they foresaw difficulties in the gun trade if controls were placed on these weapons. In fact, so far as Great Britain was concerned, such a case could better have been made out for target or sporting rifles if the committee were relying on the statistics before them.

6. Air weapons were included in the general definition of firearms and it must be concluded that the committee proposed full controls over them.

The proposed Bill of 1911 had provided that the police were to grant a certificate as a matter of course if the applicant produced a statement from a reputable householder that he was a person who could be permitted to have a weapon without danger to the public safety. The committee thought this inadequate and proposed that, subject to a right of appeal to Petty Sessions, the police should have discretion to refuse a certificate. They further proposed that all manufacturers, as well as sellers of firearms should have to be registered and that any offence should render a dealer liable to removal from the register. In considering the application of police discretion to this aspect, they took account of the remarks of the Chief Constable of Birmingham in suggesting that there should be virtually no discretion left to the police in a matter which might be construed as an arbitrary interference with trade. They thought that the powers of removal from the register after conviction were sufficient.

In the matter of police discretion on the issue of certificates to individuals, they thought that the Chief Officer of Police should satisfy himself that the applicant had made out a good prima facie case for requiring the firearms, that he was a person of good character and[3] that there was no reason for supposing that he intended to use the weapon for unlawful purposes. With regard to pistols, they thought that the ground on which a firearm certificate would be applied for would be that the applicant considered it necessary to protect himself and his household from burglars.

This ground could obviously be urged with much more force by an applicant who lived in a rural or out of the way district than by one who lived in a well patrolled street in a town . . . If the applicant were not a householder, or the circumstances were such as to make the risk of any attempt at burglary on his premises a negligible one, it would be reasonable that the police should require the applicant to show special grounds for the need of a revolver.

To assist in tracing weapons and to discourage evasions, it was recommended that all manufacturers and sellers of firearms should be required to maintain records, a duty which the 1903 Act had applied only to retailers, and they proposed that the Home Secretary should be given powers to prescribe the form and content of these records. To further contribute to the efficiency of the system, they addressed themselves to the problem of ensuring that the person who acquired the weapon was the person to whom the certificate had been granted, and, after considering a number of methods, they proposed a requirement for the dealer to notify details of the sale to the police who could, in cases of doubt, verify the transaction.

It was suggested that imports and exports of arms and munitions, including all firearms, should be the subject of a general prohibition except where a licence was issued. The committee felt that such licences should be issued freely for imports of firearms to dealers, or of sporting weapons by individuals. There was concern about illegal importation by persons arriving from abroad, and the Chief Officer under the Aliens Act, in a memorandum, made it clear that it would be impossible to prevent the smuggling of weapons into the country. Whilst accepting this, the committee suggested that specific powers to search for arms should be given under the Aliens Act.

Appendix A to the report contains the suggested 'Heads of a Bill' for the control of firearms and this is sufficiently important, particularly as it has not before been published, to reproduce in full except for the proposed penalties, references to the 1911 Bill and parts applying only to Ireland.

Appendix A

Heads of a Bill to Provide for the Control of the Possession, Manufacture, Sale, Import and Export of Firearms and Ammunition in the United Kingdom.

1. (1) The right to purchase, possess, use or carry any description of firearm (as defined in 12) or ammunition for the weapon, to be limited to persons holding a firearm certificate.

(2) Firearm certificate to be granted by the Chief Officer of Police of the district in which the applicant resides, on payment of the required fee, when such Chief Officer is satisfied that the applicant is a person who can be permitted to have the firearm without danger to the public safety. Certificate to relate to one identified firearm only, and to a definite quantity of ammunition; but a certificate may be granted for the use for bona fide sporting purposes of a rifle not identified as the property of the user.

(3) There shall be a right of appeal to a Court of Summary Jurisdiction against the refusal of a Chief Officer of Police to grant a certificate.

(4) Chief Officer of Police not to grant firearm certificate
  (i) to a person under the age of 18 years.
  (ii) to a person whom he knows, or has reasonable cause for believing to be of drunken habits.
  (iii) to a person whom he knows or has reasonable cause for believing to be of unsound mind.
  (iv) to a person whom he knows to have been sentenced to penal servitude or imprisonment for a crime of violence, or burglary or housebreaking; or to a person for the time being under recognisances to keep the peace or be of good behaviour; or to a person holding a licence under the Penal Servitude Acts; or to a person under police supervision.

(5) Firearm certificate to be subject to expiration and annual renewal, as is the case of gun licences, and, preferably on the same date. Fee on grant of a certificate to be five shillings and on annual renewal two shillings and sixpence.

(6) Firearm certificate not to be required
  (i) by any person in H.M. Naval, Military, Air or Reserve Services, or in a Police Force, for any firearm which he possesses or uses in his official capacity; or
  (ii) by any gunsmith or his servant having the firearm in the ordinary course of his trade or business as gunsmith, or by any authorised servant of a Proof House; or
  (iii) by a common carrier having or carrying a firearm in the course of his business; or
  (iv) for any firearm forming part of a ship's equipment, provided it is not brought ashore; or

(v) by any member of an approved rifle or miniature rifle club for using or carrying a firearm when engaged in target practice.

(7) Person using or carrying a firearm not to be relieved from the obligation to take out a gun licence.

2. (1) Person not to manufacture, sell, whether wholesale or retail, or expose for sale firearms by way of trade or business unless registered as a firearms dealer.

(2) Pawnbroker not to take firearms in pawn. Firearms already in pledge to be sold to registered dealer only.

(3) Person not to sell firearm except to a registered dealer unless purchaser produces a firearm certificate.

(4) Seller of firearm immediately to inform Chief Officer of Police who issued certificate of full particulars of sale.

(5) Manufacturers or dealers who sell firearms by way of trade or business, whether by wholesale or retail, to enter in a book to be kept for the purpose the particulars of each transaction set out in the Schedule to the Act. The book to be open to inspection by officers of police and any officers engaged in the administration of the Gun Licences and Game Licences Acts.

(7) This provision to be in addition to and not in derogation of any provisions of this or any other Acts which prohibit or restrict the sale of firearms to any person.

3. Person under 18 not to purchase, possess, use or carry a firearm.

4. (1) Firearms not to be sold to any person whom the seller knows, or has reasonable ground for believing to be drunk or of unsound mind even though such person may have been granted a firearm certificate.

5. (1) A person ineligible to hold a firearm certificate under Cl 1(4)(iv) not to possess, use or carry a firearm.

6. (1) The Chief Officer of Police of every Police District to keep a register, in form prescribed by Secretary of State, of persons manufacturing or selling firearms, and to register therein every person who, having a place of business in his district, desires to be registered as a firearms dealer, and furnishes such particulars as may be prescribed by the Secretary of State and pays a fee of five shillings.

(2) Court to have power to cancel registration on conviction of registered person of an offence under the Acts, or any

offence against the Customs Acts in relation to the import or export of firearms.

7. Application of fees to be provided for.

8. Court to have power to forfeit firearm or cancel firearm certificate on convicting a person of an offence under the Act, or of an offence which makes him ineligible to hold such a certificate under Cl 1(4)(iv).

9. Constable to have power to demand production of firearm certificate by any person possessing, using or carrying a firearm and on failure or refusal to produce certificate, power to seize the weapon.

10. Justice of the Peace, if satisfied by information on oath that there is reasonable ground for suspecting that an offence under the Act has been, or is about to be, committeed, or that a person is in possession of firearms imported or about to be exported without proper authority, to have power to grant a warrant authorising any constable named therein to search places or persons for firearms, and to seize the firearms if found, or to examine a registered dealer's books.

11. The Secretary of State to have power to require, by Order, and by Regulations set out in the Order, that no firearms must be removed by any means of conveyance from one place in the United Kingdom to another, unless accompanied by a permit issued by or with the authority of the police of the district whence the removal takes place. Such power to be exercisable either generally, or as respects particular kinds of firearms, or particular modes of conveyance, or removals within, or between particular districts or localities.

Police to be given power to search for and detain firearms removed in contravention of such Order and Regulations.

12. Definition Clause:

The term 'firearm' includes a firearm of any description and an airgun or any other weapon from which any shot, bullet or other missile (including any noxious liquid or gas) can be discharged, and the term 'ammunition' means ammunition for any such firearm. Provided that in Great Britain a smoothbore shotgun and ammunition therefor shall not be deemed to be a firearm or ammunition respectively unless and until sold or removed for shipment either for exportation or carriage coastwise.

13. Saving for antique pistols and guns.

14. Application to Ireland.

15. General power to Secretary of State to make Rules for the carrying out of the Act; prescribe forms for gun and pistol certificates and for record of sales, and forms of licence for import; and by order to vary or add to the Schedule to the Act.

16. Pistols Act 1903 to be repealed. Section 1 of the Unlawful Drilling Act 1819 to be amended.

Schedule

Particulars to be entered in book by registered dealer:

1. Name and address of seller.
2. Name and address of purchaser.
3. When sale is to a person not a registered dealer, district in which firearm certificate is issued and date of notification of sale to Police.
4. Description, number and calibre of firearm.

Paragraph one refers to the limitation of the right to possess firearms and this is amplified in a summary of recommendations in the report, 'The right to purchase or possess a revolver or any other description of firearm as defined in the Bill, or ammunition for such weapons, shall be limited to persons, who, in the opinion of a Chief Officer of Police, may possess a firearm without danger to the public safety'. Any constitutional problems surrounding the restriction of an ancient right appear not to have troubled the committee, but the wording is important as it indicates that the committee accepted the existence of the right at that time and also that they were not seeking to extinguish the right, but to restrict it and make it subject to the approval of an official. The use of firearms as a means of defending one's person or property was, apparently, still accepted.

So, the first steps were taken. First an Act which, though bound to fail to have any real effect, was so apparently innocuous that it reached the Statute Book, and then, in the changed climate of Britain after the First World War, proposals based as much on external as internal considerations, to control all firearms except shotguns. It remained for the Home Office to commence consultations with interested parties prior to presenting their Bill to parliament.

3 Between Committees

The Firearms Bill did not reach parliament until 19 April 1920, when it was introduced into the House of Lords, but Home Office officials had obviously been very busy in the interim consulting various interested bodies; and the suggestions of the Blackwell Committee, though retaining their original shape, were much amended in detail. One cannot but speculate that, if the committee had been more broadly based, or if (like a later committee) it had taken evidence and opinions from interested parties, much of this work might have been avoided and the subsequent Bill might not have been as imperfect as it was. Examination of the Act indicates many of the areas in which amendments were made to the Blackwell Report.

The definition of a firearm in the Act was, 'Any lethal firearm or other weapon of any description from which any shot, bullet or other missile can be discharged, or any part thereof'. Experience was to show that this was far from perfect. The inclusion of the word 'lethal', which remains in the present definition, restricts the meaning to weapons capable of causing injury and excludes mere toys, but the phrase, 'other weapon of any description' remained vague and could possibly have included such things as crossbows or catapults! It was to be a further sixteen years before the term 'lethal barrelled weapon' was to be used to give a logical definition of the word firearm in this context. The definition was reduced in scope by providing that,

A smooth bore shotgun or air gun or air rifle (other than air guns or air rifles of a type declared by the Secretary of State under this Act to be specially dangerous) shall not in Great Britain be deemed to be a firearm for the purposes of this Act, except in the provisions relating to the removal of firearms from one place to another or for export.

This part of the definition meant that shotguns and air weapons were completely outside the scope of the Act for virtually all purposes, including such matters as the criminal use of firearms and possession by children or convicted criminals. No distinction was made between the various types of shotgun and so the sawn-off shotgun was excluded from any form of control.

Ammunition was defined as, 'Ammunition for any such firearm, and includes grenades, bombs and other similar missiles whether such missiles are capable of use with a firearm or not, and ingredients and components thereof'. Excluded from the Act was, 'Ammunition for a smooth bore shotgun or air gun or air rifle'. This definition, too, was found to be inadequate. The single ball projectiles used in shotguns were excluded from control and the provision about ingredients and components of ammunition must have caused some difficulty. The ingredients of shotgun ammunition are the same as those of rifle ammunition except for the projectile—both use propellant powders and primers. Persons who reloaded shotgun ammunition and the few people who were still using muzzle-loading guns must have had some problems in purchasing powder and primers. The reference to ingredients was dropped from later legislation.

Section 1 of the Act provided that

(1) A person shall not purchase, have in his possession, use or carry any firearm or ammunition unless he holds a certificate [in this Act called a firearm certificate] granted under this Section and in force at the time.

(2) A firearm certificate shall be granted by the Chief Officer of Police of the district in which the applicant for the certificate resides, if he is satisfied that:

  (i) the applicant is a person who has good reason for requiring such a certificate, and
  (ii) the applicant can be permitted to have in his possession, use and carry a firearm or ammunition without danger to the public safety or to the peace, and
  (iii) on payment of the appropriate fee.

Provided that a firearm certificate shall not be granted to a person whom the Chief Officer of Police has reason to believe to be:

  (i) a person who is by this Act prohibited from possessing, using or carrying a firearm, or
  (ii) a person of intemperate habits or unsound mind, or
  (iii) for any reason unfitted to be entrusted with firearms.

The firearm certificate was to be in a prescribed form (the document eventually became a small booklet) and was to specify, 'The nature and number of firearms to which it relates and, as respects ammunition, the quantities authorised to be purchased and to be held at any one time'. The certificate was to be valid for three years and to be renewable for three year periods. The weapons authorised by the certificate were to be specified in it and provision was made for variations, or application to the Chief Officer of Police, so that additional weapons could be acquired or existing weapons disposed of. Revocation of the certificate by the police was authorised if a holder was found to fall into one of the classes who were prohibited from holding a certificate either by virtue of convictions or for one of the reasons set out in Section 1. Power was granted for the Chief Officer to insert conditions on the grant of a certificate, but it appears that this was rarely done. Appeal to a Petty Sessional Court lay against any refusal by the police to grant, vary or renew a certificate. The fees suggested by the Blackwell Committee were applied, five shillings for the grant of a certificate (except where the grant applied only to firearms owned prior to the passing of the Act when the fee was 2s 6d). Renewal of a certificate was to cost 2s 6d, but there was apparently no fee for variations. Possession of a firearm without a certificate, or otherwise than as authorised by a certificate, was a summary offence rendering a person convicted liable to a fine of up to fifty pounds or to three months' imprisonment with or without hard labour.

At Section 1(8), the Act made provision for a number of exemptions from the requirement to hold a firearm certificate and many of these are clear evidence of the consultations held between the Home Secretary and interested bodies during the drafting stage of the Bill. Many of the exemptions remain in present legislation in similar terms, and these are more fully dealt with in Chapter 13. The 1920 exemptions, which mainly related to possession only and did not authorise acquisition, were:

(i) Members of the armed Service or police in connection with their duties.

(ii) Carriers or warehousemen in the course of their business (auctioneers were not then included).

(iii) Persons possessing firearms or ammunition as part of the equipment of a ship, but these were not to be brought ashore without a certificate or a permit issued by the police. (The current exemption also refers to signalling equipment for aerodromes.)

(iv) Members of rifle clubs or cadet corps approved by the Secretary of State, in connection with drill or target practice.

47

(v) Persons carrying a firearm for a certificate holder for sporting purposes.

(vi) Slaughtermen were authorised both to possess or acquire 'any humane killer' without a firearm certificate. Certain models of humane killer are, in fact, no more than modified pistols firing a normal cartridge and this exemption was subsequently changed to allow of possession only and to provide for a free certificate for purchases.

(vii) The exemption relating to persons conducting or carrying on a miniature rifle range (whether for a rifle club or otherwise and to persons using weapons at such ranges was identical to the current exemptions.

(viii) A special exemption in Section 14 provided that nothing in the Act should apply to the two Proof Houses operating under the Gun Barrel Proof Act 1868, or to persons taking weapons to or from the Proof House.

(ix) The exemption in relation to antiques was shortened from that contained in the Pistols Act 1903 to its present form, 'Nothing in this Act relating to firearms shall apply to an antique firearm which is sold, bought, carried or possessed as a curiosity or ornament'. No attempt was made to define antique any further. The definition in the Pistols Act was obviously found to be unsuitable and, indeed, during the debate in the Lords, it was said by the Earl of Onslow, 'I must confess that a precise definition of that word is beyond the powers of Her Majesty's Government. I can only say that the definition must be left to common sense'.

(x) The exemption relating to firearms dealers referred to 'any person carrying on the business of a gunsmith or dealer in firearms or of testing or proving firearms' and not to a registered firearms dealer. Thus a person carrying on an unregistered business would have committed no offence under this Section by his possession of firearms and ammunition, although he would have been penalised under the provisions relating to the registration of dealers. The anomaly was later removed by exempting only registered dealers.

(xi) Provision was made for the police to grant 'temporary permits', but this was restricted to persons who had been refused the grant of a certificate or whose certificate had been revoked. This must have caused problems, for example, when an executor came into possession of firearms the owner of which had died. On a strict interpretation of the Section, such a person had to apply for a certificate and be refused before he could be granted a temporary permit. This anomaly was also removed in later legislation.

(xii) There appeared at Section 1(8)(f) an exemption in favour of, 'An officer of the Post Office by having in his possession, using or carrying a firearm or ammunition when acting in the course of his duties'. This is not the exemption which permits the postman to deliver a parcel containing a firearm, that is covered under the exemption relating to carriers. This exemption appears to have envisaged the carrying and use of firearms by postal workers for the protection of the mails and of themselves. It was not re-enacted in subsequent legislation.

(xiii) Many of the retired and reserve officers who served in the First World War and who had been required to purchase their own pistols, had retained these weapons. Section 13(2) made provision for them to retain the weapons, without ammunition, without the requirement for a firearm certificate, provided they gave notice of the fact to the police and the Chief Officer agreed to dispense with a certificate. Such agreement was not to be given if the Chief Officer was of the opinion that the owner was not a person to whom a firearm certificate would be granted. This special exemption relating to trophies of war was modified in later legislation to allow only of the grant of a free certificate.

Restrictions on the manufacture and sale of firearms and ammunition were imposed by Section 2, 'A person shall not manufacture, sell, repair, test or prove, or expose for sale, or have in his possession for sale, repair, test or proof, firearms and ammunition by way of trade or business unless he is registered as a dealer in accordance with this Act'. Chief Officers of Police were required to maintain a register of dealers and to enter therein the name of any dealer who had a place of business in his area and who supplied the prescribed particulars and paid a fee of one pound. The area of discretion left to the police was limited. First, of course, they could refuse to register a person who was not a bona fide dealer by way of trade or business as he would not fall within the Section; second, they were permitted to refuse registration if they were satisfied that the person, 'Could not be permitted to carry on business without danger to the public safety or to the peace'. A right of appeal to Petty Sessions lay against a refusal to register. All registered dealers were required to maintain records and to make them available for inspection, a requirement similar to that under existing legislation. On convicting a registered dealer of an offence under the Act, or of an offence under the Customs Acts relating to the import or export of firearms or ammunition, the Courts were empowered to order the removal of the dealer from the register and to confiscate any stock in hand.

It was an offence to sell (which was, by the definition, to include any parting with possession) a firearm or ammunition to anyone other than a registered firearms dealer unless that person produced a firearm certificate authorising his possession of the weapon, or proved that he was exempt. Every person who sold a firearm or ammunition to anyone other than a registered dealer was required to enter the particulars in the firearm certificate and, in the case of the sale of a firearm, to notify details of the sale to the Chief Officer of Police who issued the certificate within forty-eight hours.

Recognition was given in the Act to 'rifle clubs or cadet corps approved by the Secretary of State'. Members of such organisations were permitted to use firearms in connection with their activities without holding a firearm certificate and provision was made for the grant of a free certificate to the responsible officer of a club in respect of weapons held by the club. The system adopted to secure the Home Secretary's approval persists to the present. Cadet corps connected with the armed services pursued their applications through service channels. Other clubs could, if they wished, make direct approach to the Home Office, but the normal procedure was for the club to be affiliated to one of the national bodies controlling the sport, The National Rifle Association for fullbore shooting and the National Smallbore Rifle Association (then the Society of Miniature Rifle Clubs) for smallbore shooting. When the national organisation was satisfied with the organisation and constitution of the club, it would make application to the Home Office who would arrange for enquiries to be made by the police into the status of the club and its officers. If all this was satisfactory, a 'certificate of approval' would be given.

The restriction on sale to or possession by young persons referred only to children under 14 and penalised both possession by them and supply to them except in circumstances where the child was exempted by the Act from the requirement to hold a certificate. Supply of a firearm by any means to a person who was believed to be either drunk or of unsound mind rendered the offender liable to a fine of twenty pounds or imprisonment for up to three months. Certain convicted persons were, for specified periods, prohibited from possessing, using or carrying a firearm or ammunition.

(i) A person sentenced to penal servitude or imprisonment for a term of three months or more was prohibited for five years from the date of his release.

(ii) Any person
    (a) on licence from prison or
    (b) subject to police supervision, or
    (c) subject to a recognisance to keep the peace, a condition of which was that he should not possess firearms was prohibited during the term of the licence or recognisance. Because shotguns and air weapons were, under the terms the definition, outside the scope of the Act, the prohibitions did not apply to them and there was no penalty attached to the possession of a shotgun by a child, drunkard or convict.

The first reference to 'prohibited weapons' in a statute appeared in Section 6, but this referred only to weapons and ammunition 'for the discharge of any noxious liquid, gas or other thing'. Machine guns and similar weapons which now fall into the same category were not mentioned and these, therefore, were subject to the type of control applicable to pistols and rifles. The authority of the Admiralty, Army Council or Air Council was required before anyone could lawfully manufacture, deal in or possess prohibited weapons.

Efforts to prevent the use of firearms in crime were given little direct attention. Section 7 created the offence of possessing a firearm with intent to endanger life or cause serious injury to property which still exists as Section 16 of the 1968 Act. However, the 1920 Act had excluded shotguns and air weapons from the terms of this offence by virtue of the definition clause. The wording of the offence had been taken from Section 3 of the Explosive Substances Act 1883 and the 1920 Act made the offender liable to a penalty under the earlier Statute of up to twenty years' imprisonment.

Enforcement of the Act was facilitated by powers granted to the police and magistrates. Police were authorised to require the production of a firearm certificate from any person whom they believed to be in possession of a firearm or ammunition. Failure or refusal to produce the certificate, or to show that one of the exemptions applied, authorised the officer to seize the weapon and require the person's name and address. If this was not given, or if the officer suspected that the name and address were false or that the person was likely to abscond, he was empowered to make an arrest without warrant. Magistrates were authorised to grant search warrants on information on oath that an offence under the Act was being committed and Courts, having convicted a person of an offence under the Act, or of an offence which would make the convicted person ineligible to hold a firearm certificate, were empowered to confiscate any firearm involved and to order the cancellation of the firearm certificate.

Provisions corresponding to those in Section 6 of the 1968 Act gave the Home Secretary powers to make orders to regulate the movement of firearms or ammunition within the United Kingdom or for export. Other powers enabled the Home Secretary to make Orders and Rules specifying the documents to be used under the Act and the details which had to be entered; for regulating the manner in which Chief Officers of Police were to carry out their duties; and 'generally for carrying the Act into effect'. The Pistols Act of 1903 was repealed and the 1920 Act was applied, with considerable variations, to Scotland and Ireland.

The Bill was introduced in the House of Lords and, opening the debate on the Second Reading for the government, the Earl of Onslow said that it had two objects, 'Firstly to afford an effective system of control over the possession, use and carrying of firearms and, so far as possible, to secure that they did not come into the hands of criminals or otherwise undesirable persons. Secondly, to enable us to carry out our obligations under the Arms Traffic Convention recently signed in Paris.' The noble Lord's brief was obviously compiled from the Blackwell Report and he went on to recite the statistics and conclusions shown in the report, including the suggestion that the reduction in numbers of criminals using firearms during the war years was due primarily to the Defence of the Realm Regulations. The Bill received an unopposed Second Reading which indicates that it was entirely acceptable in principle—a dramatic change in attitude from that which faced previous legislation.

During the Committee Stage, concern was expressed about the sale of pistols to persons under eighteen. The Bill prohibited possession of firearms by persons under fourteen and the Earl of Onslow pointed out that Chief Officers would be able to refuse the grant of a certificate to a person under eighteen.

Besides the two obvious conditions that the person must be of good character and not likely to use his weapon for an unlawful purpose, it is the opinion of the Government that the applicant must make out a good prima facie case for acquiring the weapon. It is difficult to see how a boy of under 18 years of age is likely to establish such a case for carrying a pistol. Speaking generally, it must be assumed that the ground on which a revolver will be applied for and on which the application will be granted is for the protection of the applicant's house. By Clause 4 it will be seen that power is given to the Secretary of State to make rules for regulating the manner in which Chief Officers of Police are to carry out their duties under the Act. This provision will enable the Secretary of State to prohibit the issue of a licence to a boy under 18 except in the most unusual circumstances.

The Committee Stage concluded with no major alterations to the Bill which received its Third Reading on 6 May 1920 and was sent down to the Commons.

In the Commons, the debate on the Second Reading was opened by the Home Secretary and, in elaborating on the objects of the Bill, Mr Shortt pointed out:

The first proposals are designed to maintain greater control so that, as far as possible, criminals or weak minded persons and those who should not have firearms may be prevented from having these dangerous and lethal firearms. As far as possible we have provided that legitimate sport should not be in any way hampered, and so that any person who has good reason for possessing firearms, or as to whom there is no objection, may be entitled to have them; but we hope, by means of this Bill, to prevent criminals and persons of that description from being able to have revolvers and to use them.

Despite these reassurances, the Member for Whitechapel, Mr Kiley, had considerable misgivings. He was of the opinion that a dangerous burglar who desired to obtain firearms would find it easy to do so by burgling a place where they were kept in stock and where he could get them wholesale:

It cannot, therefore, be necessary to pass such a drastic measure as this is in order to deal with a case of that character. While it achieves no useful purpose, so far as I can see, it does interfere with legitimate traders. So far as burglars are concerned it will have no effect. These men are dangerous, but there is nothing in this Bill which will adequately deal with them.

The constitutional right to keep arms was called in question by this Bill, although it had been made clear from the outset that it was not intended that the right to keep arms for the defence of person or household should be completely extinguished. Only one Member, Lt.-Commander Kenworthy of Hull, expressed grave concern at this. He pointed out that there was

a much greater principle involved than the mere prevention of discharged prisoners having weapons. In the past one of the most jealously guarded rights of the English was that of carrying arms. For long our people fought with great tenacity for the right of carrying the weapon of the day, the sword, and it was only in recent times that it was given up. It has been a well known object of the Central Government of this Country to deprive the people of their weapons.

Other Members raised their hands in horror at what Earl Winterton called, 'This most extraordinary theory of constitutional history and law which holds that the State is an aggressive body endeavouring to deprive private individuals of the weapons which Heaven had given into their hands.' But the Commander interrupted to expound his understanding of the principles, 'The very foundation of the liberty of the subject in this country is that he can, if driven to do so, resist. You can only govern with the consent of the people'. This view was countered by Major H. Barnes, who felt that:

There could be nothing more dangerous at the present time, or indeed at any time, than to lead the people of the country to believe that their method of redress was in the direction of armed resistance to the State. The time has gone for that. We have in our methods of elections, in our access to Parliament, and in other ways, means of redress against the State which in times past were not afforded; and some of us, looking back into history, may believe that it was because at one time people were able to carry weapons and use them against the State that we are in the happy position in which we find ourselves today . . . Whenever the Executive tends to aggression, whether it be against life and liberty or against property, I think the feeling of the House is that the subject should have free appeal to the Courts, and I am quite sure that the noble

Lord [Earl Winterton] will agree that nothing should be done
to bar the subject from that redress, and it is by giving him
opportunity through Parliament and through the Courts to find
redress that we shall most effectively turn his attention away
from using weapons.

It is clear that the House as a whole did not share in the concern
felt by Kiley and Kenworthy. Many Members had reservations
about specific aspects, particularly in regard to the application of
the Bill to Ireland and the method of enforcement there. To a lesser
extent, the granting of executive powers to the police was a matter
for concern, yet it is clear that the spirit of the Bill had overwhelming
support and it passed its Second Reading by no less than 254 votes
to 6. Its remaining stages caused no difficulties, and so the first Act
to impose stringent controls on some firearms became law. Parliament had not quite extinguished the right to keep arms, for it is
clear that they believed that they had preserved a conditional right
to keep arms for the defence of the person or household. Nevertheless, so much of the right as remained was heavily bound up in the
discretion of Chief Officers of Police.

There is evidence to suggest that the police welcomed the Act and
made vigorous efforts at stringent enforcements from the start.
Before 1920 was out, there had been two complaints in parliament
about over-zealous enforcement, apparently involving both shotguns
and antiques which were excluded from the Act. The Home Secretary
admitted that he had received other complaints and found it necessary to issue instructions to the police to 'assist them in carrying out,
on a fair and reasonable basis, the administration of the Act which
was intended to restrict the possession of firearms to fit persons
having good reasons for possessing or acquiring them.'

Loopholes in the Act became apparent fairly quickly and numerous questions in parliament related to toy pistols which were made
exactly like a normal revolver, but in which the barrel was not
bored through. Many instances were given where these weapons,
bought without restriction, were bored out and subsequently involved in crimes or accidents. A Private Member's Bill was introduced
in 1928 in an attempt to bring such weapons under control, but this
was not proceeded with. The government felt unable to legislate
against toys and it was not until the definition of 'firearm' was
revised by a later committee that the Courts were able to hold that
a blank cartridge weapon which was capable of being easily con-

verted to discharge a projectile was subject to controls (see Cafferata *v*. Wilson—Chapter 13).

The scope of the controls had been widened and the number of offences increased. It is not surprising, therefore, that the number of summary prosecutions was much higher than those under the Pistols Act (26 in 1908 and 16 in 1909). According to a parliamentary reply, 1926 saw 618 prosecutions and 486 convictions of which 396 prosecutions and 313 convictions were for possessing a firearm without a certificate. The number of prosecutions and convictions in 1929 fell slightly to 386 and 290 respectively.

The controls imposed under the 1920 Act did not, as some people appear to have expected, prevent criminals from obtaining firearms. Although such statistics as exist do not allow of valid comparisons, the problem was raising its head in the House of Commons with considerable frequency in the early 1930s. Two questions in 1931 sought still stricter controls on firearms and increased penalties for criminal use. The increasing use of the motor car by criminals led to the introduction of the term, 'motor bandits' who, possibly because of their novelty, achieved some notoriety.

The failure of the 1920 Act to cater adequately for the use of firearms by criminals, for example, in completely excluding shotguns and air weapons from all its offences, finally led to an attempt to tackle the problem directly with the introduction to parliament of the Firearms and Imitation Firearms (Criminal Use) Bill 1933. In presenting the Bill for its Second Reading in the Lords, the Earl of Lucan said, 'My Lords, the profession of a gunman is, happily a novel one in this country, but latterly the combination of the revolver and the motor car has given the criminally minded a power against the community which might grow to serious proportions if it is not promptly and efficiently checked'. In attempting to efficiently check the problem, parliament addressed themselves to the criminal use of firearms and imitation firearms, but chose to ignore the criminal use of motor cars. It is by no means established which of these two elements is the more important in a modern armed crime, but there are good grounds for suggesting that it is the car that is most vital to a successful crime. Only in 1970 is parliament, on the advice of a committee, considering the power to disqualify for the criminal use of motor cars.

For the purposes of this Bill a new definition was to bring in all classes of firearm and so penalise the criminal use of shotguns and air weapons. An imitation firearm was to include anything having the appearance of a firearm, whether or not it was capable of discharging a missile. The Bill created offences which are now to be found in Section 17 of the 1968 Act:

(i) Using a firearm or imitation firearm with intent to resist arrest.

(ii) Being in possession of a firearm or imitation firearm at the time of committing, or when arrested for, certain specified offences.

It was specifically provided that the penalty for these offences should be in addition to any other penalties imposed, and the laying of either charge was a bar to the summary disposal of any other indictable offence involved in the case. The Act also provided that a firearm or imitation firearm was to be regarded as an 'offensive weapon' for the purposes of the offence of armed robbery, or the offence of possessing offensive weapons by night with intent to commit a felony.

In the following year, the law relating to the possession and acquisition of firearms by young people was tightened, by amending the provisions of Section 3 of the 1920 Act. The 1934 Act provided that a person under 17 should not purchase or hire a firearm or ammunition and, by a fairly complicated amendment of the definition, shotguns and air weapons were brought within the terms of this Section only. The prohibition on possession by persons under 14 remained in respect on firearms other than shotguns or air weapons, so that the position was that no one under 17 could purchase his own firearm or ammunition, but if they were bought for him, he could possess and use them. If under 14, a person could not use pistols or rifles except where one of the exemptions in the 1920 Act applied.

The 1920 Act had been the first effort at strict controls and it was to be expected that experience would indicate faults in the drafting of the Act. It had concentrated, in the first place, on controls applicable to everyone, but amending legislation had been required to encompass the criminal use of firearms, suggesting that controls alone were not achieving their purpose. Many of the drafting errors can, perhaps, be laid at the door of the Blackwell Committee which failed to take account of the assistance and advice which outside bodies could have given. The subsequent consultations within the framework laid down by the Report, did not eliminate all the errors and omissions. The problem was by no means solved and it was very clear that some of the basic definitions upon which the legislation had been built were inadequate. The Home Office therefore sought to rationalise and clarify the law through the medium of a committee on the 'Statutory Definition and Classification of Firearms and Ammunition'.

4 The Bodkin Committee

By a Warrant of Appointment dated 2 February 1934, the Home Secretary appointed a committee to

consider the various types of firearms and similar weapons capable of being used for the discharge of missiles or noxious substances, and ammunition therefor, and to enquire and report whether, in the interests of public safety, any amendment to the law is necessary or desirable in respect of the definition or classification of such weapons and ammunition.

The committee was rather more broadly based than had been the Blackwell Committee. Its Chairman, Sir Archibald Bodkin, K.C.B., was a recently retired Director of Public Prosecutions and, in addition to a number of civil servants, the committee had three Members of Parliament (including one whose boast was that he had left school at the age of twelve to work in a coal mine). The Chief Constable of Leeds and His Majesty's Chief Inspector of Explosives added their expertise. Several of the members are listed in the 1934 edition of *Who's Who* and three of them listed shooting amongst their major recreations. This broader base for the committee was, however, not considered sufficient by them, and they received oral evidence from 38 witnesses representing 21 organisations—gunmakers, butchers, police, lawyers, sportsmen and so on—together with written memoranda from ten other organisations or individuals. They also examined many exhibits, caused various tests to be conducted and examined statistics supplied to them by the police.

Their Report (Cmd 4758–1934), submitted on 8 November 1934, is both lengthy and, in many respects, detailed. It was made clear from the start that they were 'not required to consider whether any alterations are desirable in the general statutory scheme of control of firearms or ammunition or the manner in which it is administered' (Para. 5). In other words, they had no brief to examine the effectiveness of controls on rifles or pistols, or to suggest any major changes in the system of controls. They were merely to make suggestions about whether this or that weapon should be brought more strictly under control, or whether relaxations could be made in respect of other weapons.

After careful consideration of the legislation then current, the committee looked at some of its effects. Apart from complaints which were thought to be of a minor character, it was considered that the police had administered the Act efficiently. As to its effects on trade, they said:

> It is obvious, and it has been confirmed by evidence that the effect of the Act must have been to reduce considerably the market for firearms in this country and that the trade had suffered accordingly. Manufacturers of and dealers in firearms have nevertheless borne their losses with resignation and have loyally co-operated with the authorities in the measures for the restriction of firearms during the past 14 years.

In looking at the possible effects of the controls on armed crime, they said:

> We recognise that no scheme of controls can make it impossible for the determined criminal to obtain possessions of firearms and ammunition, or for careless persons to inflict injuries on themselves or others. So far, however, as it is reasonably possible by legislative and executive measures to reduce the risk of such evils, we think that the Statutes already referred to and the efforts of those concerned in their enforcement can be regarded as highly successful, and we are of the opinion that, in view of 14 years experience of the working of the Statute, no alteration of substance, apart from those recommended in this report, is required.

This is one of the few statements in the report which is not substantiated by evidence. The statistics supplied referred only to those weapons which were outside the controls. No comparative figures were obtained on the criminal use of all types of firearms prior to and following the introduction of controls, despite the fact that very little effort would have produced figures comparable to those supplied for 1911–13 and 1915–17 in London. It is a great pity that such information was not obtained and examined, for without something of the sort the relative success or otherwise of the controls can hardly be objectively gauged.

The figures supplied to the committee are reproduced at Appendix II of their Report and the main table refers to 'Cases known to the Police of England, Wales and Scotland involving weapons which were not controlled by the Firearms Act 1920 in the three years ended 28th February 1934' (see Table 6). It is important to note, first, that these figures relate to England, Wales and Scotland, and cannot be compared with previous figures which related to England and Wales or to the Metropolitan Police District only; and further, that they relate to a period of three years. The yearly average has been shown in brackets at the end of each line and as a separate heading at the bottom of each table. The system of classifying incidents as accident or crime is in no way comparable to the present system. It is clear from Paragraph 92 of the Report (referred to later) that instances where young people caused injuries (and in one case even death) by the improper use of air weapons were categorised as accidents. Such instances are today recorded as crimes and, in fact, make up the greater proportion of all crimes involving air weapons.

The committee considered in detail various types of weapon and the controls which they thought appropriate for them, bearing in mind the information they had concerning the legitimate uses of such weapons and the incidence of crime and accidents.

Section 1 firearms. It was recommended that all types of rifle and pistol should continue to be the subject of the strictest controls. The committee devoted considerable attention to the place of .22 rifles in these controls. They had before them a good deal of evidence about the legitimate use of such weapons and of the substantial reductions in dealings in such weapons since the passing of the 1920 Act. They noted that these rifles were, to a certain extent, privileged under the Act in that they could be used on rifle ranges and at shooting galleries without a certificate and that responsible officers of approved clubs could obtain free certificates. Strong representations were made that such weapons should be freed from control provided the barrel length exceeded twenty inches and, whilst the committee had some sympathy with this view, they found themselves unable to accept it, particularly in view of the fact that .22 ammunition was also suitable for use in pistols and they could not recommend that the ammunition should be unrestricted. They therefore recommended that these rifles should continue to be subject to controls, but they thought it,

Desirable that Chief Constables, in considering applications for

TABLE 6 *Return to the Bodkin Committee of firearms not controlled by the Firearms Act, 1920*

(*a*) *Weapons used or carried by criminals*

Weapon	Sui-cide	Discharged			Not discharged		Totals (Av.)	
		Fatal cases	Serious injury	Slight or no injury	Used to intimi-date	Found in poss'n		
Shotgun	378	28	18	20	10	18	94	(31)
Sawn-off shotgun	1		1	2	3	2	8	(3)
Smoothbore pistols	16	5	5	4	2	9	25	(8)
Toy pistol converted	2		2	12	8	28	50	(17)
Toy pistol unconverted				7	26	96	129	(43)
Air pistol			1		6	36	43	(14)
Air gun	1			2		1	3	(1)
Totals	398	33	27	47	55	190	352	
Average per year	133	11	9	16	18	63	117	

(*b*) '*Accidents*'

Weapon	Fatal injuries	Serious injuries	Slight injuries	Totals	(Av.)
Shotgun	161	111	101	373	(124)
Sawn off shotgun	—	—	—	—	
Smoothbore pistols	5	4	14	23	(8)
Toy pistols converted	1	4	12	17	(6)
Toy pistols unconverted	1†	4	20	25	(8)
Air pistols	—	9	75	84	(28)
Air guns	1	63	239	303	(101)
Totals	169	195	461	825	
Average per year	58	65	154	278	

† death from tetanus as a result of a finger wound.

firearm certificates in respect of such rifles, and ammunition therefor, should keep in view the many purposes for which these rifles may properly be used and the considerable quantities of ammunition which normally require to be expended.

Whilst accepting that the decision whether to grant or refuse a certificate was (subject to the right of appeal) one for the Chief Constable, they made it clear that they thought that certificates for .22 rifles should, in suitable cases, be fairly freely granted.

The committee also gave a good deal of attention to humane killers which, it will be recalled, were subject to a fairly wide exemption under the 1920 Act. They drew a very clear distinction between the 'free bullet' humane killer, which is simply an adapted pistol firing a normal cartridge, and the 'captive bolt' humane killer in which a blank cartridge is used to throw forward a bolt which penetrates the animal's skull. The bolt is not capable of leaving the weapon and, therefore, the committee had doubts about whether such implements were 'firearms' within the definition; further, they said, 'We do not consider it necessary that the view should be adopted that the Act applies'. Accordingly, they recommended in Paragraph 56(8), 'The captive bolt type of instrument should be free from control'. As to the 'free bullet' humane killer, they found much wrong with the framing of the 1920 exemption and suggested that a firearm certificate should be required to purchase or acquire such weapons, but that a fairly wide range of persons should be authorised to possess them in the course of their trade. They saw additional merit in this distinction in that it would tend to encourage the use of captive bolt killers where they were appropriate. 'Free bullet' killers are, of course, essential in certain circumstances and the committe made special reference to the necessary use of this type of instrument by, for example, the Royal Society for the Prevention of Cruelty to Animals.

The distinctions made by the committee still apply and the captive bolt humane killer appears to be outside any strict interpretation of the definition of firearm, but this is one of the suggestions of the committee which appears to have escaped the notice of those responsible for administering the Act. Captive bolt killers appear invariably to be subject to the weighty procedures involved in the issue of a free firearm certificate and no distinctions are made between the two types, indeed, it seems in many cases that the distinctions are either not known or not understood.

Shotguns. In considering the question of smoothbore shotguns, the committee noted the remarks of the Blackwell Report and, 'After carefully weighing the evidence, found no reason to take a different view'. They noted that the police returns had shown this class of weapon to be responsible for more suicides and accidents than any other class of weapon shown in the returns (cases involving pistols and rifles were not included, but it seems doubtful if the numbers would have even approached those for shotguns) but, they said:

> When it is considered that this is the only type of firearm (apart from smoothbore pistols) which has been sold without restriction, that in rural districts it is a common and necessary weapon, and that accordingly the numbers in almost daily use by private persons far exceeds those of any other type of firearm, the figures in the table are not surprising and cannot be regarded as excessive . . . They very general use of sporting shotguns, often in circumstances in which accidents are very liable to occur, will inevitably result in casualties more or less serious. There is no doubt that the great demand for these guns will continue and it does not seem likely that if placed under control the number in use would be materially reduced. Chief Officers of Police would not be likely, in the vast majority of cases, to find any substantial grounds for refusing to issue firearm certificates to persons genuinely requiring such guns for sporting purposes, and control would have little or no effect in reducing the number of accidents arising from the use of this very popular type of weapon.

Accordingly, the committee recommended that the ordinary sporting shotgun should continue to be excluded from any restrictions on purchase or use. Smooth-barrell pistols and sawn-off shotguns were, however, a different matter. It was noted that the definition in the 1920 Act had not made clear what class of smoothbore shotgun was exempt and, as a result, smoothbore pistols were commonly considered to be outside the controls. Despite a limited legitimate use for such weapons, the committee felt that they should be included within the controls. Sawn-off shotguns, which were also outside the scope of the 1920 Act, had been used in nine criminal cases (one of which was a suicide) in the three years reviewed, and the persons using them were all found to be over 17 years of age. No legitimate uses were seen for the sawn-off shotgun and the committee recommended, not only that they should be subject to controls, but that the shortening of shotgun barrels without authority should be made a separate offence. To cater for these recommendations, it was suggested that only those shotguns which had barrels exceeding twenty inches in length should be excluded from the controls. As to shotgun ammunition, the committee was concerned to find that considerable quantities of bulleted cartridges were being sold outside the controls because they were designed for use in smoothbore guns. These varied from .22 'BB' caps to the 12-bore rifled slug. After much consideration, they recommended that the only ammunition which should be exempted under this heading should be, 'Cartridges containing five or more shot, none of which is of a diameter greater than one half the diameter of the cartridge'. With a modification to specify the precise diameter of the pellets, this suggestion remains effective today.

Air weapons.   The committee appeared to have some special concern about air pistols and their statistics had been gathered to show these separately. The information contained in the table was elaborated on in Paragraph 92, and it must be kept in mind that the figures quoted relate to a three year period and to the whole of England, Wales and Scotland.

Air pistols: Criminal use—43 cases; in 6 the weapon was used to intimidate, but not discharged; in 36 the weapon was found in possession on arrest, but not used; and in the remaining case a lunatic shot and injured a baby and then committed suicide by disconnecting the gas meter and setting the house on fire.

Air pistols: Accidents—84 cases of accidental injury were reported, 9 being serious (8 of these being eye cases) and the remainder slight. In 70 of the 84 cases the person discharging the weapon was under 17 years of age.

Air gun, air rifles: Criminal use—4 cases occurred, one in which the air rifle was fired to avoid arrest, but no injury was caused, one found in possession on arrest; the other two were cases of suicide or attempted suicide.

Air guns, air rifles: Accidents—303 cases of accidental injury were reported; 63 cases were serious (of which 53 were eye injuries), 239 only slight. One injury proved to be fatal. This was a case of a boy improperly using an air rifle, the pellet from which entered the eye of another boy, who died under

anaesthetics during an operation for the removal of the eye.
In 233 cases, the persons discharging the weapons were under
the age of 17.

The most significant factor to emerge from these figures is a change
in reporting procedures. Those incidents where air weapons are fired
by persons under 17 (usually at persons under 17) and which resulted
in injury were then recorded as accidents. Virtually without exception
they are today recorded as crimes involving firearms.

In relation to air weapons generally, the committee concluded:

> It appears from these particulars that air weapons are little
> used by criminals. Cases of their use for intimidation may now
> be dealt with under the Firearms and Imitation Firearms
> (Criminal Use) Act 1933. As regards the number of accidents,
> those in which serious injuries were caused do not in our view
> amount to an alarming figure having regard to the very large
> number of all kinds of air weapons in use.

It was found impossible to establish even an approximate figure
of the number of air weapons in the country, but the numbers of
foreign-made weapons imported to Great Britain were 67,000 in
1931; 25,000 in 1932 and 42,000 in 1933—134,000 in three years
to be added to the very large number of weapons manufactured at
home. The committee further noted that, 'The great majority of
accidents were caused by persons under 17 years of age, a position
which the Firearms Act 1934 will, no doubt, considerably improve'.
(That Act prohibited purchase of air weapons and ammunition by
persons under 17.) It was concluded that it was neither possible
nor desirable to attempt any controls on ammunition for air
weapons.

The possibility of there being developed an air weapon of power
similar to that of cartridge weapons occupied a good deal of time.
The 1920 Act had made provision for the Home Secretary to make
rules declaring certain air weapons to be specially dangerous and
so bring them within the firearm certificate procedure. The Home
Office had apparently reached agreement with British manufacturers
to limit the power of their weapons so that, at five feet, the pellet
would not completely penetrate 7 strawboards, each $\frac{3}{64}$ in. thick
and packed tightly together. After opinions from a number of
sources and arranging for experiments to be carried out, the committee suggested that the power to declare certain air weapons

specially dangerous should be retained, and that a standard based on penetration in deal boards ($\frac{1}{2}$ in., for pistols and 1 in. for rifles) should be the criteria beyond which further consideration should be given to declaring air weapons specially dangerous.

Prohibited weapons. The committee noted with approval the special restrictions placed on any weapon 'designed for the discharge of any noxious liquid, gas or other thing', but suggested that the word 'designed' in the definition should be changed to 'designed or adapted for the discharge' so as to bring within the Section articles which, though not designed for such a purpose, were, with minor alterations, capable of being put to use. It was noted, however, that machine guns were not specially provided for, and were subject only to firearm certificate procedures. This was a matter of concern, particularly in regard to sub-machine guns which, they had been informed, 'are popular weapons in America, particularly amongst bandits'. No legitimate civilian use was seen for these weapons and it was recommended that they be categorised as prohibited weapons.

Toy and blank cartridge weapons. The problem of the blank cartridge pistol which was easily converted to fire live ammunition presented the committee with the practical difficulty of attempting to create a legislative distinction between the convertible and non-convertible types. They found this difficult and the majority suggested that the recommendations made to subject all bulleted cartridges to full controls was, when taken in conjunction with the provisions of the Firearms and Imitation Firearms (Criminal Use) Act, a sufficient answer to the problem. A minority of the committee thought that an attempt should be made to legislate specifically against convertible weapons. In the event, no such legislation was included, but the new definition of 'firearm' was so drawn that a judge was later able to decide that pistols capable of easy conversion fell within the controls (see Cafferata *v.* Wilson, Chapter 13). Whether this was the intention of the draftsman or not is a matter for speculation. The position of blank cartridges under the 1920 Act was obscure and it was recommended that these should be the subject of a special exemption.

A number of other types of weapon were considered in less detail and the recommendations can be summarised:

Antiques: to remain exempt—no attempt was made at an exhaustive definition.

Trophies: Any dispensations from the requirement to obtain a firearm certificate should be subject to triennial renewal. When legislation was introduced, the basis of the exemption was changed and the subsequent requirement was that a free firearm certificate should be obtained.

Miscellaneous weapons: A variety of weapons from 'watch chain' pistols to 'cement guns' used for shooting cement into fissures in gas retorts, were considered. It was felt that the definition clause would cater for all of them. If the article was a weapon, if it was lethal, and if it was capable of discharging a missile, the appropriate degree of control was thought to be suitable in most cases.

Silencers and sound moderators: It was recommended that these should be deemed to be 'part' of a firearm and so subjected to full controls.

Signalling apparatus: The exemption relating to ship's equipment was to be extended to include signalling devices at aerodromes. Any other legitimate user was to be entitled to a free certificate.

A number of other matters outside the strict terms of reference were also considered and the recommendations made included suggestions for clarifying the convictions which should involve prohibition under the Act; redrafting the Section which related to possession of firearms with intent to endanger life, etc.; a recommendation that a fee be charged for the renewal of a dealer's registration; removal of the anomaly which permitted certain persons to possess firearms without a certificate, but made no provision for such persons to acquire them legitimately; suggested clarification of the words 'purchase' and 'sell' in the 1920 Act; and suggestions for clarifying the form of certificate. Three other matters outside the terms of reference were covered and these are worthy of attention.

There was concern about the identification of weapons. Many of the cheaper, imported firearms did not bear a serial number and it was suggested that it would be of assistance to the police if all such weapons were numbered in such a way that they could be traced. A fairly complicated system of compelling importers to mark weapons was suggested, but this was not proceeded with and, in retrospect, it is possible to say that the cumbersome and complicated procedure would have achieved little, if anything. As the manufacture of weapons became concentrated in larger factories, the practice of numbering weapons became almost universal, though substantial numbers of older, un-numbered weapons still exist.

It was noted that the 1920 Act gave Chief Constables an implied authority to impose conditions on the grant of a firearm certificate, but this was rarely done. The committee therefore recommended the insertion of standard conditions in all certificates to require the safe custody of weapons when not in use, the reporting of any theft or loss of a weapon, and the notification of any change of address. These standard conditions were later included in the Firearm Rules and imposed on every certificate.

Complaints were made by the police about the system of appeals to Petty Sessional Courts. It was pointed out that, in some of the large force areas, there might be as many as twenty or thirty Petty Sessional Divisions and different views had been taken of similar cases within one police district. Chief Officers complained that they had difficulty in deciding how to interpret the effects of these decisions on their policies, and they suggested that it would be more satisfactory if appeals were made to a Court of Quarter Sessions, which, being a more permanently constituted court, would be more likely to adopt a more consistent attitude. No evidence was produced to support the view that Petty Sessions decisions had caused difficulty, but the committee accepted it and recommended that the venue for appeals be changed accordingly. They said, rather surprisingly, 'It does not appear to us likely that appeals of this character would involve any heavy costs, because in most cases it would not be necessary for counsel or solicitors to be instructed on either side'. In view of the representations made by the police, it might be concluded that appeals to Petty Sessions were far from rare, but since the change of venue appeals have been extremely rare. It seems unlikely that any layman would venture into a Court of Quarter Sessions without the assistance of lawyers and there is little doubt that the cost and complications of this appeal procedure have deterred people from appealing.

The Bodkin Committee Report represents a careful and detailed examination of most of the matters within its terms of reference and, in the main, its recommendations were quickly adopted. The fact that an examination of the effectiveness of legislative controls was outside the terms of reference is a matter for regret, for if the committee had approached this question with the thoroughness they applied to many other aspects, the results might well have been of the utmost value.

The Firearms (Amendment) Act 1936 amended the 1920 Act broadly in accordance with the recommendations of the Bodkin

Report, but the amending Act was longer than the amended Act and, taken in conjunction with the other two Acts in force, the result was, to say the least, untidy. Consolidating legislation was obviously envisaged when the 1936 Act was introduced and all the existing legislation was brought together in the Firearms Act 1937. This Act was to stand for 25 years and to provide a system of control which appears to have been largely accepted by the shooting community and liberally applied by the police. The Act still forms the basis of controls, but has been amended by the Airguns, Shotguns Etc., Act 1962, the Firearms Act 1965 and, with the introduction of shotgun controls, by the Criminal Justice Act 1967. Each of these Acts, and the amendments they made, will be discussed later.

Statistics relating to the criminal use of firearms during the period immediately prior to the Second World War do not appear to have been gathered, a fact which in itself indicates a satisfactory state of affairs. One set of figures was given in a parliamentary answer and these showed that in the eighteen months between 1 July 1936 and 31 December 1937 only 20 persons arrested in the Metropolitan Police District had been found in possession of firearms. Of these, 12 had air weapons and one a toy pistol. This can only be considered a very satisfactory state of affairs and the average of about 14 cases for one year compares favourably with the returns of similar cases for the periods 1911–13 and 1915–17 when the figures were 41 and 18 respectively, although it has to be borne in mind that the greater reduction—41 to 18—was achieved without any real firearms controls.

5 The Second World War and After

The outbreak of the Second World War in September 1939 moved any questions on firearms controls into the background. When the 'Phoney War' phase ended after the evacuation from Dunkirk, the government found itself making substantial demands on legitimate firearms users. Urgent appeals went out for weapons of all descriptions to arm the Local Defence Volunteers, and many thousands of privately owned firearms were handed in at police stations for distribution to the rather motley companies of elderly or very young men with their 'LDV' armbands. Rifle clubs became centres of instruction for both reserve and regular forces. The plea for weapons was not restricted to this country and appeals were made to American civilians for certain firearms. As time passed the weird assortment of shotguns, sporting rifles and even pikes with which the LDV were armed were slowly replaced with more suitable weapons and the name of the unit was changed to the 'Home Guard'. By the time of the invasion of Europe, this was a relatively well armed body.

During this time millions of men of many nationalities were under arms in this country and, in addition to the regular soldiers, such reserve units as the Home Guard were fully equipped with rifles, sub-machine guns and other small arms, many of which were kept in the men's homes. Government requests for certain weapons continued all through the war and as late as March 1945, the Secretary for War was explaining that the government was still requesting civilian owners of automatic pistols to either give them or sell them to the government because no such weapons were made in the United Kingdom and the government relied on the United States and on civilian owners in this country to meet their requirements (parliamentary reply 20 March 1945).

When the war ended in 1945 large numbers of returning servicemen retained weapons as souvenirs, a fact which was disputed by the Home Secretary who claimed that the military authorities had instituted stringent checks to ensure that weapons were not brought in from abroad. Nevertheless, when an amnesty (under which illegally-held weapons could be surrendered without fear of prosecution) was held for a six-week period in 1946, 75,000 illegal weapons were surrendered, including 59,000 pistols and 1,580 machine guns or sub-machine guns. There is evidence to suggest that the end of the war saw a tightening of police policy on the issue and renewal of firearm certificates, and a number of questions were addressed to the Home Secretary about refusals to renew certificates. One reply clearly indicated the substantial change of policy within the executive on the ownership of firearms for protection of person or household, when on 17 October 1946, the Home Secretary said, 'I would not regard the plea that a revolver is wanted for the protection of an applicant's person or property as necessarily justifying the issue of a firearm certificate.'

From time to time questions relating to firearms controls were asked in parliament, and in most cases these followed isolated incidents which were headline news in the national press. On 11 November 1952 the House of Lords held a short debate on the subject on a question by Lord Lawson:

> To ask Her Majesty's Government whether the attention of the
> Home Secretary has been drawn to the increasing possession
> of revolvers and other weapons by civilians, whether he is
> taking steps to put an end to this dangerous situation, and, if
> so, the nature of the action taken.

The Lord Chancellor, replying, said that he presumed that reference was being made to the unlawful possession of firearms and their use in crimes of violence. He went on, later, to say that such evidence as was available did not point to a significant increase in the use of firearms in crime, and quoted figures for 'The number of cases in the Metropolitan Police District in which possession of firearms, whether used or not, has come to light'. These were: 1948, 48; 1949, 28; 1950, 39; 1951, 14 and in the first nine months of 1952, 17.

The fact that these figures indicated a relatively steady pattern with a downward trend appears to have escaped their Lordships. Lord Lawson thought it would, 'not give the public very much satisfaction to learn that while there had been—I think this is admitted—more crimes in which the use of firearms was involved, the Home Secretary is not going to take any steps other than to depend on the police.' He later suggested that 'Undoubtedly, the public mind is much disturbed on this question at the present moment.' What was the situation which so disturbed their Lordships and, according to them, the public? If, as is suggested in Chapter 11, the only reliable index of the criminal use of firearms has been the numbers of robberies in the Metropolitan Police District in which firearms were involved, the real picture was that the rate of armed crime was plunging to what is probably the all-time low of 1954! This short debate, inconsequential in itself, is yet a further illustration of the way in which the legislature has been ill-informed of the real state of armed crime and has been totally unable to interpret such information as it had.

Their Lordships returned to the same lists in November 1961 on a motion by Lord Mansfield. Lord Mancroft was worried about the 'apparent ease' with which pistols and revolvers could be legally and illegally come by, and proposed the principle that the fewer people who own a revolver, the better. He hoped that the Home Office would ask Chief Constables to accept higher standards of requirements before they issued licences. Lord Cottesloe entered a strong defence of the sport of target shooting as run by the national associations, but Lord Windlesham thought that such organisations had outlived their usefulness and were a possible source of illegal weapons. He thought they should lay aside their rifles and pistols: 'Why cannot they shoot at clay pigeons . . . using a weapon which is of no danger to anybody' (a shotgun!). Lord Swinton found himself unable to agree that 'England would in future be sufficiently defended by those members of the Liberal Party who engage in clay pigeon shooting'. He felt that the rifle associations had a useful role in providing sport and possibly in national defence. Others of their Lordships joined the debate which was wound up by Earl Bathurst who briefly expounded the effect of the controls then current and assured the House that the matter was being kept under careful scrutiny. Lord Mancroft withdrew his motion—and they all went home for tea!

During the late 1950s a small number of questions had been asked in the Commons about the use of air weapons by children. The Home Secretary had indicated that he had no evidence that further legislation was required and that, 'It had been the view of successive governments that the responsibility for deciding, if at all, and on what conditions children should handle firearms must remain with the parents.' (Reply—19 April 1956.) The questions appear to have been paving the way for the rather oddly named 'Airguns and Shotguns Etc., Bill 1962', a Private Member's Bill introduced by Mr Brian Harrison. The Bill was short, and its provisions were re-enacted in Sections 22 to 24 of the 1968 Act.

F

On the Second Reading of the Bill it was emphasised that the promoters were concerned with injuries and damage caused by young people using air guns and shotguns which, although they were prohibited from buying for themselves, they could be given and could carry with little restriction. Sir Barnett Janner, speaking in support of the Bill, mentioned the statistics obtained for the Bodkin Committee which indicated that in the three years ended 28 February 1934 there were 390 reports of injuries resulting from air weapons. Further information supplied by the police indicated that the comparable figure for the three years ended 1 December 1958 was 2,712; which appears to represent a sevenfold increase. Unfortunately, such figures cannot be compared, due primarily to changes in reporting procedures. During the 1930s, the reporting of less serious crime, or other incidents, by the police was a haphazard affair following no set pattern and, according to police officers who served in the late thirties, dependent largely on the whim of the individual officer or his immediate superior. The important factor appears to have been that the 'crime state' had a suitable appearance at the end of the year. It seems likely that there had been a substantial increase in the number of injuries caused by air weapons, but it is not possible to quantify this by comparing police statistics gathered in the early 1930s with those of the 1950s. The need for further control was also illustrated by reference to a number of specific incidents involving injury to humans or animals. The Bill had a large measure of support in the House and also from outside bodies ranging from the Association of Municipal Corporations to the National Farmers' Union.

It was in attempting to settle the ages at which restrictions should be imposed that difficulty was encountered. The government and the Bill's supporters were anxious not to have too many different ages involved, but various members tried to change the ages at which prohibitions would be imposed. The results are discussed in Chapter 13, but it is fair to say that a well intentioned and useful Act lost a little of its impact by creating complications which must be beyond the understanding of those to whom it is supposed to apply. Despite the problems caused by the different age limits, the Act was quickly effective against the problem to which it was addressed. During a later debate on the Firearms Bill 1965, one of the Under Secretaries of State at the Home Office indicated that in the two years after the passing of the Act there were more than 1,000 prosecutions or cautions and the number of injuries caused by air weapons fell from 946 in 1961–2 to 815 in 1962–3 and 804 in 1963–4. These figures are strictly comparable and show a reduction of 142 cases in two years. Neither has the Act lost its impact, for, according to the Home Office publication *Firearms in Crime*[1] the total number of indictable offences involving injury in which air weapons were concerned during 1968 was 292. Although this figure is not strictly comparable to the 1961–4 figures, the difference cannot be great. Injuries involving air weapons very rarely come to the notice of the police unless they are very serious, or it is a case of one person shooting at another, in which case it is regarded as an 'indictable offence involving a firearm' in almost all circumstances. Even allowing for the difference in classification, the figures undoubtedly indicate a substantial reduction.

If the figures relating to armed robberies involving firearms represent a reasonable guide, the criminal use of firearms was rising in the late fifties and early sixties to a level at, or just above that of the late forties. The exceptionally low figures obtained around 1954 accentuated the rise and a number of the more dramatic cases were making headline news. The Home Office were apparently still concerned with those weapons not subject to strict controls and a reply in the Lords on 22 November 1960 indicated that, in conjunction with the police, a review was being held of the law relating to shotguns and air weapons. An indication of the results of the review can be found in later statements by the Home Secretary. In January 1965, no less than ten supplementary questions were addressed to the Home Secretary on various aspects of firearms controls and, in reply, he said that he was examining the adequacy of present legislation in consultation with Chief Officers of Police. On 4 February a series of twenty supplementary questions drew from Sir John Hobson the query:

> Will the Home Secretary bear in mind that, in principle, it is much more effective to hit hard those who are in illegal possession of firearms, or who use them in the course of crime, rather than to set up complicated administrative machinery which affects ordinary innocent citizens and is usually wholly ineffective? In particular will he bear in mind the experience of New York City where there are the most elaborate provisions for the licensing of firearms, but where 22% of the crime is committed by persons carrying firearms?

Sir Frank Soskice replied:

75

The Right Honourable and learned gentleman has put his finger right on one of the central points of the enquiry. One has obviously to make any steps one takes completely effective and not put immense burdens on people who could not in any sense be said to be suspect.

By 11 February, the Home Secretary was ready to make a statement in the House concerning his proposals for legislation. He said, 'Our object has been to strike at the criminal, the potential criminal and the hooligan while limiting as much as possible the restrictions placed on law abiding citizens and the burden placed on the police.' He went on to outline in some detail the main proposals and, referring to shotgun controls, he said:

The Government have considered carefully the possibility of extending to shotguns the firearm certificate procedure, but have decided against it. There are probably at least 500,000 shotguns in legitimate use throughout the country and the burden which certification would put on the police would not be justified by the benefits which would result.

In questions which followed, Sir Frank was asked if, in view of the presence before parliament of the Bill to abolish the death penalty for those classes of murder for which it could still be imposed (which included murder by shooting, in the course or furtherance of theft, or of police) he would try to have all the necessary discussions on the Bill before the conclusion of proceedings relating to the proposed abolition of the death penalty. In reply, Sir Frank said, I do not necessarily accept that there is a close connection between the two Bills', but he nevertheless agreed to try to arrange parliamentary discussions before the Second Reading. The Firearms Bill, which at this stage had not even been presented to the House, became law in August 1965—three months before the Murder (Abolition of the Death Penalty) Bill, which was already at the Committee Stage in February.

The tremendous haste with which the Bill was rushed through parliament is best illustrated by its timetable in the Commons:

21 January: Home Secretary announces that he is proposing to examine the adequacy of present legislation.
11 February: Announcement of proposals
28 February: Introduction of Bill
2 March: Second Reading

12 May: Report Stage and Third Reading
5 August: Royal Assent

Between the Second Reading and the Report Stage, the Bill had been considered in Committee; and between the Third Reading and the Royal Assent it had passed through its various stages in the Lords, been returned to the Commons for consideration of the Lords' amendments, and returned to the Upper Chamber.

The provisions which reached the Statute Book have been re-enacted in the 1968 Act and their legal implications are discussed in Chapter 13, but the Bill presented to parliament bore little resemblance to the Act which received the Royal Assent. The exceptionally high number of amendments which were accepted—many of them to remedy defective drafting and many more to prevent unforeseen consequences—are a further indication of the tremendous urgency apparently placed on this measure. Even during the Third Reading, the Home Secretary found it necessary to propose a number of further amendments. By and large, the Act concentrated on the criminal use of firearms and did not increase restrictions on legitimate users, although some of its provisions were concerned with dealers and others had effects, which appear not to have been foreseen, on a small number of legitimate users.

The offence of carrying firearms with intent to commit an indictable offence, which is now Section 18 of the 1968 Act, caused a lot of difficulty in drafting and was the subject of a number of amendments. As finally passed, it was intended to enable the police to act before an armed crime was committed, but the problem of proving that a person intended to commit an indictable offence, or resist arrest, is frequently insurmountable until the intention is transformed into action.

The restrictions on carrying firearms in public places, first mooted in the unsuccessful Bill of 1883 and now Section 19 the 1968 Act, was also subject to a number of amendments, but in its final form it made reasonable provision for the legitimate user, and was likely to be effective and useful to the police when persons were found carrying firearms under suspicious circumstances. The offence of armed trespass was not included in the original Bill, but was the subject of a Private Member's Bill which was having an extremely difficult passage for want of time. The government were pursuaded to adopt it as part of their Bill and the Private Member's Bill was dropped. The proposals had the backing of a large number of organisations concerned with the countryside, including almost all the shooting organisations. The powers of the police were extended to enable them to require that weapons be handed over for inspection, to empower them to search persons and vehicles suspected of carrying arms, and extending their powers of arrest without warrant. The maximum penalties imposed by the 1937 Act were increased, in many cases, quite severely.

Controls over registered firearms dealers were increased by authorising Chief Officers of Police to impose conditions on registration, and these were generally imposed in relation to security of the premises and the precautions to be taken against thefts of weapons. For the first time persons whose dealings were limited to shotguns were required to be registered, and dealers were required to maintain a record of all transactions in shotguns and components. The speed with which the Bill was brought before Parliament caused those responsible for its drafting to overlook some of the problems this would cause to many of the gun trade outworkers who made various components for shotguns, but did not make complete weapons. An amendment proposed at a late stage exempted such persons from the requirement to keep such records in certain circumstances.

The exemption to the 1937 Act relating to shotguns had specified a barrel length of 20 in. to be the dividing line between shotguns and Part I firearms in law. There were no provisions in the original Bill to change this, but on the Second Reading, Mr Maxwell Hyslop drew attention to the existence of one make of .410 shot pistol which had a barrel of barrel of 20⅛ in. He suggested that the minimum barrel length should be 24 in. which would cater for the majority of sporting shotguns. Both he and Mr W. F. Deedes saw no reason for permitting anyone to shorten the barrels of shotguns below 24 in. and suggested that the exemption which permitted a registered dealer to do this, provided he subsequently dealt with the weapon as a Part I firearm, should be removed. The Home Secretary hurriedly introduced another amendment, but was then informed that shotgun barrels were being repaired on a relatively large scale by cutting off the old tubes and sleeving on new ones—so the amendment had to be ʼmended. The final result was to change the minimum barrel length ⸱ shotguns from 20 to 24 in. and to absolutely prohibit the shorten-
ʼf them except in the case of a registered dealer who was replac-
⸱ barrels by sleeving. This produced a number of anomalies.
ʼnaker can still make a shotgun with barrels less than 24 in.

in length, provided he deals with it as a Section I firearm, but he cannot convert one. One well-known gunmaker specialises in shotguns with 25 in. barrels and if one of these is damaged, say $1\frac{1}{4}$ in. from the muzzle, the gunsmith cannot trim off the tubes to leave a perfectly serviceable gun subject to firearm certificate procedure. A number of small calibre shotguns frequently used for killing vermin in confined places have barrels 23 in. long and these were suddenly Section I firearms, though it is doubtful if many owners have so declared them. The criminal using a sawn-off shotgun cuts it down to 12 in. or less, and is unlikely to go to a registered firearms dealer to have this work done. It is difficult to see what useful purpose this hurried amendment could serve.

Under the 1937 Act, the prohibition on the possession of firearms by persons who had received specific sentences was for a period of five years from the date of their release from prison. This was amended to provide a lifelong prohibition on persons who had served three years or more, and to bring within the five year ban persons sentenced to Borstal training or to detention in a detention centre.

All in all, the Act did what it set out to do in providing heavy penalties for the criminal use of firearms and arming the police with useful additional powers against the unlawful use or carrying of firearms. Some of its provisions reflect the haste and urgency with which it was rushed through parliament, and the extremely lengthy debates, coupled with the vast number of amendments to such a short Bill (a mere eleven sections including interpretation and short title), clearly indicate a lack of consultation and preparation of the sort which normally preceeds this type of legislation.

The statistics quoted to support the Bill were those for 'indictable offences involving firearms' and these have been shown to be very misleading, but even these figures did not show a pattern of increasing use of firearms. On the Second Reading, the Home Secretary had said, speaking of the figures for the Metropolitan Police District, 'During the years 1961 to 1963 the numbers had declined slightly from 127 to 118 and then to 103, but they rose again in 1964 to 172'. For the provinces, the figures quoted were from 425 in 1961 to 559 in 1964. Bearing in mind what these figures represent, all indictable offences and not just 'crimes', they might well have been a cause for concern in respect of the apparent increase in 1964 which followed on decreasing figures, but they were no justification for the virtual panic behind this Act. There is no doubt that the Bill was rushed

79

6 And so to Shotguns and Airguns

Following the 1965 Act shotguns and airguns remained outside the firearm certificate procedures, although heavy penalties existed for their misuse in any way. On 18 December 1965, a gang of five men armed with a revolver, a sawn-off shotgun and iron bars broke into the office of a dairy in North London. An employee, Mr Alfred Philo, was disturbed and when he intervened he was shot and later died. On 22 December, Mrs Joyce Butler, MP, asked the Home Secretary if, in view of this murder, he was satisfied with the workings of the Firearms Act in relation to shotguns. An Under Secretary of State replied, 'The full provisions of the Firearms Act 1965 did not come into operation until 1 November 1965 and it is too soon to assess the effect of those directed against the misuse of shotguns. Possession of a sawn-off shotgun without a firearm certificate is already illegal.'

Late in 1965, Sir Frank Soskice was replaced at the Home Office by Mr Roy Jenkins and when, on 3 March 1966, the new Home Secretary was asked if he would amend the Firearms Act 1965, he replied, 'No. The 1965 Act created new offences relating to the carriage of firearms and prescribed heavy penalties. I do not consider that a further change in the law along the lines suggested would produce worthwhile results. I am, however, actively considering new legislation in relation to shotguns.'

In May 1966, in a further reply, Mr Jenkins made known the numbers of indictable offences involving firearms for 1965 (see Table 7), bringing the previously published figures up to date. The basis on which these figures were collected is discussed in Chapter 8, and it is clear that they were not a reasonable indication of the growth of the criminal use of firearms and, in particular, the rise in the figure relating to shotguns is just as likely to have been caused by differences in police interpretation of the word 'involving' when submitting their returns, as it is to reflect a real increase in the use of these weapons.

The figure for 1965 had been obtained from police forces early in 1966 and was, presumably, one of the factors taken into account in Mr Jenkins's 'active consideration' of legislation relating to shot-guns. By 23 June, consideration was completed and, in reply to a further question, the Home Sectetary said:

> The type of shotgun which is freely available and which can be used without special exemption was considerably restricted under the Firearms Act. I must pay some regard to the burden of inspection which would be put on the police. The police do not consider that it would be right to make an extension at the present time.

TABLE 7 *Indictable offences involving all firearms and shotguns, 1961–5*

Year	Indictable offences involving All firearms	Shotguns
1961	552	107
1962	588	122
1963	578	144
1964	731	215
1965	1,140	318

The situation appears to have been that the controls on shotguns had again been carefully considered by the Home Secretary in conjunction with the police, and their conclusion was the same as that conveyed to parliament by Sir Frank Soskice in 1965: the burden which certification would place on the police would not be justified by the benefits which would result.

But there was to be a change—a sudden and dramatic about-face! About mid-afternoon on Friday 12 August 1966, three police officers were patrolling in a car in the Shepherds Bush area of London. In a quiet back street, Braybrook Street, they saw a vehicle containing three petty criminals and two of the officers left their car to check on the three men. They cannot have known that there were three loaded pistols in the car until, suddenly, shots rang out and the two officers fell dead. One criminal then left the car and ran over to the police car where he shot the driver through the head. In a few seconds it was all over—three policemen dead and the criminals had made their escape, at least temporarily. Two of the three were arrested shortly afterwards, but the third eluded the police for some three months before he, too, was arrested.

Shock and horror swept the country, to be supplemented by anger and revulsion. There was a huge wave of protests about the abolition of capital punishment, with many people expressing the view that the tragedy of Braybrook Street would not have occurred if the threat of the rope had still existed for murders of police. The calls for the reintroduction of capital punishment became louder and were strongly voiced by the police, for whom the Home Secretary has a special responsibility, through their Federation. They issued an immediate statement demanding the restoration of capital punishment and maintained this demand strongly. Mr Jenkins visited the scene and there spoke to pressmen. When asked about the Police Federation's statement and the effect it might have on Home Office policy on the abolition of capital punishment, he was reported by a number of newspapers to have said, 'I can well understand the reaction and feeling of policemen at the present time, but it would be quite wrong for me to take a major policy decision in the shadow of one event, however horrible that may be.' Mr Jenkins had been an abolitionist and he maintained his position throughout the storm of protest which followed.

On 12 September 1966, Mr Jenkins was speaking at Hounslow to a Labour Party conference on 'Crime and Society' and he chose that platform to announce that he was (according to the *Daily Telegraph* report of the following day) 'Endeavouring to draw up plans to end the unrestricted purchase of shotguns. They can', he said, 'be purchased far too easily, by mail order or other means, and there is evidence that the criminal use of shotguns is increasing rapidly, still more rapidly than that of other weapons. Between 1961 and 1965 the numbers of known indictable offences involving firearms as a whole doubled, but those involving shotguns trebled.' Could it be that a Home Secretary did not know that the 'criminal use' of shotguns was in no way reflected in the figures of indictable offences involving firearms? Equally, it would appear that the Home Secretary did not know that the basis on which these figures had been gathered made them extremely unreliable. The weapons used at Shepherds Bush had been pistols, but the proposed course of action was shotgun controls. In relation to capital punishment, Mr Jenkins felt that it would be quite wrong to take a major policy decision in the shadow of one event, but he was apparently quite happy to take a major policy decision in relation to shotgun controls and, indeed, to completely reverse his policy just seven weeks after reaching a considered conclusion. The fact that this was irrelevant to the incident which sparked off the major policy decision seems not to have been important. The Home Secretary said that, 'He realised that his plans to end the unrestricted purchase of shotguns would be bound to involve a little inconvenience for some legitimate users and suppliers. With crime offering its present challenge, this would be a small sacrifice which it might not be unreasonable to demand.'

The vehicle which the Home Secretary chose for the introduction of his proposals was the Criminal Justice Bill 1967. That this was a strange vehicle appears to have occurred to few people at the time, but Criminal Justice Acts have been a fairly regular feature of modern legislation and, invariably, they have been confined to matters concerning the administration of justice or the treatment of offenders. The Criminal Justice Act 1921 contained important changes in the probation system, the jurisdiction of the courts and court procedure. The Criminal Justice Act 1948 abolished hard labour and whipping in prisons, made further important changes in probation, introduced corrective training and preventive detention for persistent offenders, and made many changes in administrative arrangements and procedures. The Criminal Justice Act 1961 made important changes in the Borstal system, introduced detention centres for young offenders, dealt with treatment in approved schools and with such matters as transfers and recalls of prisoners. Nothing outside the field of the administration of criminal justice had been included in any of these previous Acts.

The Criminal Justice Bill dealt, for the most part, with precisely the same considerations and it contained a number of extremely important—almost revolutionary—changes in British Criminal procedure. Just some of the more important topics will give an indication of the scope and importance of the Bill:

Totally new and complicated procedures for avoiding, in many cases, the need for a full hearing of evidence before examining justices prior to trial by jury.

New restrictions on newspaper reporting of committal proceedings.

A change in the law relating to the proof of criminal intent, substituting the subjective for the objective test.

Admission in evidence of written statements.

Requirement for the defence to give notice of an alibi.

Majority verdicts in criminal trials.

Restrictions imposed on the rights of magistrates to refuse bail.

Abolition of preventive detention and corrective training and
the substitution of extended sentences.

Introduction of suspended prison sentences.

Introduction of the parole system for the early release of
prisoners.

Abolition of corporal punishment in prison.

Changes in the legal aid system.

All this had been in the course of preparation for a long time. Each one of the provisions mentioned had been, and in many cases still was, the subject of controversy. Many of them, for example the changes in committal proceedings or the introduction of majority verdicts represented nothing less than the reversal of hundreds of years of legal practice. Debates on all the topics raged both inside and outside parliament, and it was into the middle of all this—possibly the most important Criminal Justice Act ever—that Mr Jenkins slipped his proposals about shotguns. Part V of the Bill contained those provisions which have been re-enacted in the 1968 Act and still apply. Broadly, it introduced a system of licensing in which persons were licensed and then permitted to acquire shotguns as and when they pleased.

The Second Reading of the Bill in the Commons was on 12 December 1966 and, as was to be expected, the debate was opened by the Home Secretary, who outlined the main proposals. Speaking for over an hour, Mr Jenkins did not have one single word to say about Part V, and in this he set the pattern for the House. At this Reading, which is the time when the principle of a Bill should be challenged, or when important issues concerning it should be raised, Part V was mentioned three times. Once, Mr Richard Sharples made a half-hearted query about the administrative burden placed on the police; once Mr W. F. Deedes said one short sentence in favour of 'checking the use of shotguns' and once when Mr Charles Doughty made a short comment that he agreed with shotgun controls. Of a debate covering 57 columns in the official report, about $1\frac{1}{2}$ columns referred to this part and these were inconsequential remarks.

On the Report Stage, two minor drafting amendments were proposed by the Home Secretary, but there was no other mention of Part V in 207 columns of report. The Third Reading occupies only

7 columns, one of which is taken up with a relatively obscure aspect of carriers possessing shotguns in the course of their business. When the Lords' amendments were returned, 18 columns of report refer to Part V out of a total of 102 columns. Thus it can properly be said that the shotgun controls were never debated in the House of Commons, yet previous firearms legislation had always provoked lengthy debates and had been the subject of much concern by many members. Could it be that this is what was anticipated when Part V was wrapped up in the midst of vital and controversial legal reforms?

The Lords, on 13 June 1967, delved a little more deeply into the problem. Lords Swansea, Bowles and Derwent were concerned about the various grounds upon which a Chief Officer could refuse a certificate and the original suggestions were amended to give the present situation where the grounds for refusal are relatively specific. They, and several other Members, questioned whether the proposals would do anything to prevent criminals acquiring shotguns and Lord Mansfield thought the first parts of the Bill could well be described as the 'Criminal Justice (Encouragement of Evildoers) Bill' and Part V as the 'Criminal Injustice (Harassment of Citizens) Bill'.'In short,' he said, 'this Part of the Bill, however well intentioned is not going to do one iota of good as far as prevention of crime is concerned . . . [it] is so bad that it cannot be amended and I hope, therefore, that your Lordships will throw it out in toto.' Lord Swansea then raised the question of the amount of attention given to this Part of the Bill:

> For the first time since the Bill came before either House, Part V of the Bill is the subject of proper debate, not in Committee, but on the Floor of the House . . . I submit that neither in another place nor here has this Part of the Bill received proper consideration . . . It is simply due to the fact that this Bill within a Bill has been wrapped up and heavily disguised in a Bill of much wider application.

A number of other Members added similar views and doubted that the Bill would have any effect on criminals who wished to acquire shotguns.

Lord Stonham, Under Secretary of State at the Home Office, replied at length and with several interruptions. He said:

> The purpose of Part V—and this is the main point—is to limit the present unrestricted sale of shotguns. Of course a deter-

mined criminal can get one illegally, as he can get a pistol despite the 1937 Firearms Regulations, stringent though they are. Of course he can; and this Bill will not stop a determined criminal from getting a shotgun. But it will make it that much more difficult, it will assist the police in tracing the criminal and I think it will increase the public awareness of this problem.

His Lordship did not explain how the Bill would help trace a criminal—a very questionable proposition in view of the fact that it was not proposed to record details of weapons. Lord Stonham then started to give figures for indictable offences involving firearms in England and Wales: 1961—552, of which 107 involved shotguns, and he was then interrupted by Lord Swansea who asked if the latter figure was for all shotguns or for shotguns which were not sawn off. Lord Stonham was unable to differentiate, but went on:

So far as crimes are concerned they are frequently committed with shotguns which are not sawn off—and I mean crimes of violence and not poaching. The figures stayed fairly steady for 1961, 1962 and 1963. In 1966 the shotgun offences jumped from 107 to 215; that is to say, in four years they had doubled. In the next year, 1965, they jumped to 318. By then they had trebled. In 1966, they had jumped to 404. So, in five years—I should say six years to be fair—the number of indictable offences involving shotguns had almost quadrupled. I think these figures provide justification for one dealing with this matter as soon as we could.

As Under Secretary of State at the Home Office, Lord Stonham should surely have known that the figures relating to indictable offences involving firearms could not be equated in any way to 'crimes of violence and not poaching' (in fact they include a large selection of offences, one of which is night poaching) and he should also have known that the entire basis of the figures was such as to make them extremely unreliable. It was these same figures (except those for 1966) that the Home Office had considered just a year before when they reached the conclusion that controls were not justified. Two other comments made by Lord Stonham may give some indication of the reasoning behind the controls. He said, 'This provision as to certification is the beginning of our plans, and the one which we thought would best give us control.' Finally, at the end of this speech, he said, 'I think, in principle, it deserves your Lordships' support because it is an honest attempt, the best we can make, to deal with a real problem and in that attempt I feel we deserve the support of the Committee.' Their Lordships were somewhat mollified by these remarks and returned to making amendments to various clauses. No further attack was made on the principle of Part V and thus, the Bill became law.

The suggestions for controls were made just seven weeks after the Home Office decision that such controls would not be justified, and they were based on statistics which the Home Office officials and Ministers must have known to be inaccurate and misleading. There can be little doubt that there was a measure of panic behind this legislation and that one of its purposes was as a sop to public opinion, to draw attention away from the insistent demands for the re-introduction of capital punishment. That the provisions were unlikely to be effective in preventing criminals from obtaining shotguns was admitted, but Lord Stonham may have revealed something of the thinking behind the legislation when he said that this was the best they could do, but certification was the beginning of their plans. If this is so, how very reminiscent it is of the circumstances surrounding the Pistols Act.

Questions on the control of air weapons had been raised at intervals, and on 17 November 1966, in answer to a question from Mrs Joyce Butler, the Home Secretary had said that he was considering using his powers under the Firearms Act to subject to the firearm certificate procedure certain classes of specially dangerous air weapon. On 5 May 1967, Mr Jenkins was able to announce that he proposed to make rules which would bring under the full firearm certificate procedure air weapons capable of developing more than prescribed levels of power output. The Firearms (Dangerous Air Weapons) Rules were made on 13 January 1969 and came into operation on 1 May 1969. Part of the difficulty encountered appears to have been in expressing the level of power at which controls should apply. The Bodkin Committee's suggestions about using a specified quality of deal board to assess the powers of penetration was difficult to express in legal terms because deal boards vary considerably in density of grain, and the latitude available in testing light, low velocity projectiles is very small. Eventually it was decided to specify a kinetic energy for the projectiles, and the level was fixed at 6 ft-lbs for air pistols and at 12 ft-lbs for air rifles. This was a convenient figure which left domestic products unaffected, but imposed the weighty firearm certificate procedure on some imported weapons which were capable of being pumped up to pressures which would produce rather more than the prescribed energy levels. One of the higher levels of energy was found in an American weapon capable of producing energies, with a .22 in. pellet, of just over 20 ft-lbs. To put these figures into perspective, the common .22 in. cartridge (.22 long rifle) produces well over 100 ft-lbs (158 ft-lbs in the case of high velocity rimfire) and powerful full bore rifle cartridges can produce over 4,000 ft-lbs). The 6 ft-lbs limit set for air pistols can be achieved by using a sizeable ball-bearing in a catapult, or by a normal man throwing half a brick.

The weapons brought within the controls were the more expensive imported air rifles. Extensive enquiries from every source available have failed to produce a single case of a 'specially dangerous air weapon' having featured in a crime or accident. On the contrary, air weapons used in crime appear to be the cheaper models and, in fact, are usually little more than imitation firearms. The figures quoted in Chapter 5 indicate that injuries caused by air weapons have shown an almost incredible drop. If air weapons generally were being brought so well under control, and the so called dangerous air weapons were not shown to have featured in any way in crime or accidents, it is difficult to understand why the rules were created. The power to do so had remained dormant for fifty years and the fact that a relatively small number of imported weapons were a little more powerful than the domestic product hardly justifies the efforts of the police and the few owners of such weapons in implementing the rules.

The last changes in legislation to date have been two Orders in 1969 and 1970 varying the fees payable under the Act. The charges were originally set by the Blackwell Committee and details of the charges, and the increases, are set out in Chapter 13. The charges effective from 1 January 1971 of £3 10s (£3·50) for a grant and £2 10s (£2·50) for the renewal or variation of a certificate are very high. They appear to have been based on the overall cost of the system of controls, but in the case of many applicants, whose certificates are granted without difficulty, the cost is much less than this. It appears that such an applicant is being made to pay for the difficult applications and for the refusals. Firearm controls are, allegedly, for the protection of the community at large and not just for the benefit of certificate holders. There is nothing to suggest that the cost to the police was the criteria on which fees were first based, or that parliament had such a criteria in mind when it authorised the collection of fees. It is difficult to avoid the conclusion that the new fees are, to some extent, intended to price out some legitimate users.

Although the Variation of Fees Orders are the last legislation, the matter does not rest there, for on 15 December 1970, the Earl of Cromartie raised the question of shotgun controls yet again in the House of Lords on a motion,

> To ask Her Majesty's Government, in view of the use of shotguns, sawn-off or otherwise, by criminals, to consider asking for the following additional information on application forms for shotgun certificates issued under the Firearms Act 1968:
> (1) The maker's registered number stamped on each shotgun, and
> (2) The number of shotguns in the holder's possession.

Lord Windlesham, a Minister of State at the Home Office, informed the House that the Home Secretary had asked Her Majesty's Chief Inspector of Constabulary to review arrangements for the control of all kinds of firearms in consultation with chief officers of police. The Earl of Shannon considered that the distinctions made between shotguns and Section 1 firearms were an anachronism and appears to have considered that shotguns should be subjected to the full firearm certificate procedure. Lord Windlesham said that note would be taken of the suggestion.

And so, over the years since 1903, firearms controls have been built up to their present state, and the pattern formed is distinctly repetitive. The announcement of a further review of the problem at least displays a desire to know a little more before bringing in further controls. It can only be hoped that the study which was announced will look at the problem in a little more depth than have some of its predecessors.

7 Common Law Rights

In following the progress of firearms controls through the twentieth century, the fate of the common law right for every Englishman to keep arms for his own defence has not been made clear. The existence of this right has been established up to the beginning of the twentieth century and the Pistols Act 1903 contained an exemption which makes it clear that the right was not affected by that Act. It was not until the passing of the Firearms Act 1920 that the legislature saw fit to place any restraints on the right (see Chapter 3). It is important to establish the precise nature of the restraints which the 1920 Act imposed. It is clear from the debates that parliament believed that the right was to be continued, subject to the overriding requirement for a firearm certificate; but it is equally clear that the right was considered to be in relation to defence against intruders into the Englishman's home, and in no way as a defence against supposed aggression by the state. The position after the 1920 Act appears to be that the right to keep arms for personal defence existed only in respect of a person who was not prohibited by the Act from possessing firearms by virtue of convictions, who was not of unsound mind, intemperate habits, or for any reason unfitted to be entrusted with a firearm and who could satisfy the chief officer of police that he could be permitted to have a firearm without danger to the public safety or to the peace. In other words, the common law right provided that personal protection or protection of the household was a 'good reason' for requiring a firearm. This view might be supported by the wording of the Section, which has been continued to the present, 'A firearm certificate SHALL be granted by the chief officer if he is satisfied', etc. If the area of discretion left to chief officers had been intended to override the common law, the statute would have had to expressly provide for this, and one would have expected to see the word 'may' in place of 'shall'.

Legislation since 1920 has not changed this situation. The wording of the various Acts has retained the use of 'shall' in relation to the granting of certificates and nowhere has either parliament, or the courts, expressly changed the common law. During the intervening years, chief officers of police, either at the suggestion of or with the support of the Home Office, have withdrawn this right by purely executive decisions until the present position is that any claim to have a firearm for self-defence is certain to fail except in the most unusual circumstances. Clearly, neither chief officers of police nor officials at the Home Office have any authority to change the common law, and a superficial examination of the problem might lead one to suggest that their actions have been unlawful, and that anyone wishing to possess a firearm for personal protection must be granted a certificate if the remaining requirements of the Act are satisfied. Certainly, parliament is aware of the change which these executive decisions have made. In a reply in October 1946, the then Home Secretary made it clear to the House of Commons that his department no longer considered that personal protection provided a good reason for requiring a firearm.

The fact that parliament has recognised the existence of a particular practice does not, however, mean that it has approved it, and certainly does not bind the courts to uphold it. Speaking in the case of West Midland Baptist (Trust) Association (Incorp) v. Birmingham City Corporation (1968 1 All ER 205) Lord Justice Salmon rejected an argument that a long-standing administrative practice relating to compensation in the compulsory purchase of land had been affirmed and recognised by the legislature.

> No doubt the legislature must be taken to have recognised that
> the practice existed—a practice founded on no statutory
> enactment or decision of the courts, but merely on obiter
> dicta pronounced long ago without any consideration of the
> problems and injustices to which the practice now gives rise. . . .
> The legislature did no more than to recognise the existence of
> the practice. It did not, in my view, intend to take away from
> the courts the power of altering the practice should the courts
> conclude that the practice rested on obiter dicta, had no legal
> validity and was, in modern conditions, unjust.

The practice of denying firearms for personal protection is not even based on obiter dicta and has no statutory or judicial backing. It is therefore safe to say that the mere fact that parliament has enacted further legislation, probably with full knowledge of the practice, does not lend any validity to the executive decision.

To conclude from this that the common law right remains unchanged and that, subject to his fulfilling the other requirements, an applicant for a firearm certificate can demand its grant if it is in respect of a firearm for personal protection, may well be to take too rigid a view of the nature of the common law. In discussing one aspect of the changing nature of the common law, D. G. T. Williams wrote:[1]

> A significant and often overlooked feature of judicial legislation is that English judges mould the law in a negative as well as a positive direction; that is, they 'repeal' as well as 'enact'. . . . There are several old common law offences which, despite the inaction of Parliament, have been skilfully narrowed down from precedent to precedent, often to the point of virtual extinction. In theory a doctrine of desuetude is not overtly recognised in English law, but in practice, it is submitted, such a doctrine clearly does operate.

In support of this contention, Williams quotes such common law offences as blasphemy, the scope of which has been narrowed by judicial decisions, and the offence of maintenance which, prior to its abolition by the Criminal Law Act 1967, was similarly narrowed to an almost non-existent point.

This changing nature of the common law is enlarged upon in two further cases which, although in no way related to the right to keep arms, may be relevant is assessing the state of the law. Speaking in the House of Lords in Shaw *v.* D. P. P. (1961 2 All ER 452), Viscount Simonds said:

> In the sphere of the criminal law, I entertain no doubt that there remains in the courts of law a residual power to enforce the supreme and fundamental purposes of the law. . . . [and, further] The law must be related to the changing standards of life, not yielding to every shifting impulse of the popular will but having regard to fundamental assessments of human values and the purposes of society. Today a denial of the fundamental Christian doctrine, which in past centuries would have been regarded by the ecclesiastical courts as heresy and by the common law as blasphemy, will no longer be an offence if the decencies of the controversy are observed.

In Attorney General *v.* Butterworth (1962 3 All ER 329) a lower court had refused a motion to commit for contempt a person who had penalised a witness after he had given evidence. No precedent could be found to support the contention that such

93

actions were a contempt. In the Court of Appeal, Lord Denning, Master of the Rolls said, 'It may be that there is no authority to be found in the books, but, if this is so, all I can say is that the sooner we make one the better.' Supporting his view with precedents which, though not strictly to the point of the case, pointed to the fundamental purposes of the law of contempt, the Court enlarged the scope of the offence to meet the needs of the case before it.

Thus, the common law can change and develop to a considerable extent to keep in step with the times. It does not seem that the right to keep arms has been asserted by anyone in recent times; and no precedent on this point has come to light. In speculating on what course the Court of Criminal Appeal might take in a case brought to them on a point of law from Quarter Sessions, there appear to be no binding precedents. But the court would be bound to take into account the changing pattern of life since the doctrine was expressed by Blackstone. Having regard to what seems to be the generally accepted state of opinion in this country, it seems likely that the court would feel that the need for this right had, to a large extent, passed. Whilst they might feel unable to extinguish the right completely, they might well feel able to narrow it to an almost non-existent point and so confirm the practice which the police have adopted. The outcome of such a case cannot be prejudged, but it would be entirely unsafe to assert that the common law right to keep arms still exists in this country.

Those organisations which have been concerned with representing the legitimate user of firearms on questions relating to controls have never advanced the right to keep arms for defence as part of their platform, possibly because they were not aware of its existence. What they have advanced, though perhaps not in precise terms, is another common law right. Blackstone expressed it, with his almost Biblical turn of phrase, 'For all of us have it in our choice to do everything that a good man would desire to do; and are restrained from nothing, but what would be pernicious either to ourselves or to our fellow citizens.' More recently, the eminent judge, Lord Justice Salmon, speaking at the Haldane Memorial Lecture to the Law Society, and quoted from the *Daily Express* of 4 December 1970, expressed the rule more prosaically, 'It is the right to think what you like, and to do what you like—provided that in doing so you do not injure your fellows.'

The argument of those concerned with the legitimate use of firearms is that they have a right to follow the sport of their choosing, provided that, in doing so, they do not endanger the community. One of the problems of firearms control legislation is to find the balance between the rights of individuals to follow pursuits requiring the use of firearms, and the danger to the community, if any, of the presence of these firearms. It is to assessing the possible danger presented by these legitimately held firearms that a part of this study is directed.

Part II Criminal and Illegal Use of Firearms

8 Measuring the Problem

The size and scope of any problem created by the illegal ownership or use of firearms in England and Wales has, in recent years, been judged mainly on figures published by the Home Office under the heading, 'Indictable offences known to the police in England and Wales in which a firearm was involved'. In this chapter, the Home Office figures will be examined in detail to check their validity as a year-by-year index of the problem, and to establish precisely what each year's figures might indicate. To further illustrate the true meaning of the figures, a sample of cases in 1969 has been examined in detail. These cases have been classified according to the circumstances of the offence and, in this and the following chapters, various aspects of each class of offence are related to the current firearms controls.

In November 1970, the Home Office published a booklet, *Firearms in Crime*[1] in which was attempted a detailed statistical survey of indictable offences involving firearms for 1967 and 1968. Table 1 of the booklet reproduces the total of indictable offences in which a firearm was involved for the years 1961–8, with the percentage change over the previous years. The figures are shown here in Table 8 and the figure for 1969 has been added from a parliamentary reply on 4 February 1971.

In presenting the table, the compilers of the booklet said, 'It appears from this table that there were large increases in the involvement of firearms in crime in every year from 1964 until 1967 but, owing to changes in methods of obtaining the information, described in paragraph 11, comparisons with previous years' figures are misleading. The comparison between 1967 and 1968 is, however, believed to be reliable.' The figures for 1967 and 1968 were believed to be reliable, but those for 1969 appear to be thought less so, for when details were given on 4 February 1970, the Home Secretary added, 'It is thought that improved reporting partly accounts for the increase in the figure'.

If the Home Office believes comparisons made prior to 1967 to be misleading, and thinks that the increase shown by the 1969 figure may be due to 'improved reporting', we are apparently left only with the comparison between 1967 and 1968 which is believed to be reliable. It would appear, therefore, that the manner in which the figures were collected is worthy of very close examination, but before such an examination can be made, it is necessary to establish

TABLE 8   *Indictable offences known to the police in England and Wales in which a firearm was involved*

Year	Number of offences	% change from previous year
1961	552	
1962	588	+6·5
1963	578	−1·7
1964	731	+26·5
1965	1,140	+56·0
1966	1,511	+32·5
1967	2,339	+54·8
1968	2,503	+7·0
1969	3,298	+31·0

precisely what the term 'indictable offence in which a firearm was involved' might mean. This is the term which has been used throughout to label the published figures, despite references by ministers and others to other titles and despite the unfortunate use of such phrases as 'the involvement of firearms in crime' used in the quotation above, and the title of the booklet, *Firearms in Crime*.

The term 'indictable offence' is far from synonymous with the word 'crime' as generally used. An indictable offence, strictly speaking, is an offence which is triable before a jury at Quarter Sessions or Assize Courts, as distinct from a summary offence which is triable before magistrates. The distinction is not clear-cut. A summary offence may carry a right of trial before a jury if the punishment exceeds certain limits and indictable offences are, in many cases, triable summarily with the consent of the accused. In addition, a number of offences are triable either summarily or on indictment (frequently at the choice of the prosecutor). A list of those indictable offences which are included in Home Office statistics, showing the classification number, is supplied by the Home Office and is reproduced in the annual criminal statistics at Appendix IV. Matters recorded in this way include all offences which the layman might call crime—murder, robbery, burglary, theft, etc., but amongst those listed, and in particular under the heading 'other indictable offences' will be found matters which the layman might be surprised to see, for example, poaching in the daytime is a summary offence which does not feature in these statistics, but poaching at night (one hour after sunset to one hour before sunrise) is an indictable offence and would be included. In fact, one of the latter group, which involved the use of a firearm, features in a sample which was analysed during the present study. Detailed examination of the indictable offences recorded under the various headings covered in this study will give a broad indication of the sort of conduct which will be labelled 'an indictable offence'.

The meaning which should be ascribed to the word 'involved' is made clear in paragraph 10 of *Firearms in Crime*: 'Involved is defined as used, carried, stolen, received or fraudulently obtained, or otherwise misappropriated.' Thus, a shotgun fired during the commission of a robbery is involved, but so too is an unusable antique pistol stolen during the course of a burglary. The same paragraph defines 'firearm' as 'Any lethal barrelled weapon of any description from which any shot, bullet or other missile can be discharged. The term is used to include imitation firearms and devices so closely resembling firearms as to be easily mistaken for them, e.g. starting pistols'. Thus, if anything which could possibly be called a firearm, or which could be mistaken for one, is in any way concerned with the commission of an indictable offence, then the offence is brought into the Home Office figures. The term 'criminal use of firearms' could perhaps be defined as the use or carrying of a firearm to further the commission of a crime, whether it was the use of a firearm to commit a robbery at gunpoint, or to resist arrest after the crime. It will be seen, therefore, that this term has little in common with 'indictable offences involving a firearm'.

The figures in the booklet, *Firearms in Crime* were originally published as parliamentary replies. The first such figures, for 1961, 1962, 1963 and 1964, were made public in a reply on 20 January 1965. They showed the figures under separate headings for the Metropolitan Police, County Force, and City or Borough Forces, with a separate figure in brackets to indicate the number of cases in which a shotgun was involved. In May 1966, a parliamentary reply added similar figures for 1965. By February 1967, the 1966 figure was available, but without the breakdown by police area. Two replies in March 1969 gave the figures for 1968, together with a breakdown showing the number of cases in which various categories of weapon were 'used or presented', together with the number of cases involving wounding or killing.[2]

The first returns of the Home Office figures were for the years 1961–4, and the fact that they were given to parliament on 20 January 1965 means that no time was lost by police forces in supplying the 1964 figure. Conversations with a number of statistical officers, coupled with the writer's personal experience, indicates that, in some forces, the figures required for the first three years were not easily available at headquarters level, and varying methods were adopted to compile the returns. In a number of cases, the request in respect of the first three years was sent down to local section level, and a large variety of officers were put to wading through records for the period to sort out those offences which involved a firearm. In many cases the records for 1964 were then current at headquarters, but there was no way of extracting details of those cases involving a firearm without checking through every crime report manually. Therefore, someone (and it must frequently have been a cadet) was given the job of manually sifting the reports to extract those involving a firearm.

One of the problems lay in deciding just what information was required by this urgent request from the Home Office for figures. The 'indictable offences' part posed no great problem, but it seems that neither 'firearm' nor 'involved' were clearly defined in the request. It appears, therefore, that hundreds of different people were involved in extracting these figures, at different levels, and there seem to have been just as many different interpretations of these two words. Certainly, few people could have included air weapons amongst their definition of 'firearms'. A parliamentary debate on the Firearms Act 1965 (see Chapter 5), revealed that in one year (1961–2), 946 cases of injuries caused by air weapons came to the notice of the police. As is explained later, it may be that not every one of these was an indictable offence, but it seems clear that a large number were. The total figure for 1961 was 552, so that few of the air weapons offences can have been included.

Perhaps a few forces submitted returns showing all indictable offences in which a firearm was involved for all four years, but in some, the results of the enquiries sent to lower levels were based on a hurried run through the section records in many different stations, with widely differing degrees of application to the task. Significantly, the figures for 1961, 1962 and 1963, gathered to a large extent at section level, but at the same time, were relatively constant. The 1964 figure of 731, primarily gathered at headquarters level, showed a dramatic increase, but it seems likely that this is due almost entirely to a more efficient search of current records. Reference to following years shows clearly the significant problem of interpreting the requirement. The Home Office figure for 1964 was 731, but 731 what? Certainly it did not mean all the indictable offences in which a firearm was involved, and equally certainly it was not the criminal use of firearms. It seems, unfortunately, to have been a tangled mixture of the two which cannot now be untangled.

The information for 1965 was collected early in 1966 when the records were current. This time a number of forces appear to have anticipated the request and included an appropriate heading in their records system. However, just what type of offence was so labelled is not clear, and the confusion about what was required remained. The 1965 figure of 1,140, shows another dramatic rise, but much of this can be accounted for by a recording system which labelled offences as they came in, instead of sorting through thousands of files to supply an answer as had been done for the previous return.

In 1966 the system changed again and, to quote from *Firearms in Crime*:

> In 1966 it was decided that the information should be collected regularly and a system of monthly returns from each force was introduced and used in that year. But in 1967 this method was discontinued for two reasons: firstly the method allowed only a superficial analysis of the statistics, and secondly, there was some evidence to suggest that there was some variation in the way different police forces interpreted 'involved'.

The figure produced for 1966 was 1,511, showing a rise of 371 over 1965. It is likely that the greater proportion of the rise was due to the different methods of collecting statistics.

For 1967 the method of collecting the figures was changed yet again, and each force was asked to submit a report to the Home Office in respect of each indictable offence in which a firearm was involved. It seems from the figure that fresh instructions were given, attempting to make clear exactly which type of offence should be included, and what each part of the requirement meant. The figure for 1967, gathered in this manner, showed an increase over 1966 of 828, to give a total of 2,339, an alarming 54·8 per cent rise, due almost entirely to the changed method of collecting the figures. The system was continued and it should therefore follow that, as quoted in *Firearms in Crime*, 'The comparison between 1967 and 1968 is, however, believed to be valid'. It should also follow that the figure for 1969, collected on a newly devised form for computer processing should be equally valid.

The comparison between 1967 and 1968 was, in fact, 2,339 to 2,503, a rise of 164 cases. The validity of the comparison is called in question when it is learned that at least one large force was still concluding that what was required was a return solely on the use of firearms in crime. During the period January to September 1967, just one report was submitted from this force. During the period October to December, presumably following a reminder or clarification from the Home Office, 50 such reports were submitted. If this last figure was reasonably representative, the total for the year should have been around 200 and not the 51 recorded. The difference of 149 accounts for almost all of the supposed rise between 1967 and 1968. If, as announced in parliament, it was found that 'improved reporting' partly accounts for the further increase in 1969, it would appear that other forces were under the same misapprehension as the large force quoted above, and the comparability of the figures for 1967 and 1968 must be further called in question.

The supposed rise in indictable offences involving a firearm since 1961, which has been used as a basis for legislation, and which has certainly caused a great deal of public anxiety is, therefore, attributable mainly to differences in the methods of collecting information year by year. It is now impossible to extract from these figures anything which might give even the vaguest information about what has been happening in this field. As a means of judging any rise in the criminal or unlawful use of firearms over the years, these statistics appear to be useless. Fortunately, however, there is one source which does supply useful information, and this will be discussed in Chapter 11.

If the Home Office figures do not represent a valid indication of the rise in the illegal use of firearms from year to year, it might be expected, now that the method of collection has settled down, that a single year's figure will give a clear picture of the problem for that year. In the presentation of his results, a statistician has, surely, a duty to do more than present a mathematically correct analysis. The overall picture presented by the statistics should be something which truly represents the problem to the layman. In presenting its statistics, the Home Office has carefully used the term 'indictable offences in which a firearm was involved', but what is important is how this has been interpreted by the public. An article which appeared in the *Daily Mirror* on 27 July 1967[3] is perhaps representative of the view taken of these figures by the general public, by politicians and even by police officers.

Gun law has increased dramatically in Britain. Criminals used guns 1,511 times last year. This is 361 more than in 1965 and the figures for that year were more than double those in 1964. This Chicago style trend continues despite recent amnesties in which thousands of guns and millions of rounds of ammunition were handed in to the police.

Now, of course, that statement is simply not true. These figures would not even vaguely suggest to the informed student (of whom there seem to have been remarkably few in this field) that criminals used guns 1,511 times in 1966; nor, as we have seen, was the rise in the figures indicative of anything except a change in the method of collecting the statistical data. Yet this was the impression gained by an experienced journalist and imparted by him to his millions of readers. This journalist was far from alone in placing that sort of interpretation on the figures. According to his report, he checked with the Home Office and, far from correcting matters, the ubiquitous 'Home Office spokesman' is reported as having said, 'The Home Secretary is very concerned about the increase'.

This figure of indictable offences in which a firearm was involved lumps together under one heading a case of night poaching and a serious armed robbery, a burglary in which an antique pistol was stolen and a bank hold-up. This system has been continued in the statistical survey for 1967 and 1968, and under this one heading were included cases such as one in which a small boy fired 'Plasticene' from an air rifle causing a small bruise on the leg of a girl, and a case where a man, intent on raping a woman, shot her in the back with a shotgun (both these being actual cases in 1969). Clearly, such totals mean little or nothing. The very important distinctions which arise in the various cases under one heading are not taken into account, and so the child shooting 'Plasticene' from an air rifle

H

is listed as 'An offence in which a firearm was used—motivated by violence'.

In an attempt to establish just what these figures might mean, and how they might affect, or be affected by, firearms controls, a more detailed study with sample cases has been made. With the kind permission of the Chief Officers concerned, a study has been made of the full file, including statements, prisoners' records, etc., relating to all indictable offences in which a firearm was involved in selected areas of the country. The year selected was 1969, simply because the study commenced during 1970 and this was the last complete year. The areas selected were intended to provide a reasonable cross-section of England and Wales outside the Metropolitan Police District:

1. The City of London: the square mile in the centre of London with a low resident population, but with a very high risk in terms of business premises and cash available.

2. The Cities of Manchester and Salford: a large provincial city area as representative as any of the problems of that type of conurbation.

3. The Mid-Anglia Police Area: an almost entirely rural area with no large conurbations and no heavy industry.

4. Nottinghamshire: the City of Nottingham and the surrounding County area, largely urban with mining, industrial and some rural areas.

5. West Yorkshire: one of the largest county areas, with a number of large towns such as Wakefield, Dewsbury, Barnsley, etc., and a great deal of heavy industry, including mining, steel and textiles, and some rural areas.

The total population of these areas (see Table 49) is 4,472,250, 9·15 per cent of the population of England and Wales. Previous studies have indicated that the Northern areas have a strong tendency to be more violent than much of the country.[4]

The total number of cases examined was 367, representing an 11 per cent sample of the figure of 3,298 offences for England and Wales. Excluded from the examination were eight cases which, on investigation, had proved to be a 'no crime'. For example, a reported theft of a .22 rifle from an army cadet unit in which, on investigation it was found that the rifle had been properly issued to another unit. Reports which are believed to be false, but cannot conclusively be proved so, remain undetected and are included in the study. The

Home Office figures appear to include a number of cases subsequently marked 'no crime' and this accounts for the discrepancy in each case. Two other cases have been excluded—the theft and the handling of a substantial number of Section 1 firearms stolen by a police officer from surrendered weapons. The majority of the weapons concerned were recovered and none fell into criminal hands. Such a case is, of course, extremely rare. This case would have so distorted the picture for Section 1 firearms that the total would not have been in any way representative. Table 9 shows the total number of cases examined in each force area. Detailed examination of the offences

TABLE 9 *Sample of indictable offences in which a firearm was involved—by force area*

Force	Thefts of firearms & ammn.	Handling stolen firearms	Others	Totals
City of London	3	—	7	10
Manchester & Salford	42	3	26	71
Mid-Anglia	30	2	4	36
Nottinghamshire	30	2	24	56
West Yorkshire	133	5	56	194
Totals	238	12	117	367

included in the survey has led to the use of a method of categorising the offences which will, it is hoped, give a clear indication of the type of conduct involved, the size of the threat which such conduct might pose to society and the likely effect of firearms controls on that class of offence (see Table 10). Offences falling into each category are analysed in detail. In the more serious cases, brief details are given of each incident so that the reader can judge the merit of the classification, and make an independent assessment of the problem involved. The manner in which various aspects of firearms controls might affect, or be affected by, the offences is reflected in Tables for each category, showing the type of weapon involved and the nature of its use, how the weapon was acquired and the previous record of the offender in terms of the possibility of his obtaining such a weapon legally. A total of eleven categories have been used, and offences have been classified under these headings irrespective of the offence recorded by the police. The method of classifying the offences will be discussed in detail under each heading.

TABLE 10 *Classification by circumstances of offences in the sample*

Type of offence	Number	% of total	Number detected	Detection rate (%)
Thefts of firearms	238	64·8	108	45·3
Handling stolen firearms	12	3·2	12	100·0
Juvenile assaults with air weapon	51	13·8	39	76·4
Adult assaults with air weapon	11	2·9	11	100·0
Domestic assaults	16	4·3	16	100·0
Non-domestic assaults	3	0·8	2	66·6
Robberies and attempts	16	4·3	8	50·0*
Burglary and attempts	9	2·4	3	33·3†
Possession with intent	3	0·8	3	100·0
Resisting arrest	6	1·6	4	66·6
Miscellaneous	2	0·5	2	100·0
Totals	367		208	56·6

* Four of the complaints are believed to be false—see under that heading.

† 6 of the complaints are matters in which the so-called use of the firearm was very questionable. See under that heading.

Thefts of Firearms

Clearly, thefts of firearms form the greater part of these indictable offences. Thefts and handling account for 68 per cent of the total sample, which is slightly higher than the 63·1 per cent and 61·6 per cent indicated for the national figure in the Home Office survey for 1967 and 1968. This is accounted for to a large extent by the fact that the Metropolitan Police District (not covered in the survey) shows a disproportionately high number of robberies in the national table, an aspect which will be discussed later. Taking account of this fact, the proportion of thefts and handling of firearms in the sample is in line with that in the national figures for the earlier years.

A detailed examination was made of the cases in which weapons were stolen, and Tables 11 and 12 show the number of cases broken down by type of firearm. The definitions of the firearms involved are those used in the Firearms Act (see Chapter 13), thus a sawn-off shotgun will be included under Section 1 firearms. Where more than one type of firearm was stolen, the case has been shown under the higher heading. For example, if a rifle and a shotgun were stolen in one burglary, the case has been shown under Section 1 firearms, but the shotgun involved is recorded under the appropriate heading when the numbers of weapons are considered.

TABLE 11   *Thefts of firearms—number of cases*

Type of firearm	Number of cases	% of total thefts	Number detected	Detection rate (%)
Section 1	17	7·1	7	41
Shotguns	61	25·6	25	40
Air weapons	114	47·9	59	51
Starting pistols	21	8·8	12	57
Antiques	20	8·4	3	15
Ammunition only	5	2·1	2	40
Totals	238		108	45·3

TABLE 12   *Thefts of firearms—number of weapons*

Type of firearm	Number stolen	Number recovered	% recovered
Section 1	21	13	61·9
Shotguns	77	27	35·0
Air weapons	143	67	46·6
Starting pistols	23	13	56·6
Antiques	28	3	10·7
Totals	292	123	42·1

TABLE 13   *Thefts of weapons by circumstances of theft*

Place and circumstances	Section 1 firearms		Shotguns		Air weapons		Starting pistols		Antiques		Totals	
	Stolen	Rec'd	Stolen	Rec'd	Stolen	Rec'd	Stolen	Rec'd	Stolen	Rec'd	Stolen	Rec'd
Dwelling												
(a) Where substantial amount of other property stolen	4	2	27	8	23	6	0	0	13	0	67	16
(b) Where little or no other property stolen	2	2	11	5	10	4	3	1	4	2	30	14
Huts, outbuildings etc.												
(a) Where substantial amounts of other property stolen	—	—	—	—	2	0	—	—	—	—	2	0
(b) Where little or no other property stolen	—	—	19	7	30	14	4	2	—	—	53	23
In transit												
(a) Weapon stolen from car	2	1	8	3	12	2	3	2	—	—	25	8
(b) Car stolen with weapon	—	—	1	0	2	2	—	—	—	—	3	2
Other premises												
(a) Reg'd firearms dealer	1	0	3	2	5	3	—	—	—	—	9	5
(b) Other shop	—	—	—	—	43	25	—	—	4	—	47	25
(c) Other building	10	7	4	0	9	7	13	8	7	1	43	23
Others												
(a) Left unattended	—	—	2	2	2	1	—	—	—	—	4	3
(b) Other	2	1	2	0	5	3	—	—	—	—	9	4
Total	21	13	77	27	143	67	23	13	28	3	292	123

Shotguns. The greatest number of weapons were taken during burglaries in which other property of considerable value was also stolen. Bearing in mind that a best shotgun can cost £1,500, and that very few decent guns are worth much less than £100, it is not surprising that a burglar will add to his haul an easily portable, easily disposable item of such value. There is little doubt that in the majority of the cases falling into this category, the shotgun was taken as an item of value and not as a weapon for criminal use. Nineteen shotguns were stolen from huts on allotments, outbuildings on farms, etc. In all cases these were cheap, old guns, many of them virtually unserviceable. They had been left in these outbuildings and the circumstances of the thefts indicate that either juveniles or other casual thieves were responsible. Seventy-seven shotguns were stolen, but only one was subsequently used in crime. This gun was stolen from a gunsmith's shop and used in the shooting of a taxi driver (see Chapter 10, classification 7, no. 8). A small number of shotguns were abandoned close to the scene of the theft.

Air weapons. Of the 143 air weapons stolen, three main categories appear. Twenty-three were stolen during the course of burglaries in which substantial amounts of other property were stolen, indicating, again, that the weapon was taken as an item of value rather than as a weapon. Thirty air weapons were stolen from places such as huts on allotments, farm outbuildings, etc., and as in the case of shotguns, these were invariably old, cheap weapons, many being barely serviceable. Forty-three weapons were stolen from sports shops, or second-hand shops. In both the latter sets of circumstances, juveniles were responsible for virtually all detected crimes. In two cases, air weapons reported stolen featured in further 'crimes'. In one case a man arrested for burglary had an air pistol in his possession (see Chapter 10, classification 8, no. 3). There was no attempt to use the weapon. He stated that he had borrowed it from a friend, but when seen by the police the friend said (not unnaturally) that the man had no authority to take it and a crime of theft of the weapon was recorded. In another case, a juvenile who had stolen an air pistol fired it at another child, causing slight injury and this is one of the offences discussed under juvenile assaults with air weapons.

Starting pistols. These weapons have, of course, no significance in relation to causing injury, and rank as imitations so far as their use in crime is concerned. By far the greatest number of these were stolen from schools and the detected cases indicate that juveniles were almost entirely responsible for this class of theft. In no case was there any evidence to suggest that any of the stolen weapons were subsequently used in crime.

Antiques. All the antiques were stolen in circumstances which show that the value of the item was the point of interest. The value of such weapons can be very high and the low recovery rate indicates a good market for disposal. The low recovery rate, the low detection rate and the very high value of the property stolen in the housebreaking cases indicates that many of these were the work of a better class of thief. None of the weapons subsequently featured in crime and it is difficult to understand why these figures have been included in the Home Office statistics in relation to the 'involvement of a firearm'.

Theft as a source of weapons used in crime. There has been a theory that a major source of weapons used by criminals has been thefts from certificate holders or from dealers. This survey suggests that any such presumption is without foundation, and the figures relating to the traced sources of weapons used in other offences in the survey support this suggestion. Of 292 weapons stolen, only one (a shotgun stolen from a dealer) featured in a serious crime. Two air weapons were subsequently used in the commission of an indictable offence, but in one case the alleged theft was questionable and in the other case, the offence was one of irresponsible use only. The efficiency of the police system for identifying stolen weapons is illustrated in two cases in the survey. A shotgun stolen during a housebreaking in Huntingdonshire was found in a hotel room in Yorkshire and was traced back to its source immediately. A rifle stolen in Yorkshire was found in a hotel room in Glasgow and this too was traced back to its source without difficulty. If a weapon which was used in any of the offences studied had been stolen anywhere in Great Britain, the enquiries which would have been made about each weapon would almost certainly have traced the source of the weapon. If any of the stolen weapons had been used in a crime in another part of Great Britain, it would have been traced back and the fact recorded on the files. No system can be infallible, but, in relation to firearms, this system is extremely efficient. If the theft of firearms were a major source of the weapons used by criminals, it is to be expected that a far greater number of the weapons covered in this survey would have been identified. It is clearly possible, however, that a stolen weapon has featured in crimes which have remained undetected or in which the weapon has not been recovered.

Handling Stolen Firearms

The 100 per cent detection rate for this offence is not an indication of the vigour with which the police pursue these cases, but is a product of the fact that an offence of handling is not recorded until it is known that all the ingredients of the offence are present. This cannot be known until the offence is detected. When considering the number of indictable offences, it must be remembered that a 'handling' concerns weapons which must have been reported stolen. Thus, two indictable offences indicate two aspects of what could be the same incident. Twelve handlings were reported: five of these were concerned with air weapons which had been stolen by juveniles, and two were concerned with starting pistols also stolen by juveniles. Three of the air weapons and both starting pistols were handled by juveniles and the remaining two air weapons were handled by youths of 19. This tends to confirm the proposition raised by the study of thefts of this class of weapons, that such offences are generally the work of juveniles. Three of the cases of handling stolen firearms involved shotguns and in each case the value of the weapons was under £20. One case involved a .22 rifle which was found on a refuse tip, having previously been stolen. A woman found it on the tip and kept it. She later handed it over to her husband who was reported for handling the rifle after his wife had stolen it (by finding it on the tip and failing to take steps to trace the owner). The final case involved the handling of a stolen revolver and ammunition by a man of 29 and his wife aged 24.

Having, then, studied in detail the 250 cases of stealing and handling firearms which form 68 per cent of the total indictable offences in the survey, it might be thought that the remaining 117 cases, involving the carrying or use of a firearm, would form the serious criminal aspect of the study. These cases will be examined in considerable detail in the following chapters to see if such thoughts could be justified.

9 Assaults with Firearms

It has been shown that thefts of firearms form the greater part of the offences recorded by the Home Office, and the remainder have been labelled by the statisticians, 'Offences in which firearms were used or carried'. Under this broad heading are included so many different types of use that a sensible analysis is not possible unless the offences can be categorised in a manner which takes account of the variety of circumstances. Offences are categorised by the police according to the legal classification of the offence disclosed and this may not be indicative of the circumstances of the offence. Even in the most serious offence, murder, the classification merely indicates that someone was killed. A murder could be the result of a person having been killed in the course of a robbery, or it could be that an argument between husband and wife has had a tragic ending. Whilst both may be murder, the circumstances differ greatly. In many cases, the classification of the offence is dependent to some extent on the practice in a particular police force. For example, if a man were to force his way into a house at gunpoint and steal cash, the offence recorded would almost certainly be robbery, but it could be recorded as aggravated burglary. In categorising the assaults with firearms discussed in this chapter, reference has been made to the full circumstances of the case, and the offence has then been classified according to the circumstances, independently of the offence recorded by the police. The headings are listed in Table 10 and the method of classifying offences is discussed under each separate heading. Classifications 1 and 2 (Theft and Handling) have already been dealt with.

Classification 3—Juvenile Assaults with Air Weapons

Offences have been included under this heading if the offender is known or reliably believed to have been under the age of 17, and has used an air weapon to commit an offence of causing actual or grievous bodily harm. In none of these assaults is there any suggestion of any other class of offence; thus the use of an air weapon by a juvenile who was stealing would be categorised as robbery and not under this heading. The assaults are all without sensible motive and represent only the irresponsible use of an air weapon. Cases where such irresponsible use of an air weapon resulted in injury to animals, or in damage to property which amounted to £100 or more (at which level the offence becomes indictable) have also been included.

Fifty-one cases fell within this classification and the following examples indicate the type of conduct reflected in this figure. Example number five was included as the only case which involved serious injury.

Example 1. Two girls, aged 10 and 11, were walking in a quarry when a thirteen-year-old boy shot at them with an air pistol. Both girls were hit on the leg, causing red marks and bruising. There had been no contact between the girls and the boy prior to the offence. Two indictable offences were recorded, one in respect of each of the two girls.

Example 2. A 14-year-old boy had been talking in the street to his 12-year-old friend who had an air rifle. As the older boy rode away on his cycle, the younger boy shot at him with the air rifle, causing bruising to the thigh.

Example 3. Three boys, aged 13 to 15 were playing together in a field, shooting at various objects with air rifles. Without any reason, one boy fired at another, causing bruising to the body.

Example 4. A 14-year-old boy fired an air rifle from the window of his home, hitting a 13-year-old boy who was cycling in the street and causing slight injury.

Example 5. A 14-year-old boy who was playing in the street with an air rifle, fired a shot at another boy as he approached. The pellet hit the boy in the eye, causing serious injury. This case represents the one serious injury in 51 cases.

To relate these offences to the provisions of Sections 19, 20 and 22 of the Firearms Act 1968, which refer to possessing loaded firearms in public places, trespassing with firearms and restrictions on the possession of firearms by persons under 17 (see Chapter 13), the offences have been categorised according to the age of the offender and the location of the offence (see Table 15).

TABLE 15 *Juvenile assaults with air weapons—circumstances of cases*

(a) *Offenders under 14*

| Location | None | Injuries caused | | Total |
		Slight	Serious	
(i) Unsupervised on highway	—	6	—	6
(ii) Unsupervised in field etc.—trespassing	—	4	—	4
(iii) Unsupervised on own private property	—	1	—	1
Total offences by persons under 14	—	11	—	11

(b) *Offenders aged 14 to 17*

| Location | None | Injuries caused | | Total |
		Slight	Serious	
(i) With uncovered air weapon on highway etc.	1*	14	1	16
(ii) In fields etc.—trespassing	—	7	—	7
(iii) On own private property	—	5	—	5
Total offences by persons aged 14 to 17	1	26	1	28

(c) *Offenders described as under 17 but not traced*

| Location | None | Injuries caused | | Total |
		Slight	Serious	
(i) On highway etc. with air weapon not covered	—	5	—	5
(ii) In fields, etc.—trespassing	1†	5	—	6
(iii) Believed on own private property‡	—	1	—	1
Total offences by persons not traced	1	11	—	12

* Case of malicious damage to windows.
† Shooting at a cow and causing injury to the animal.
‡ Shots fired from a block of flats.

117

Of the 51 offences committed by juveniles, Table 15 shows that 45 (all except (b)iii and (c) iii) were committed in circumstances where the offender could have been dealt with for an offence under the Act before the assault took place.

Classification 4—Adult Assaults with Air Weapons

These offences are similar in many ways to those in classification 3, except that the offender is known or believed to be over the age of 17. No offence has been included which amounted to more than the irresponsible use of an air weapon in circumstances similar to those in the juvenile cases. Eleven cases fell into this category, and it is significant that, in 8 of the cases the offenders were aged 18 or under. The following examples show clearly the type of conduct under consideration.

Example 1. A 32-year-old man was shooting an air rifle from the kitchen window of his home at a target in the garden, when he irresponsibly fired at a woman in the next garden, causing bruising to the buttocks.

Example 2. A 21-year-old youth, who was a passenger in a motor car, fired an air rifle from the car window, hitting a youth who was walking in the street.

Example 3. A 13-year-old girl was walking in the street when an 18-year-old boy fired an air rifle at her, causing bruising to the thigh.

Example 4. A 17-year-old boy firing an air rifle from the window of his home hit a 14-year-old boy who was walking by, causing slight injuries.

An analysis of the offences by location and injuries will assist in assessing the value of the provisions of the Firearms Act in preventing this type of offence (see Tables 16 and 17).

In Table 16, in the one case under (ii), action could have been taken prior to the commission of the offence for trespassing with a firearm contrary to Section 22 of the Firearms Act. In the four cases in which the offender was on a highway, action could only have been taken

TABLE 16 *Adult assaults with air weapons—circumstances of cases*

Location	None	Injuries caused Slight	Serious	Total
(i) Offender on highway	—	4	—	4
(ii) Offender trespassing in fields	—	1	—	1
(iii) Offender on own private property	—	6	—	6
Totals	—	11	—	11

TABLE 17 *Adult assaults with air weapons—ages of offenders*

Years	No. of offenders
17	4
18	4
21	1
22	1
32	1
Total	11

if he had been found with the air weapon loaded (Section 19). In the other cases, no action could have been taken by police until shots were fired.

General Comments on Classifications 3 and 4

Whilst conduct of the type revealed in classification 3 and 4 is not to be condoned, it is hardly the type of conduct which the layman would label 'serious crime'. The details given in Chapter 5 indicate that the provisions of the Airguns, Shotguns, Etc., Act 1962, as continued by Section 22 of the 1968 Act, have very substantially reduced offences of this type. No doubt the provisions of Sections

119

19 and 20 of the 1968 Act, relating to possession of loaded air weapons in public places and to trespassing with a firearm, have further assisted. It is clear from the tables given that a slightly better enforcement of these provisions would reduce the number of offences still further. The number of air weapons in circulation in this country cannot be estimated with accuracy, but there is no doubt that it runs to several millions.[1] Bearing this in mind, the incidence of this type of offence might be thought to be at a remarkably low level. According to *Firearms in Crime* (Tables 14 and 19) the total number of injuries, both serious and slight, caused by the use of air weapons in all indictable offences (not just those falling within these classifications) in England and Wales during 1968 was 292, and 268 of these were slight injuries.

There appears to be one area in which the legislation could usefully be strengthened and that is in circumstances where irresponsible conduct is revealed, but no offence under Sections 19, 20 or 22 has been committed. In this present survey that would involve 12 or 16 cases. It may be that a provision which penalised the wilful use of any firearm (including an air weapon) in such a manner or in such circumstances that danger was likely to be caused to any person, would enable the police to take action before injury was sustained in a few cases. If the penalty for such an offence included the forfeiture of the weapon and, perhaps, a prohibition on the possession of firearms, it could have an effect on the small number of people involved.

Thefts, handling and the irresponsible use of air weapons have disposed of no less than 84·7 per cent of the total number of indictable offences involving firearms (312 of the 367 offences in the sample), without yet having reached 'the criminal use of firearms'.

Classification 5—Domestic Assaults

A method of classifying offences of violence by the relationship between attacker and victim was set out by McClintock in his 1963 study *Crimes of Violence*.[3] The following classification of such relationships was used in that survey:

1. Family relationship:
   Husband and wife (including permanent cohabitation)
   Relatives (including in-laws and step-children)
   Lodgers or friends living in the same household

2. Previous relationship of some duration:
   Sweetheart, mistress or lover (including former sweetheart, etc.)
   Friends or rivals
   Members of the same club
   Neighbours
   Persons working together

For the purpose of this survey, the domestic relationship has been defined a little more closely, and a domestic assault is taken to be one in which there is a close domestic association between the two parties, and where the assault is directed at the other party and has arisen from a dispute relating to the domestic situation. Thus, if a son were robbing his father, this would not be a domestic assault, but if, during a family argument, the son used a firearm to shoot or threaten his father, this would be categorised as a domestic assault. For this purpose, McClintock's two sub-headings, 'Members of the same club' and 'Persons working together' have been included only if the two parties were friends of some standing and could properly be said to have a domestic relationship. The offence recorded by the police in such cases varies, and might include murder, attempted murder, aggravated burglary, possessing firearms with intent to endanger life and causing grievous or actual bodily harm. Sixteen offences were categorised as domestic assaults and to illustrate the variety of circumstances to be found, brief details of each of them follow.

1. A woman, who had been living with the accused, left him and went to live with another man. The accused went to the home of the other man with a loaded pistol and threatened to kill him. When the other man entered into a conversation, the accused was persuaded to take the magazine out of the pistol and eventually to hand the weapon over to the man he had threatened to kill. The accused was also in possession a knife, and this too, he handed to the other man. When the police arrived, the accused was unarmed. The pistol was a 7·65 mm automatic, illegally held. The accused refused to supply information about where he got it.

2. A man separated from his wife travelled 150 miles to the house where she had previously lived. He was in possession of a loaded shotgun. When the door was answered by the woman occupant, the accused pushed his way inside, but when he discovered that his wife no longer lived there, he left at once. He was found in his vehicle near his home, still in possession of the shotgun, but this had been

I

dismantled. The shotgun was illegally held and he had owned it since before the introduction of controls.

3. Two boys aged 15 and 16, both close friends, were in a room at a farm and were examining a shotgun owned by the 16-year-old. The older boy pointed the gun at his friend's head and pulled the trigger without checking to see if the gun was loaded. It was loaded and the friend was killed. The older boy was charged with manslaughter, but the charge was dismissed. He was the holder of a shotgun certificate.

4. A 74-year-old man was living with his sister whom he had nursed through a serious illness. The sister's daughter and son-in-law visited and during an argument about the sister's will, the man picked up a loaded .22 rifle and threatened the younger couple. He said he thought he was about to be attacked. He was the holder of a firearm certificate.

5. The accused had an invalid wife and had frequent arguments with a neighbour about children playing near his home. During one such argument, the accused went into his home and returned with a .410 shotgun, which he fired at the neighbour, wounding him in the head and arm. The neighbour ran to call the police and when he returned, the accused shot at him again, hitting him in the left side. When the police arrived, the accused went out to meet them unarmed. The shotgun was his own, illegally held since before the introduction of controls.

6. Two men who were neighbours and who worked for the same employer, had an argument about which of them was to use the employer's van. The accused followed the second man into a nearby town with a shotgun and fired a shot into the air. A fist-fight followed and the police arrived. The shotgun was discarded before the start of the fist-fight. The gun was owned by the accused, illegally held by him since before the introduction of controls.

7. A man was arguing with his girlfriend about how she became pregnant. Her father interceded and the man produced a shotgun and ordered the father to leave. The father complied and reported the matter to the police. The accused was arrested without any form of resistance. The gun was found, but there was no trace of ammunition and the accused insisted that the gun was never loaded. The accused was not the holder of a shotgun certificate and had bought the gun recently from a local man.

8. The accused, who was of previous good character, was the owner of a 9 mm pistol for which he held a firearm certificate. He

had been living with a woman who left him to return to her father. The accused visited her parents' home and when the girl refused to have anything further to do with him, he asked to be driven to a nearby town. The girl and her father went in their car. During the journey the accused produced a pistol and ordered the car to be driven elsewhere, his apparent intention being to abduct the girl. There was a struggle between the accused and the girl's father, during which the girl escaped. The accused then ran off. He was later stopped in his own car by the police and he then shot himself in an unsuccessful suicide attempt.

9. Two gypsies in the same encampment had an argument about the treatment of the accused's wife who was the sister of the witness. A fist-fight followed and later, when the witness returned to the encampment, the accused fired a shotgun at him from a caravan, causing slight injuries. When the case was brought to court, the witness failed to identify the accused as the person who fired the shot and the case was dismissed. The accused was not the holder of a shotgun certificate.

10. Two friends argued in a club and when one of them became violent, he was ejected by a club official. In the early hours of the following morning, the official was awakened by the accused who asked that the official accompany him to the other man's house to witness a fight. The accused had a shotgun which he said was only to ensure that the other man came out for a fair fight. When the official refused to have anything to do with the matter, the accused walked off. The police were informed and they found the accused near his own home and nowhere near the other man's house. He had hidden the shotgun. The gun was his own, held without a certificate since before the introduction of controls.

11. A married man was associating with a woman who also had an association with a second man, all parties being known to each other. The second man saw the accused and the woman together and accosted them. During the argument, the second man struck the accused who pulled out an automatic pistol and shot the second man in the leg. The accused told the police that he had bought the pistol illegally two years before. He was the holder of a firearm certificate for other weapons, but was unlawfully in possession of the pistol used.

12. A young man and woman living together had a domestic argument in the home. The man picked up an air rifle and fired it at the woman, hitting her in the leg.

123

13. A wife had been out late and when she returned home, her husband was waiting for her and an argument developed. The husband picked up an air rifle and a shot was fired. The woman later said that a slight puncture wound to her hand was caused by the foresight when she grabbed the barrel.

14. The defendant went to the home of a friend whom he believed to be associating with his wife. With the aid of a starting pistol, he forced his way into the friend's bedroom. He found no one there and left immediately.

15. Two men had been business partners, but the business broke up and the accused was dissatisfied with the arrangements made. The accused walked into a snack-bar where he saw his ex-partner and asked if the partner had been responsible for changing the locks on the business premises. When the partner said he had, the accused shot him in the stomach with a .38 revolver. The accused said he had 'found' the weapon two years before. It was in excellent condition and well maintained and was believed to have been bought illegally.

16. The accused approached a neighbour and argued about noise caused by the neighbour's children. When the neighbour tried to reason with him, the accused produced a pistol and shot the neighbour in the neck. The pistol was a home conversion from a starting pistol and had to be muzzle loaded. It imparted so little energy to the bullet that it only just penetrated the skin of the neck.

Domestic assaults account for 4.3 per cent of the total of indictable offences involving firearms in the present sample, but once thefts, handling and the irresponsible use of air weapons have been eliminated, they form a significant part of the remainder—16 out of 55 offences. The effects of firearms controls on this class of offence is indicated to some extent in Tables 18, 19 and 20.

The numbers and seriousness of the injuries caused might well give some indication of the intention of the attacker. In the one fatal case, the circumstances and the eventual verdict of a jury, indicate that this was much more an accident than a crime. In a number of cases, it is plain that no injury was intended. Where the weapon was an air weapon or an imitation firearm, the risk of serious injury was either non-existent or very slight. In a number of cases, however, it is clear that the risk of causing a death was certainly present and there can be no doubt that such domestic assaults result in death in a number of cases each year. One of the most significant factors in considering this type of offence is the 100 per cent detection rate.

TABLE 18   *Domestic assaults—weapons used and injuries caused*

| Weapon | Fired without injury | | | Injuries caused | | | Total | Injuries caused by weapon other than firearm* |
	Threats only	Injury not intended	Injury intended	Slight	Serious	Fatal		
Pistol	2	—	—	1	2	—	5	—
Rifle	1	—	—	—	—	—	1	—
Shotgun	3	1	—	1	1	1	7	—
Sawn-off shotgun	—	—	—	—	—	—	—	—
Air weapon	—	—	—	2	—	—	2	—
Blank or imitation firearm	1	—	—	—	—	—	1	—
Others	—	—	—	—	—	—	—	—
Total	7	1	—	4	3	1	16	—

* Includes cases where the weapon was used to strike, but was at no time used as a firearm.

TABLE 19 *Domestic assaults—how the weapon was acquired*

Weapon	No restrictions on purchase	Held on cert.	Illegally held and			Not established	Total stolen	Total
			Owned before restrictions	Illegally 'bought'	Home-made*			
Pistol	—	1	—	3	1	—	—	5
Rifle	—	1	—	—	—	—	—	1
Shotgun	—	1	5	1	—	—	—	7
Sawn-off shotgun	—	—	—	—	—	—	—	—
Air weapon	2	—	—	—	—	—	—	2
Blank or imitation firearm	1	—	—	—	—	—	—	1
Others	—	—	—	—	—	—	—	—
Total	3	3	5	4	1	—	—	16

* Includes conversion of blank pistol to fire ammunition.

TABLE 20   *Domestic assaults—previous record of offender in terms of likelihood of grant certificate prior to offence*

Weapon	No cert. required	Cert. held for weapon	Prohibited	Unlikely to be granted	No known reason for refusal*	Not known	Total
Pistol	—	1	—	3	1	—	5
Rifle	—	1	—	—	—	—	1
Shotgun	—	1	—	3	3	—	7
Sawn-off shotgun	—	—	—	—	—	—	—
Air weapon	2	—	—	—	—	—	2
Blank or imitation firearm	1	—	—	—	—	—	1
Others	—	—	—	—	—	—	—
Total	3	3	—	6	4	—	16

* Taking account of character only, and not taking account of the requirement to establish good reasons for requiring a firearm certificate.

Reference to the details of the cases will show that this was not fortuitous, nor was it the product of efficient police work. In every case it would have been impossible for the offender to avoid responsibility for his actions, and in no case was there any effort to escape at the time. Acting as they did, amongst people who knew them, each offender must have realised, if he had given any thought to the question, that it was inevitable that he would be called to account for his actions. The high rate of detection is not, of course, limited to domestic assaults with firearms. The McClintock study[3] showed that of all domestic assaults reported to the police in London during 1950 and 1957, the detection rates were 99 per cent and 98·2 per cent respectively. This one factor sets domestic assaults apart from many other classes of crime.

A further significant factor is the background of the defendants. None of them had convictions which amounted to a prohibition under the Firearms Act, although six of them had backgrounds (convictions, mental history or other aspects) which would make the grant of a certificate unlikely. Three held firearm certificates and had been subjected to the close scrutiny which this entails. Comparison with Table 28, produced in respect of robberies involving firearms, further illustrates the significance in distinguishing domestic assaults from other offences.

In considering the effectiveness of firearms controls in relation to this class of offence, three questions might usefully be asked:

1. Have controls prevented unauthorised persons from acquiring and using firearms, bearing in mind the certainty of detection?

2. How far could certificate procedures have gone in preventing the offenders from obtaining firearm or shotgun certificates prior to the commission of the offence?

3. Would the absence of a firearm have made any significant difference to the outcome of the assault?

On the question of how controls affected the acquisition of firearms, it is significant that of the cases where pistols were used, three were purchased illegally, one was illegally converted at home and only one was lawfully held. Two of the men who bought pistols illegally and the man who converted the weapon were unlikely to have been granted a firearm certificate. One of the men who bought a pistol illegally was the holder of a firearm certificate for other weapons. Fifty years of strict controls on pistols did not prevent these people from obtaining them. So far as shotguns were concerned, six of the seven were illegally held, five having been owned since before controls were imposed. In three of the latter cases, the offenders were unlikely to have been granted a certificate. Of course, it can be said that controls on shotguns have been operating for a short time only, but clearly, the mere existence of controls had not previously brought these weapons to light. Unless these men drew attention to themselves in some way, their ownership of the shotguns was unlikely to come to light. It cannot, therefore, be claimed that firearms controls have been effective in these cases. That the number involved in the sample is small is beyond argument, but there is no reason to suppose that it is not representative.

A number of the people concerned were the holders of firearm or shotgun certificates before the offences were committed, and with regard to some of the others, there was no reason why a certificate should not have been granted. How, then, can people like this slip through the type of enquiries which are made, particularly with regard to firearm certificates? The simple answer is that, in these cases, there was nothing in the person's background to indicate that he might commit an offence of this type, unlike the armed robber who has often graduated from a lesser crime.

It would be easy to say of such cases, that if no gun had been available (legally or illegally), the outcome of these asaults would have been less serious; to suggest, as did the compilers of *Firearms in Crime*[2] in paragraph 31, '. . . the violence depends on the availability of a weapon,' and again, in paragraph 32, 'It is also more likely that a shotgun will be ready to hand than a pistol or rifle for an offence of violence which, as mentioned above, is likely to be a spontaneous event, relying on the availability of a weapon'. An examination of the cases in the survey shows that such a suggestion appears rather superficial and is, to say the least, questionable.

Professor Marvin E. Wolfgang discussed this problem in relation to homicides in general, following a lengthy and detailed study in Philadelphia, the results of which are contained in *Patterns in Criminal Homicide*.[4] He concluded:

> Several students of homicide have tried to show that the high number of, or easy access to, firearms in this country [the U.S.A.] is causally related to our relatively high homicide rate. Such a conclusion cannot be drawn from the Philadelphia data. Material subsequently reported in the present study regarding the place where the homicide occurred, relationship between victim and offender, motives, and other variables, suggest that

many situations, events and personalities that converge in particular ways and that result in homicide do not depend primarily upon the presence or absence of firearms . . . More than the availability of a shooting weapon is involved in homicide. Pistols and revolvers are not difficult to purchase—legally or illegally—in Philadelphia. Police interrogation of defendants reveals that most frequently these weapons are bought from friends or acquaintances for such nominal sums as ten or twenty dollars. A penknife or a butcher knife, of course, is much cheaper and more easily obtained. Ready access to knives and little reluctance to engage in physical combat without weapons, or to 'fight it out', are as important as the availability of some sort of gun. The type of weapon used appears to be, in part, the culmination of assault intentions or events and is only superficially related to causality. To measure quantitatively the effect of the presence of firearms on the homicide rate would require knowing the number and type of homicide that would not have occurred had not the offender—or in some cases, the victim—possessed a gun. Research would require determination of the number of shootings which would have been stabbings, beatings or some other method of inflicting death had no gun been available. It is the contention of this observer that few homicides due to shooting could be avoided merely if a firearm were not immediately present, and that the offender would select some other weapon to achieve the same destructive goal. Probably only in those cases where a felon kills a police officer, or vice versa, would the homicide be avoided in the absence of a firearm.

Wolfgang's conclusion was challenged to some extent by another American, Franklin E. Zimring,[5] when he attempted to show that an attack with a gun was about five times more likely to result in death than an attack with a knife. This was done by adding together the numbers of serious assaults and homicides with each class of weapon and then relating the numbers of subsequent deaths to the respective totals. Using Zimring's formula it can be demonstrated that, in America, a gun is more dangerous than a knife; but it can also be demonstrated by exactly the same method that bare hands are more dangerous than a blunt instrument. Such a comparison was made by Mark K. Benenson[6] using figures taken from the F.B.I. Uniform Crime Reports for 1968 (see Table 21).

TABLE 21   *Relative danger of attack by different weapons*

	Gun	Knife	Blunt instrument	Bare hands	Miscellaneous & unknown	Total
Homicide	5,660	2,134	516	896	346	9,552
Aggressive assault	43,583	77,893	51,697	58,651	n/a	231,824
Total	49,243	80,027	52,213	59,547	n/a	241,376
% Homicide	11·5	2·7	1·0	1·5	—	—

Applying Zimring's formula to these figures, Benenson showed that a gun is likely to cause death in 11·5 per cent of the attacks made with it, whilst a knife is likely to cause death in only 2·7 per cent of the attacks. If, however, we draw from that the conclusion that an attack with a gun is 4·25 per cent more dangerous than an attack with a knife, we must also draw the conclusion that an assault with bare hands is 50 per cent more dangerous than an attack with a blunt instrument. Zimring's hypothesis fails to take account of the many differences between assaults, and of what is suggested as the most important factor in determining the degree of injury, namely, the seriousness of the attack in terms of the degree of premeditation and the anger or passion of the assailant. Nothing in Zimring's suggestion detracts in any way from the validity of Wolfgang's arguments.

It might be useful to speculate on how any one of the cases in classification 5 (see pp. 121–4) might have ended had a firearm not been available. Only in the cases 12 and 13 where husbands used air weapons against their wives, could it be said that the absence of the air weapons would have prevented the assaults. On the other hand, is it not just as likely that the assaults would have continued with bare hands or with some handy weapon such as a poker? In either case, the possibility of injury to the woman would have been increased rather than decreased. If the gypsy involved in case 9 had not had a shotgun, would the dispute have ended there, or would he have lain in wait with a club, an axe, or a knife? If the latter, would the injuries have been as slight as those actually caused by the shotgun? In case 11, if the accused had been carrying a knife instead of a pistol to protect himself from his lover's other man, would the result have been a wound in the leg— or a more serious stab wound? Consider case 15, if the accused had not had a revolver, would he have resorted to a knife, and if so, would the injury have been any less serious? The circumstances of each case are set out and the reader must judge for himself.

It is suggested that, in this class of offence at least, the presence or absence of a firearm, or of any other type of weapon, is of far less importance to the outcome than the passion generated in the attacker. The man who has lost control will cause serious injuries in many cases, quite irrespective of the weapon he uses and regardless of the certainty of detection and punishment. Where the anger or passion is less, the attack is frequently more of a demonstration of anger than an assault carried to a conclusion.

Classification 6—Non-Domestic Assaults

Offences have been placed in this category if the person whom it was intended to assault does not have the domestic relationship mentioned in classification 4 and the use of the firearm is not connected with a crime other than the assault. This includes assaults which may have started as domestic assaults, but which later came to include persons with no domestic association as the objects of the assault. It does not include any assault which is connected with the commission of another crime or offence, or assaults committed to evade arrest. Also excluded are those assaults falling into classifications 3 and 4, in which air weapons were used to cause injury or damage in circumstances which indicate irresponsible use with no real motive. Only three cases, each quite different, fall into this category:

1. The accused, aged 21, was involved in an argument with his brother in a club. When there was a threat of violence, the accused was ejected. He ran to his brother's home, took a shotgun and returned to the club. He burst past the doorman, entered a crowded room and fired a shot into the ceiling before he was overpowered. Although this started with a domestic argument, the object of the assault appears not to have been the brother but rather the club in general. No injuries were caused. The shotgun had been owned by the brother for some years. Neither man held a shotgun certificate.

2. The accused, aged 59, was on a garage forecourt when he was approached in the late evening, by three youths asking for water. When they refused to leave, he took an airgun to them and fired at

TABLE 22 *Non-domestic assaults—weapons used and injuries caused*

Weapon	Threats only	Fired without injury		Injuries caused			Total	Injuries caused by weapon other than firearm
		Injury not intended	Injury intended	Slight	Serious	Fatal		
Pistol	—	—	—	—	—	—	—	—
Rifle	—	—	—	—	—	—	—	—
Shotgun	—	1	—	1*	—	—	2	—
Sawn-off shotgun	—	—	—	—	—	—	—	—
Air weapon	—	—	—	1	—	—	1	—
Blank or imitation firearm	—	—	—	—	—	—	—	—
Others	—	—	—	—	—	—	—	—
Total	—	1	—	2	—	—	3	—

* Includes cases where the weapon was used to strike, but was at no time used as a firearm.

TABLE 23   Non-domestic assaults—how the weapon was acquired

| Weapon | No restrictions on purchase | Held on cert. | Illegally held and | | | Not established | Total stolen | Total |
			Owned before restrictions	Illegally 'bought'	Home-made*			
Pistol	—	—	—	—	—	—	—	—
Rifle	—	—	—	—	—	—	—	—
Shotgun	—	—	1	—	—	1	—	2
Sawn-off shotgun	—	—	—	—	—	—	—	—
Air weapon	1	—	—	—	—	—	—	1
Blank or imitation firearm	—	—	—	—	—	—	—	—
Others	—	—	—	—	—	—	—	—
Total	1	—	1	—	—	1	—	3

* Includes conversion of blank pistol to fire ammunition.

TABLE 24 *Non-domestic assaults—previous record of offender in terms of likelihood of grant of certificate prior to offence*

Weapon	No cert. required	Cert. held for weapon	Prohibited	Unlikely to be granted	No known reason for refusal*	Not known	Total
Pistol	—	—	—	—	—	—	—
Rifle	—	—	—	—	—	—	—
Shotgun	—	—	—	1	—	1	2
Sawn-off shotgun	—	—	—	—	—	—	—
Air weapon	1	—	—	—	—	—	—
Blank or imitation firearm	—	—	—	—	—	—	—
Others	—	—	—	—	—	—	—
Total	1	—	—	1	—	1	3

* Taking account of character only, and not taking account of the requirement to establish good reasons for requiring a firearm certificate.

one, causing slight injury. Although this was an assault with an air weapon, it does not fall into classification 4 as it amounts to more than the irresponsible use of the weapon. The defendant was apparently using the weapon, to some extent, in self-defence.

3. The complainant, who had been drinking, became involved in an argument with three strangers in a city street. One of the men produced a shotgun from a car and struck the complainant over the head with it. The men escaped detection. It is difficult to establish the strength of this report and it may be that the full story was not told to the police. There was no use of the shotgun other than to strike the man over the head.

Tables 22, 23 and 24 analyse the use of the weapons, etc., in the same manner as the tables for domestic assaults so that, if it is thought desirable, the two can easily be added together. Certainty of detection is clear in cases 1 and 2 and the remarks made about the effectiveness of firearms controls on domestic assaults apply equally to these two cases. Case 3 is clearly of a different type and in that offence, it seems that it would not have mattered if the attacker had been carrying a cricket bat in his car instead of a shotgun.

The assaults under classifications 3, 4, 5 and 6 account for 81 of the 117 cases involving the 'use' of firearms, leaving only 34 cases to be considered under the 'criminal use of firearms', plus two cases classified as miscellaneous. Of the 34 cases ($9 \cdot 1$ per cent of the total indictable offences involving a firearm), ten will be seen to be either false complaints or to be of questionable validity, leaving just 24 cases ($6 \cdot 5$ per cent of the total of 367 cases). These cases are examined in detail in the following chapter.

10 The Criminal Use of Firearms

Of an original sample of 267 indictable offences involving a firearm, only 36 remain to be examined. Two of these have been classified as miscellaneous:

1. A conspiracy to acquire firearms illegally, allegedly for the Irish Republican Army. In this case a number of men attempted to persuade a firearms dealer to sell substantial quantities of military weapons. No weapons were sold and all the parties to the conspiracy were arrested.

2. A case of night poaching. Poaching in most circumstances is a summary offence, but certain poaching offences are indictable. The case reported was nothing other than poaching and there was no use of firearms other than in that connection. Although such a case falls strictly within the definition of 'indictable offences involving a firearm', it is hardly what the average person would call 'crime'.

Remaining for consideration are the following cases which could be called the 'criminal use of firearms' (see Table 25).

TABLE 25   *Criminal use of firearms*

Class	Type of offence	Number	% of sample	Number detected	Detection rate (%)
7	Robberies and attempts	16	4·3	8	50·0
8	Burglaries and attempts	9	2·4	3	33·3
9	Possession with intent	3	0·8	3	100·0
10	Resisting arrest	6	1·6	4	66·6
Total criminal use		34	9·1	18	53·0

Each class will be examined separately, and it will be seen that the seriousness of the offences varies substantially. There are offences which represent a serious danger to the persons concerned, whilst others are, almost certainly, false complaints and others are trivial. The number of robberies in the sample is almost certainly an understatement of that part of the problem and this will be explained under the appropriate heading. Even allowing for this, it would seem that the figure for the criminal use of firearms is something just over one tenth of the Home Office's figure of indictable offences involving a firearm. Even within that tenth, not all cases represent serious criminal activities.

Classification 7—Robberies and Attempts

Robbery is defined in Section 8(1) of the Theft Act 1968 as follows: 'A person is guilty of robbery if he steals, and immediately before, or at the time of doing so, and in order to do so, he uses force on any person or puts or seeks to put any person in fear of being then and there subjected to force.' As has previously been mentioned, some offences could be alternatively classed as robbery or burglary. Where the ingredients of robbery are present the offence has been so categorised in this sample. This appears to follow the general police practice, particularly so far as offences involving a firearm are concerned. Attempts to rob, assaults with intent to rob and conspiracies to rob would also fall into this category. Sixteen offences were placed under this heading and these represent the most significant proportion of the criminal use of firearms. Brief details of each case are given so that independent conclusions may be reached.

1. Five men entered the registered parcels section of a post office where they attacked the staff by spraying ammonia in their eyes and coshing them. They took mailbags and ran to a parked car. A passer-by made towards the vehicle and one of the gang produced a shotgun and fired towards the man's legs. Two pellets hit the man in the leg, suggesting that the shot was wide. The case has not been cleared up.

2. A postman delivering registered mail was attacked by two men. He was struck over the head by one man who was carrying a pick handle, whilst the second attacker fired a shotgun into the air, apparently to prevent any interference from bystanders. A sack of mail was taken and the men escaped in a waiting car. Serious injuries were caused by the blows with the pick handle. No injury was caused by the shotgun. The case has not been cleared up.

3. Four men aged 26, 28, 30 and 44 went to a good class house,

one armed with a shotgun, one with a pick handle and one with an ammonia spray. The woman of the house was attacked and the house searched. When the husband returned, he too was attacked. Both occupants received serious injuries from blows to their heads with the pick handle and from the ammonia sprayed into their eyes. No injuries were caused by the shotgun. The men escaped at the time, but were later arrested. It appears that the shotgun was not loaded. All the men were prohibited from possessing a firearm by virtue of their previous convictions. The shotgun had been recently bought by one member of the gang.

4. A hotel porter was called to a room during the night. There he was attacked by four men, one of whom pointed what the porter later described as a .303 rifle at him (the description of the weapon is unreliable). He was struck on the head with coshes, and was bound and gagged. The men then went into the hall of the hotel where they similarly dealt with a second porter. They then broke open the safe and escaped with cash. Both porters received serious injuries from the coshes. No injuries were caused by the firearm. The case has not been cleared up.

5. A messenger carrying money was walking in the street when he was forced into a shop doorway by two men, one of whom pointed what was believed to be an air pistol at him. The messenger was struck on the head with the pistol and money was taken from him. Slight injuries were caused by striking him. No shots were fired. The case has not been cleared up.

6. An escaped prisoner aged 23 forced his way into an inn at gunpoint and, when the occupant retreated upstairs, the accused tried to shoot his way through a door. The occupant fired his own shotgun and the accused escaped. The accused's motive was established as theft.

7. Following the incident referred to in case 6, the escaped prisoner stopped a car and compelled the driver to drive him away. Later, he ordered the driver out of the car at gunpoint and took the vehicle. He was subsequently stopped by the police (see classification 10, no. 1, p. 148) but escaped and was arrested later, having committed a number of other offences involving the use of firearms in other police areas. The accused was prohibited by law from possessing firearms. He had acquired the weapon illegally following his escape from prison a few weeks before.

8. A 17-year-old youth hailed a taxi and asked to be taken to a point some miles away. On arrival, he produced a shotgun (which

he had recently stolen from a dealer's premises) and demanded the car keys. When the driver refused, the accused shot and seriously wounded him. The accused escaped on foot, threatening bystanders with the gun, but he was later arrested.

9. Three youths aged 19, 19 and 18, entered a newsagent's shop armed with an unloaded automatic pistol, and demanded the contents of the till. When the owner pressed the alarm bell, the youths ran off, dropping the pistol outside the shop. All three were subsequently arrested. The pistol had been bought in a snack bar for £10 a short time before. All three were prohibited from possessing firearms.

10. Three youths broke into a house during the night, one of them armed with what was described as an air pistol. They threatened the occupants who were in bed, searched the house and stole property valued at over £200. The case was not cleared up.

11. Two men aged 21 and 22 entered a sub-post office armed with a starting pistol. When the postmistress shouted for help, the men ran off, but were later arrested. Neither man was prohibited from possessing firearms, but both had numerous previous convictions.

12. A 15-year-old youth armed with an air pistol accosted a cinema manager in the street and demanded money. When the man told him to 'clear off', the boy did so. He was later arrested. He had bought the air pistol from a second-hand shop.

13. An employee (aged 20) in a jeweller's shop took a shotgun (held on certificate) to show another employee who was interested in purchasing it. Whilst the prospective purchaser was looking down the detached barrels, the accused hit him over the head with the butt and took jewellery. He escaped in a car driven by an accomplice, but was later arrested. At no time was the shotgun used as a firearm, it was simply a device for distracting attention, and any other object might well have served the same purpose. The accused had no previous convictions, but the accomplice had a substantial number of convictions.

14. A vehicle driver reported an armed hold-up involving the theft of a substantial amount of money taken from him at pistol point. Extensive police enquiries proved many aspects of the driver's story to be false and it is believed that it was concocted to cover a theft in which the driver was involved.

15. A shopkeeper in his seventies reported an attempted armed hold-up. Extensive police enquiries showed that many aspects of

his story could not have been true. The complaint was almost certainly a figment of the old man's imagination. He had made a previous similar complaint and this had also been shown to be false.

16. An employee, sleeping in the basement of a café, reported that he had been disturbed during the night and, when he went to investigate, he found a man robbing the till. The man produced a revolver and held him at gunpoint whilst he made his escape. Police enquiries showed that there had been no forced entry to the shop and it transpired that the employee had failed to lock the door and a sneak-thief had emptied the till without disturbing him. When he discovered the loss, he made up the story of the gunman to cover his negligence.

Of sixteen robberies, therefore, three were almost certainly false complaints and case 13 did not involve a firearm being used as such. Tables 25, 27 and 28 presented in the same form as those used in Chapter 9 help illustrate some aspects of the effects of firearms controls on robberies involving firearms. The last four cases (13–16), being to say the least questionable, have been excluded from these tables and from those shown later in the chapter. Possibly the most surprising fact to emerge is the very low level of injury caused by shooting. Only in case 8 was serious injury caused by shooting and in case 1, slight injuries were caused. In case 5, slight injury was caused by striking with the firearm, but in cases 1–4—all of them being what could be described as 'professional robberies'—serious injuries were caused by coshes and ammonia. This aspect of the criminal use of firearms is discussed further in Chapter 11.

There is no doubt that the proportion of robberies involved in the sample understates the problem for the whole of England and Wales. This is due entirely to the fact that a disproportionate number of firearms robberies occur in the Metropolitan Police District. Figures supplied by the Home Office clarify this (see Table 29).

To give an indication of the size of the understatement, Table 30 shows the proportion of indictable offences involving a firearm which are robberies.

If the proportion of robberies in the sample is an understatement, it appears that the detection rate suggested may well be an over-statement. The detection rate for all robberies in the Metropolitan Police District for 1969 was 32 per cent. The problem of robberies in which a firearm is involved is largely over-shadowed by the problem in London, and this will be dealt with in depth in Chapter 11.

TABLE 26 *Robberies and attempts—weapons used and injuries caused*

| Weapon | Fired without injury | | | Injuries caused | | | | Injuries caused by weapon other than firearm |
	Threats only	Injury not intended	Injury intended	Slight	Serious	Fatal	Total	
Pistol	1	—	—	—	—	—	1	—
Rifle	1	—	—	—	—	—	1	1
Shotgun	2	1	1	—	1	—	5	2
Sawn-off shotgun	—	—	—	1	—	—	1	1
Air weapon	2	—	—	1*	—	—	3	—
Blank or imitation firearm	1	—	—	—	—	—	1	—
Others	—	—	—	—	—	—	—	—
Total	7	1	1	2	1	—	12	4

* By striking only. No shot fired.

TABLE 27   Robberies and attempts—how the weapon was acquired

Weapon	No restrictions on purchase	Held on cert.	Illegally held and			Not established	Total stolen	Total
			Owned before restrictions	Illegally 'bought'	Home-made*			
Pistol	—	—	—	1	—	—	—	1
Rifle	—	—	—	—	—	1	—	1
Shotgun	—	—	—	3	—	1	1	5
Sawn-off shotgun	—	—	—	—	—	1	—	1
Air weapon	3	—	—	—	—	—	—	3
Blank or imitation firearm	1	—	—	—	—	—	—	1
Others	—	—	—	—	—	—	—	—
Total	4	—	—	4	—	3	1	12

* Includes conversion of blank pistol to fire ammunition.

143

TABLE 28 Robberies and attempts—previous record of offender in terms of likelihood of grant of certificate prior to offence

Weapon	No cert. required	Cert. held for weapon	Prohibited	Unlikely to be granted	No known reason for refusal*	Not known	Total
Pistol	—	—	1	—	—	—	1
Rifle	—	—	—	—	—	1	1
Shotgun	—	—	3	1	—	1	5
Sawn-off shotgun	—	—	—	—	—	1	1
Air weapon	2	—	1	—	—	—	3
Blank or imitation firearm	—	—	1	—	—	—	1
Others	—	—	—	—	—	—	—
Total	2	—	6	1	—	3	12

* Taking account of character only, and not taking account of the requirement to establish good reasons for requiring a firearm certificate.

Classification 8—Burglaries and Attempts

Burglary is defined by Section 9 of the Theft Act 1968 as follows:
A person is guilty of burglary if:

(a) He enters any building or part of a building as a trespasser with intent to commit any such offence as is mentioned in subsection (2) below: or

(b) Having entered any building or part of a building as a trespasser he steals or attempts to steal anything in that building or that part of it or inflicts or attempts to inflict on any person therein any grievous bodily harm.

TABLE 29 *Proportion of firearm robberies in London, 1967–9*

Year	Firearm robberies England and Wales	London	% of firearm robberies which occur in London
1967	265	201	75
1968	372	268	72
1969	484	345	71

TABLE 30 *Firearms robberies as a percentage of indictable offences involving a firearm, 1967–9*

Year	Total firearm offences	Total firearm robberies	% of total formed by robberies
1967	2,339	265	11·3
1968	2,503	372	14·8
1969	3,298	484	14·6

The offences referred to in subsection (2) are offences of 'stealing anything in a building or part of the building in question, of inflicting on any person therein any grievous bodily harm or raping any woman therein, and of doing unlawful damage to the building or

145

anything therein'. Aggravated burglary, as defined by Section 10, includes any offences of burglary committed when the person has with him any firearm or imitation firearm.

Offences involving firearms committed in a building can, in many cases, be alternatively classified as robbery or burglary. For the purpose of this study, they have been classified as burglary when all the ingredients of robbery were not present. For example, when the motive was other than theft, where the theft was completed before the firearm was produced, or where it was established that a firearm was carried, but was not used 'immediately before, or at the time of stealing'. This would include cases where a person was arrested at the scene of a burglary and found to have a firearm in his possession.

Nine cases were so classified, but it will be seen that the last six of these hardly qualify for the description:

1. Two men aged 38 and 40 broke into a cashier's office in an office block. The caretaker was disturbed and he detained one man. The second man returned and, at the point of a pistol, compelled the caretaker to release his prisoner. Both men escaped, but were later arrested. When arrested, two pistols and a sawn-off shotgun were found in their possession. The pistol carried during the burglary had, according to the accused, been bought in Ulster a short time before. Both men were prohibited from possessing firearms.

2. Two boys aged 13 and 16 were poaching with a .410 shot pistol. They entered an empty farmhouse with the suspected intention of stealing, but were disturbed by the owner. In making their escape, one of them fired a shot at the owner (see classification 10, no. 4, p. 148). One boy was detained by the owner and the other was later arrested by the police. The shot pistol had been bought recently from another youth. From its description it may well have been in circulation since before 1920. Both boys were prohibited by virtue of their ages from acquiring firearms.

3. The accused, aged 29, committed a burglary at a factory and was found on the roof by the police. He was in possession of an air pistol but he made no attempt to use it. According to the accused, the pistol had been borrowed from a friend. When seen by the police the friend said the accused had no authority to take the air pistol.

4. Six cases of burglary were committed during a short period of time on one council estate and, to judge from the methods used and the property stolen, they were the work of juveniles. The only use of a firearm was in the method of entry which had involved shooting

a hole in a window with a .22 air weapon in order that an instrument could be inserted to release the catch. The cases were not detected.

Of the nine cases of burglary, therefore, it can be said that in six the firearm was not used as such, but was merely an instrument to facilitate entry. These six cases have been excluded from Tables 31–4 at the end of this chapter.

Classification 9—Possession with Intent

Offences under this heading fall into three sub-classifications:

(a) Possession of a firearm with intent to commit an indictable offence, that is, no attempt had been made to commit an offence, but the accused was found in possession of a firearm and it could be shown that he intended to commit an offence.

(b) Possession or use of a firearm when committing an indictable offence other than robbery or burglary.

(c) Possession of a firearm when being arrested for an indictable offence when there was no use of the weapon to resist arrest and where the person was not arrested at the time he was committing the offence. Three cases fell into this classification, coincidentally, one under each sub-classification:

1. A 19-year-old youth had made telephone calls to a wealthy person living some distance away. He was admitted to hospital at his own request and was found to be in possession of a large knife and a starting pistol. The police were called and he told them that he had made the telephone calls and that the knife and starting pistol were to be used in robbing the wealthy person. He was detained for psychiatric treatment.

2. A 21-year-old man waited for a woman in a lane near her home. When she approached he fired a shotgun at her, hitting her in the shoulder. When she fell to the ground, he jumped on her, held her by the throat and produced a knife. The woman remained fairly calm and spoke to the man, who then went away and left her on the ground. He was traced to his home and arrested without difficulty. When arrested, the man admitted that he had intended raping the woman. The shotgun was his own, held on a shotgun certificate. Although his mental condition was called in question by this incident, he had no previous convictions and there was nothing in his background to suggest any mental disorder except what was described as a 'lone-wolf' tendency.

3. A 16-year-old boy arrested for a number of thefts was found to

147

be in possession of an air pistol. There was no suggestion that he had used it in any of the thefts and he was charged only with possessing an uncovered air weapon.

Classification 10—Resisting Arrest

This classification includes all offences of using firearms against the police or other persons for the purpose of resisting arrest after the commission of an offence. Where the use of the firearm was at the scene of a robbery or burglary, the offence is included under that heading. Where the use was removed from the scene, they are included in this classification. Two sub-categories emerge.

(a) The use of firearms against the police, and occasionally against civilians, to avoid arrest following the commission of a crime.

(b) The use of firearms to avoid arrest for relatively minor summary offences such as poaching. Six incidents are recorded:

1. The escaped prisoner involved in classification 7, nos 6 and 7 was seen by a police officer driving the stolen vehicle. The police car forced the other car off the road, but as the officer got out he was held at gunpoint. Despite this, the officer tackled the man and a shot was fired at him. There was a struggle and the man escaped but was later arrested.

2. A police officer saw a man trying the doors of cars in a car park. When he approached, the man drew a revolver and threatened the officer. The officer drew his truncheon and disarmed the man but he escaped following a struggle. He was not arrested. The revolver left at the scene was found to be an imitation.

3. An 18-year-old boy had made a pistol from odds and ends of metal and was seen by a police officer shooting at windows. When the officer approached, the boy threatened him with the pistol and then ran off. The boy hid the pistol and then returned to his place of work where he was arrested. The pistol was home made but functioned well. The ammunition had probably been obtained from a shooting gallery, it being of a special type used for gallery shooting.

4. Two boys aged 13 and 16 had been concerned in a burglary (see classification 8, no. 2, p. 146) when they were disturbed by the owner of the property and ran off. When the owner pursued them a shot was fired at him and one pellet struck him in the leg. One boy was detained by the owner and the other later arrested by the police. The weapon was a .410 shot pistol recently bought by one of the boys.

5. A youth, aged 17, was poaching and when pursued by the land owner, he fired a shot into the ground in front of his pursuer and threatened to shoot again. He escaped at the time, but had been recognised and was later arrested. He was the holder of a shotgun certificate and had no previous convictions.

6. A part-time gamekeeper disturbed two men poaching. They ran off and when he pursued, one man fired a shot into the ground in front of the keeper. Both men escaped.

Tables 31–4 show the various aspects of all cases of criminal use of firearms, including those for armed robbery which have previously been shown in Tables 26–8. Table 33 refers to the background of the offenders in terms of prohibitions, etc., under the Firearms Act. This table refers to the number of cases and, it will be recalled, there are instances where one man has featured in more than one case, for example, the escaped prisoner in classification 7, nos 6 and 7 and classification 10, no. 1. In no case was more than one gun used, but in a number of cases, particularly the robberies, more than one man was involved. Table 34 looks at the same problem in terms of all the individuals involved, whether or not they were carrying the weapon and irrespective of the type of weapon involved. It will be seen that the 24 offences involve 43 individuals, of whom 21 have not been traced. Of the remaining 22, 14 were prohibited from possessing a firearm and 5 were unlikely to have been granted a certificate, due in every case to previous convictions. Of the 21 untraced men, two were concerned in resisting arrest for poaching and one in resisting arrest when seen attempting to steal from cars. The remainder were all concerned in robberies, and it will be shown in Chapter 11 that the major proportion of persons concerned in robbery have previous convictions. It would be reasonable to assume that a substantial proportion of the untraced persons were prohibited from possessing firearms.

In relating firearms controls to these offences, it might be useful to ask again the three questions posed in relation to domestic assaults:

1. Have controls prevented unauthorised persons from acquiring and using firearms?

2. How far could certificate procedures have gone in preventing offenders from obtaining certificates prior to the commission of an offence?

3. Would the absence of a firearm have made any significant difference to the outcome of the crime?

TABLE 31 Criminal use of firearms—weapons used and injuries caused

Weapon	Possess only	Threats only	Fired without injury: Injury not intended	Fired without injury: Injury intended	Injuries caused: Slight	Injuries caused: Serious	Injuries caused: Fatal	Total	Injuries caused by weapon other than firearm
Pistol	1	3	—	—	1	—	—	5	—
Rifle	—	1	—	—	—	—	—	1	1
Shotgun	—	2	3	2	—	2	—	9	2
Sawn-off shotgun	—	—	—	—	1	—	—	1	1
Air weapon	2	2	—	—	1*	—	—	5	—
Blank or imitation firearm	1	2	—	—	—	—	—	3	—
Others	—	—	—	—	—	—	—	—	—
Total	4	10	3	2	3	2	—	24	4

* Used to strike only, no shots fired.

TABLE 32 *Criminal use of firearms—how the weapon was acquired*

Weapon	No restrictions on purchase	Held on cert.	Illegally owned and			Not established	Total stolen	Total
			Owned before restrictions	Illegally 'bought'	Home-made*			
Pistol	—	—	—	4	1	—	—	5
Rifle	—	—	—	—	—	1	—	1
Shotgun	—	2	—	4	—	2	1	9
Sawn-off shotgun	—	—	—	—	—	1	—	1
Air weapon	4	—	—	—	—	—	1†	5
Blank or imitation firearm	3	—	—	—	—	—	—	3
Others	—	—	—	—	—	—	—	—
Total	7	2	—	8	1	4	2	24

* Includes conversion of blank pistol to fire ammunition.
† Questionable case of theft, see burglary number 3.

151

TABLE 33 *Criminal use of firearms—previous record of offender in terms of grant of certificate prior to offence (by number of cases)*

Weapon	No. cert. required	Cert. held for weapon	Prohibited	Unlikely to be granted	No known reason for refusal*	Not known	Total
Pistol	—	—	4	—	1	—	5
Rifle	—	—	—	—	—	1	1
Shotgun	—	2	5	1	—	1	9
Sawn-off shotgun	—	—	—	—	—	1	1
Air weapon	3	—	2	—	—	—	5
Blank or imitation firearm	2	—	1	—	—	—	3
Others	—	—	—	—	—	—	—
Total	5	2	12	1	1	3	24

* Taking account of character only, and not taking account of the requirement to establish good reasons for requiring a firearm certificate.

TABLE 34 *Criminal use of firearms—background of individual offenders*

Cert. granted	Prohibited	Unlikely to be granted	No known reason for refusal*	Not known	Total
2	14	5	1	21	43

* Taking account of character only, and not taking account of the requirement to establish a good reason for requiring a firearm certificate.

In no less than 12 of the 24 cases, the persons using the firearms are known to have been prohibited by the Act from possessing firearms and it seems likely that this would apply to most of the cases in which the offenders were not traced. Of all the individuals concerned, it can be shown that the greater number were prohibited. Table 32 shows that the major source of weapons was the 'black market' and not theft or acquisition from certificate holders. Two weapons are shown to have been stolen, but in one case the theft was questionable. It would seem fair to conclude that firearms controls have been largely ineffective in preventing these offenders from obtaining and using firearms.

In only two cases was the offender the holder of a shotgun certificate and neither case is in the normal run of crime. In the case of the man who shot a woman intending to rape her (classification 9, no. 2), he was of previous good character and there was nothing in his background which would have given the slightest indication of the likelihood of his committing this type of offence. The second case (classification 10, no. 5), concerns a boy of 17 poaching and shooting into the ground to prevent the land owner catching him. Once again, the youth had no previous convictions and there was nothing in his background to suggest that he would commit an offence of this nature. It will be seen from Chapter 15, that Chief Officers of Police are very slow to grant certificates to persons with previous convictions even when these do not amount to a prohibition on the grant of a certificate. The present procedures ensure that, with the exception of the type of case mentioned above which no one could foresee, certificates are not granted to the individual likely to commit crimes of the type considered here.

As to whether the presence or absence of a firearm would have

L

made any difference to the outcome of the offences, it is easy, on a superficial examination of the cases, to conclude that it would. However, it must be noted that serious injury caused by shooting occurred in only two cases and if these are examined (classification 7, no. 8 and classification 9, no. 2) it might be asked if the offender would have been deterred from committing the offence by the absence of a firearm, and whether the substitution of some weapon such as a knife or an axe would have resulted in injuries any less severe. Slight injuries were caused in three cases. In one this was only by striking with the weapon (classification 7, no. 5), in another a shot was fired during a robbery (classification 7, no. 1) and in the third a shot was fired by juveniles resisting arrest (classification 10, no. 4). In four cases serious injuries were caused by coshes and ammonia. In relation to robbery only, this problem is discussed further in Chapter 11, but it is possible to question, in most cases, whether the injuries actually caused would have been more or less serious if no firearm had been present. In the cases of resisting arrest, it seems that the extended range of a firearm when compared to such weapons as a knife or blunt instrument, is a significant factor. Professor Wolfgang's conclusions, quoted in Chapter 9 may be found to be wholly applicable.

11 The Real Measure

In the foregoing chapters it has been established that the published figure for indictable offences in which a firearm was involved do not provide a reliable guide to any growth in the criminal use of firearms; and it has been shown in Chapter 10 that armed robberies represent the largest category of criminal use. As a class of offence, robbery is comparatively reliable as an index of criminal activity. Much has been made recently of the 'dark figures' in crime—that proportion of crime which is not, for various reasons, reported to the police. All detailed studies of reported crime reveal that a proportion of the reports relate to questionable or trivial matters, changes in the reporting habits of the public and the recording methods used by the police. All materially affect the figure of reported crime to a greater or lesser extent. It is suggested that the figures for robbery, and in particular, for robbery in which a firearm was involved, are less likely to be affected by these factors than almost any other class of crime. Only rarely will the victim of a robbery feel that it is not worth reporting the matter to the police, or will the police, on receiving the report, fail to record it correctly. Robbery, therefore, is relatively uncomplicated by such problems and the figures over a period of years are, for all practical purposes, comparable.

To measure any trend in the criminal use of firearms with any degree of certainty, it is essential that a study extends over a substantial period of time, particularly if the trend is to be related to the effectiveness of firearms controls. The figures for indictable offences involving a firearm do not represent a true picture of the trend in the criminal use of firearms; indeed, as will be shown, the indication given for recent years may well be positively misleading. The most reliable guide to the extent of the growth of the criminal use of firearms lies, it is suggested, in the figure for robberies in which a firearm was used or carried. Whilst this will not establish the full level of criminal use, it will, over the years, provide a reliable index which will illustrate clearly the relative levels of the criminal use of firearms. The figure for armed robberies for the whole of

England and Wales is available only from 1966 onwards—a period too short to permit of sound conclusions. The figure for the Metropolitan Police District has been made available by the Commissioner in his annual report since 1946, and it is this figure which represents the only reliable index to the rise in the criminal use of firearms. Throughout this chapter, reference will be made to robberies in London, and this should be taken to mean all robberies, assaults with intent to rob and conspiracies to rob in the Metropolitan Police District.

It has been shown in Chapter 10 that, even when a firearm is involved, offences recorded as robbery vary substantially between the extremes of violent and carefully planned crimes and the young boy making a very amateurish and ineffective attempt to obtain money. These extremes are also present in the figures for London but it is not now possible to refine the classification over the whole period from 1946. A great deal of work on this subject has been done by McClintock and Gibson[1] in their study of the robberies in London between 1950 and 1960. Although any rise in the rate of robbery, including the rate of robbery involving a firearm, must include cases at each end of the scale of seriousness, McClintock and Gibson found:

> The most important absolute increase was in robbery of persons who, as part of their employment, were in charge of money or goods. This group includes the premeditated and carefully planned raids on banks, post offices and large stores, and the seizure of money in transit from banks or business premises (p. 16).

The rise in question was from 95 cases in 1950 to 174 in 1957. The estimate for 1960, based on the number of cases in six months, was 433, indicating that the rise in this class of robbery continued. It seems, therefore, that whilst robberies in London will contain an element of relatively minor crime, the serious robberies continue to be a substantial (and possibly increasing) part of the total. Although the figures do not represent a particular level of serious crime, it is suggested that their reliability as an index is acceptable.

Robbery, as a class of crime, has a number of distinctive features. Many of the points brought out in Chapter 10 are confirmed in the McClintock and Gibson study. Robbery is not generally an amateur's game. The previous study found, 'Robbery is not, in general, a first offender's crime; in both 1950 and 1957 about two thirds of the offenders had previous convictions, and many of those who were first offenders were associated with recidivists in the commission of the offence'. The detection rate for robbery is low. In 1969, 32·2 per cent of robberies and assaults with intent to rob in the Metropolitan Police District were detected, but this figure does not tell the full story. McClintock and Gibson found that, in cases not cleared up, 'The proportion of male victims was higher, the use of cars greater, the prevalence of gangs was greater, and the offenders tended to be older. All these differences stem from the fact that these cases include a higher proportion of planned robberies.' What this really means is that the low-class or amateur robber is more easily caught. The chances of detection for the 'professional' criminal committing a robbery of the type shown in cases 1–4, classification 7, Chapter 10 are extremely low.

From the figures given in Table 29, it will be seen that, in 1969, robberies involving a firearm in London represent 71 per cent of all those in England and Wales. The Home Office booklet, *Firearms in Crime* shows that the proportions in 1967 and 1968 were 75 per cent and 72 per cent respectively. Thus, the figures for armed robbery in the Metropolitan Police District over the years represent a very substantial proportion of all criminal use. Table 35 gives figures extracted from the Commissioner's Annual Reports for robberies in the Metropolitan Police District. From 1962, cases of conspiracy to rob are included, and these amount to about twenty in each year. The circumstances in which such a crime would be recorded are illustrated in the following example in 1969: two men, both with previous convictions, were seen watching an office where wages were due to be paid. They had a car and one of them was found to be in possession of a .410 shotgun. They admitted intending to rob the office, but they were interrupted before they had gone far enough for a charge of attempted robbery to be brought.

The rates of robbery, armed robbery and robbery involving a firearm have been rising rapidly, but not steadily, a factor which is illustrated by Figure 1. The graph is divided into six-year periods, as are later graphs, and there are significant differences of level between the latter two and the first two periods, the differences of level being common to each of the three lines on the graph. The rise in the criminal use of firearms is clearly indicated by the figures in Table 35. Taking known firearms only, the numbers start with 25 cases in 1946, fall to a low of just 4 cases in 1954, and rise to no less than 272 cases in 1969. When compared to cases in which a blunt instru-

TABLE 35   *Robberies in the Metropolitan Police District, 1946–69*

WEAPON USED OR CARRIED*

Year	Total cases	Firearm†	Supposed firearm‡	Blunt instru- ment	Sharp instru- ment	Irritant	Total armed robberies
1946	299	25	19	n/a	n/a	n/a	n/a
1947	354	46	15	(71)		n/a	132
1948	373	28	20	(62)		n/a	110
1949	290	13	20	(50)		n/a	83
1950	256	19	15	34	12	n/a	80
1951	214	10	4	29	20	n/a	63
1952	298	19	8	51	18	3	99
1953	295	17	13	48	22	5	105
1954	241	4	8	46	15	3	76
1955	237	13	10	24	33	4	84
1956	314	19	12	58	35	9	133
1957	398	20	10	63	39	4	136
1958	558	35	14	99	71	5	224
1959	671	51	49	125	74	13	312
1960	763	39	31	149	66	22	307
1961	963	53	36	207	95	16	407
1962	1,017	62	49	191	76	29	407
1963	973	43	32	218	58	29	380
1964	1,266	92	40	250	85	68	535
1965	1,609	114	53	366	104	65	702
1966	1,992	142	84	348	161	117	852
1967	2,012	165	40	266	175	145	791
1968	1,910	225	54	258	229	72	838
1969	2,236	272	70	278	279	51	950

* A case in which weapons were used is recorded under the most 'serious' weapon involved. Thus, if four men involved in a robbery had stocks or coshes, and the fifth man had a firearm, the case would be recorded under 'firearm'. It will be noted from the cases discussed in Chapter 10 that in many of the cases in which firearms were involved, blunt instruments were also employed. The figure for blunt instruments, therefore, represents only those cases in which there was no firearm involved. The total number of cases in which blunt instruments were used includes a substantial number of the cases recorded under 'firearm'.

† 'Firearm' means any type of firearm including air weapons and imitation firearms, when it can be shown that such a weapon was used or carried.

‡ 'Supposed firearm' refers to cases where the thieves appeared to have a firearm, but it was not possible to verify this.

ment only was used, the rise has taken place much later, and the hundred mark is not passed until 1965 in the case of firearms, while it was passed in 1959 for blunt instruments. From 1965–9, however, the cases involving a firearm have more than doubled and are now about level with those involving only a blunt instrument and with those involving a sharp instrument. The graph in Figure 1 is on a

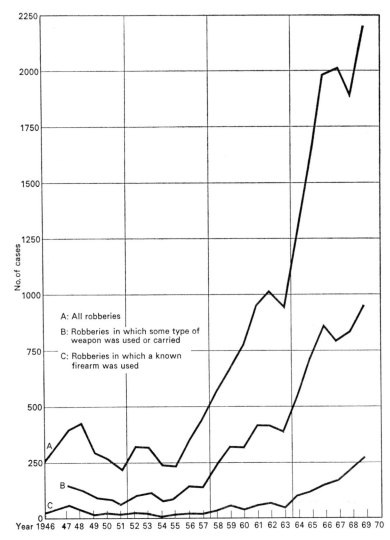

FIGURE 1   *Robberies in the Metropolitan Police District*

scale too small to show clearly just how this rise in the involvement of firearms in robbery has taken place but Figure 2 illustrates this on a larger scale. The significance of the latter two periods of time is also made clear on this graph.

These figures clearly indicate a very serious and continuing rise in the criminal use of firearms in recent years and help illustrate

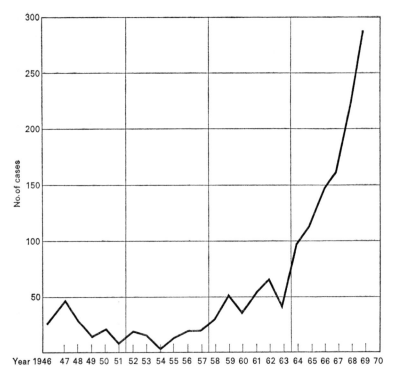

FIGURE 2 *Robberies in London in which a firearm is known to have been carried or used*

one of the dangerous features of the Home Office figures for indictable offences involving a firearm. The figures for 1967 and 1968 are considered by the Home Office to be reliable, and they indicate a levelling off of the problem—2,339 cases in 1967, 2,503 cases in 1968. The figure for 1969, 3,298 cases, suggests a sudden change in the problem. Because the figures for the criminal use of firearms are lost amongst the mass of thefts of weapons and of children causing slight injury with air weapons, the serious and dangerous trends which are shown clearly in Figure 2 are lost to sight. The true picture would seem to be that indicated by Figure 2 which shows that the criminal use of firearms has continued to rise steeply since 1964, but that the numbers are in hundreds rather than in thousands.

The figures relating to robberies in which a firearm was used or carried are worthy of close examination. There is a temptation to jump to the conclusion that more firearms have somehow become available to the criminal, and that the mere availability of firearms represents a substantial part of the problem. Such a conclusion would, it is suggested, be a gross over-simplification, and would be erroneous. Figure 2 shows that the number of cases fell during the first six year period, and stayed very low throughout the second period, with just four cases in 1954. From 1957, there was a positive rise, despite yearly fluctuations, and from 1964 the rise was so steep as to be almost vertical, ending with 272 cases in 1969. In Table 36 the twenty-four year period has been broken into six-

TABLE 36   *Robberies in London in which a firearm was invovled —6-year averages*

Years	Cases
1946–1951	23·5
1952–1957	15·3
1958–1963	47·1
1964–1969	168·3

year stages, and if the average number of cases in each of these stages is examined, the differences between the periods are more clearly shown.

In what way could firearms controls, or the availability of firearms have affected these figures. The evidence produced in Chapter 15 shows clearly that throughout the entire period there were vast numbers of illegal pistols in circulation. Until May 1968, shotguns were completely free from controls; persons with certain convictions were prohibited from possessing shotguns throughout the period, but it is clear that any criminal who wished to acquire one could have done so. With thousands of illegal pistols on the market and with shotguns free of control, any criminal who wanted a gun could certainly have got one, yet, in 1954, only four criminals chose to use a firearm in robbery. In 1969 firearms were certainly no more readily available (though probably no less) and yet there were 272 cases in which criminals used firearms. The rise does not feature only the recently controlled shotgun. The Home Office figures indicate that, in England and Wales, shotguns featured in 20 per cent of the robberies in 1967, 25 per cent in 1968, and 20 per cent in 1969, whilst pistols featured in 47 per cent, 36 per cent and 35 per cent respectively. In other words, the pistol, which has been subject to the strictest controls for fifty years, was used far more frequently than the more easily available shotgun.

How, then, can firearms controls be related to these figures? The truth of the matter appears to be that the guns were always there, available to any criminal who chose to use them, but that criminals have only chosen to use them in significant numbers during the later periods. Firearms controls do not appear to have stopped this class of criminal from obtaining a gun when he felt that he could use one.

All this, and indeed, all the argument recently made public on this question, presupposes that the answer to the problem lies in making it more difficult for the criminal to acquire firearms. Reference to Chapter 15 on the numbers of weapons illegally in circulation, and an examination of the figures just given, clearly indicate that firearms controls have failed to do this. The presumption has been that the problem lay in the availability, or use, of firearms and the question asked appears to have been, 'How can we stop criminals obtaining firearms?' From the evidence so far supplied, the answer appears to be that we cannot. Further study of the problem may, however, indicate that we have been asking the wrong question. If this is so, it is hardly surprising that we have failed to find the right answer.

Robbery, as a crime, always involves a degree of technical violence and is, in fact, simply stealing by means of threats or violence. There are many other ways of stealing: property can be stolen by burglary, or by a variety of methods of simple stealing, such as sneaking into property, and so on. Using figures extracted from the reports of the Commissioner of Police for the Metropolis, a total for all forms of stealing in each year has been found. This includes all forms of breaking offence, including attempts, all robberies and attempts, assaults with intent to rob etc., and all the various forms of stealing. The entries excluded were possession of house-breaking implements, taking motor vehicles without consent (where the vehicle is recovered), frauds and receiving. This figure has been contrasted with the incidence of robbery to establish whether, of those persons willing to steal, a greater number have been willing to use violence in their thefts, and so convert the crime from theft to robbery. Table 37 shows that whilst all forms of stealing have

TABLE 37   *All forms of stealing contrasted with robbery—Metropolitan Police District, 1946–69*

Year	All types of theft	Robbery	% of theft which is robbery
1946	119,944	299	0·249
1947	118,155	345	0·299
1948	101,509	373	0·367
1949	96,007	290	0·302
1950	90,205	256	0·283
1951	80,234	214	0·266
1952	99,122	298	0·300
1953	89,386	295	0·330
1954	69,516	241	0·346
1955	85,451	237	0·277
1956	97,921	314	0·320
1957	113,365	398	0·351
1958	138,091	558	0·404
1959	151,844	671	0·441
1960	171,320	763	0·445
1961	178,815	963	0·538
1962	194,518	1,017	0·522
1963	207,672	973	0·468
1964	231,519	1,266	0·546
1965	251,752	1,609	0·639
1966	255,545	1,992	0·779
1967	238,650	2,012	0·843
1968	241,380	1,910	0·791
1969	257,142*	2,236	0·869

* Introduction of the Theft Act.

increased, 2·14 times in the twenty-four year period, robbery has increased by no less than 7·47 times in the same period. Figure 3 illustrates the percentage of all stealing formed by robbery through the period. Once again, the latter two periods show distinct changes in pattern (see Table 38 for six year averages).

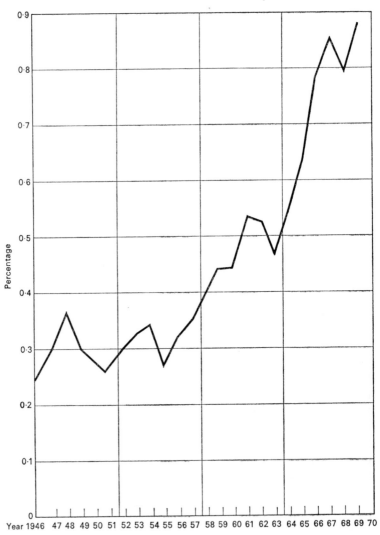

FIGURE 3   *Robbery as a percentage of all stealing—Metropolitan Police District, 1946–69*

A conclusion which might be drawn from this is that, of all the people who are willing to steal, a significantly greater number are now prepared to use some violence in doing so. That this is not a feature peculiar to London is illustrated by repeating the exercise with figures extracted from the criminal statistics for England and

TABLE 38 *Robbery as a percent-age of all stealing—Metropolitan Police District—6-year averages*

Year	%
1946–51	0·294
1952–57	0·320
1958–63	0·469
1964–69	0·744

Wales, shown in Table 39. We see from this that, for the country as a whole, the incidence of stealing has increased threefold, whilst the incidence of robbery has increased 6·55 times, confirming the conclusion reached in relation to the London figures. Taking England and Wales as a whole, the increase in robberies has not been as high as in the Metropolitan Police District, but it is none-theless significant.

The figures used in Tables 37 and 39 are 'crude', that is to say, they are taken from the published returns without being refined, or allowance being made for such factors as changes in reporting habits of the public, etc. There is little doubt that such under-reporting as occurs is disproportionately present in 'all types of theft'. Various studies suggest that, whilst robbery is nowhere near one hundred per cent reported, the published figure is much nearer to the true figure than is the case, for example, with thefts of items of small value. The figure for 'all types of theft' could be, and probably has been, affected by changes in public reporting habits, but there is no reliable way of estimating just how much of the rise represents a true rise in all types of theft. A further check has there-fore been made of robbery contrasted with breaking offences and thefts where the value of the property stolen exceeds £10. The

165

pattern was found to be similar, though less pronounced, and this tends to further confirm the previous suggestions.

Figure 4 shows the percentage of stealing which is robbery in England and Wales in the form of a graph. Once again the levels of the figures rise by distinct steps at 1957 and 1964.

By dividing the twenty-four years into six-year periods, the averages obtained again indicate the significance of the changes (see Table 40).

TABLE 39 *All forms of stealing contrasted with robbery in England and Wales, 1946–69*

Year	All types of theft	Robbery	% of theft which is robbery
1946	425,937	921	0·216
1947	439,370	979	0·222
1948	462,790	1,101	0·237
1949	393,793	990	0·251
1950	394,585	1,021	0·258
1951	451,670	800	0·177
1952	440,027	1,002	0·227
1953	397,782	980	0·246
1954	361,558	812	0·224
1955	370,437	832	0·224
1956	409,993	965	0·235
1957	466,742	1,194	0·255
1958	561,317	1,692	0·301
1959	581,120	1,900	0·326
1960	642,891	2,014	0·313
1961	698,149	2,349	0·336
1962	782,585	2,517	0·321
1963	856,237	2,483	0·289
1964	940,113	3,066	0·326
1965	949,576	3,736	0·393
1966	1,055,151	4,474	0·424
1967	1,053,602	4,564	0·433
1968	1,116,764	4,815	0·431
1969	1,300,051*	6,041	0·464

* Introduction of Theft Act.

Robbery, as has been said, is simply stealing by violence. The degree of violence eventually used may be affected by factors partially outside the criminal's control. Thus, in one robbery the victim may, through fear, hand over the property without a real

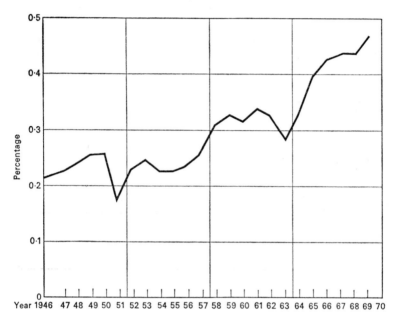

FIGURE 4   *Robbery as a percentage of all stealing—England and Wales*

struggle but in another identical case, the victim may be willing to resist and injuries may be caused. The number and nature of the injuries caused in robbery may not, therefore, be a true reflection

TABLE 40   *Robbery as a percentage of all stealing—England and Wales—6-year averages*

Years	%
1946–51	0·226
1951–7	0·235
1958–63	0·314
1964–9	0·411

167

of the criminal's intentions, or of his willingness to use violence. One factor which may be a good indicator of the degree of violence which the criminal is prepared to use is the proportion who arm themselves before committing a robbery. The fact that a robber takes with him a pick handle (a favourite weapon), or a gun, is often an indication of his willingness to use a high degree of violence if this becomes necessary. Table 41 shows the number of robberies in London together with the number which involved the use of a weapon and the proportion which these form of the whole. Figure 5

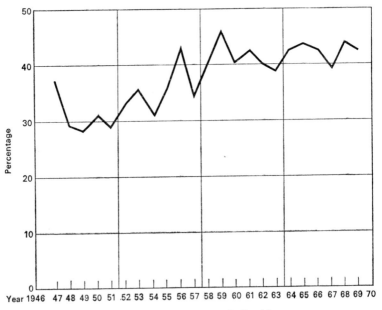

FIGURE 5 *Armed robbery as a percentage of all robbery*

shows in the form of a graph the percentage of robberies in which arms were used. Several features stand out: one is the apparent peaks showing a rise in the use of weapons in 1947–8 and in 1956, and then, once more, the general level rises after 1957 and again after 1964. Using the same six-year periods used for other figures, the rises in levels are clearly indicated (see Table 42).

Thus, the proportion of stealings which are robbery and therefore involve a degree of violence has risen sharply, and the proportion of robberies in which there was probably a premeditated willingness

TABLE 41 *Percentage of robberies in London in which weapons were used or carried, 1946–69*

Year	Number of robberies	Number of armed robberies	Percentage of robberies in which weapons were used
1946	299	n/a	n/a
1947	354	132	37·2
1948	373	110	29·4
1949	290	83	28·6
1950	256	80	31·2
1951	214	63	29·4
1952	298	99	33·2
1953	295	105	35·5
1954	241	76	31·5
1955	237	84	35·4
1956	314	133	42·3
1957	398	136	34·2
1958	558	224	40·1
1959	671	312	46·4
1960	763	307	40·2
1961	963	407	42·2
1962	1,017	407	40·0
1963	973	380	39·0
1964	1,266	535	42·2
1965	1,609	702	43·6
1966	1,992	852	42·7
1967	2,012	791	39·3
1968	1,910	838	43·8
1969	2,236	950	42·4

to use violence, evident by the carrying or use of a weapon, has also increased within the robbery classification. It is commonly supposed that a firearm must be the most dangerous weapon available to the robber, but in terms of actual injury caused, this is not so. Home Office figures[2] indicate that in 261 robberies involving a firearm in 1967, only 8 people were seriously injured and 20 people slightly injured, whilst in 1968, 5 were seriously injured and 15 slightly injured in 372 firearms robberies covering the whole of England and Wales. In the two years, injuries occurred in only 8 per cent of the firearm robberies. Even these figures overstate the

TABLE 42   *Percentage of robberies in London in which weapons were used or carried—6-year averages*

Year	%
1946–51	31·2
1952–7	35·3
1958–63	41·3
1964–9	42·3

problem, for in a number of cases the injuries reported were caused by striking and not by shooting.

A study of the circumstances of the 'professional' robberies typified by cases 1–4 (classification 7, Chapter 10), shows strong evidence of careful pre-planning, together with a quite remarkable ability to calculate the risks involved. In situations where the inexperienced would say that it was virtually impossible, they have used the correct number of men and the most efficient (and most ruthless) tactics to rush into difficult situations, grab their haul of cash or valuables and escape. The use of weapons is obviously an important part of the plan. When firearms are involved, the pattern which seems to emerge is for the minimum number (most frequently, one) to carry a gun, and for the others to be armed with coshes, pick handles or ammonia. Shooting is rare and the role of the gun is to intimidate. It is clear that much emphasis is placed on shock and on the relatively short period when all those around will be stunned into inactivity. The blunt instruments and ammonia are often used to increase the shock and to incapacitate those who are in the way at the outset. In addition to its shock-producing role, the firearm appears also to be used to prevent interference and to facilitate escape and, in most cases, it is only when the firearm is being used in this role that shots are fired at people. In its earlier role of inducing shock, the firearm is, on some occasions, fired into the air or towards the ceiling. The carrying of firearms and other weapons is, therefore, often a premeditated part of the calculations made at the planning stage of this 'professional' type of robbery.

The first four cases of robbery described in classification 10, Chapter 10, indicate a typical pattern for the more serious type of robbery and an examination of a substantial number of further cases in the Metropolitan Police District confirms that this is representative. In the four cases, the serious injuries were caused by criminals armed with coshes, pick handles or other blunt instruments. In only one case was slight injury caused by shooting. The proposition that firearms are used mainly as a means of intimidation is confirmed by these facts. Nevertheless, the fact that a criminal planning a robbery is willing to use firearms, or that one of the gang is to be so armed, indicates a willingness to accept an extremely high degree of violence if this is thought necessary. From the point of view of the victim, the firearm may present a low chance of injury in practical terms; from the point of view of the criminal, it can represent an expression of ruthlessness of the highest order. Table 43 shows the proportion of all armed robberies in which a firearm is known to have been used or carried. It will be seen that from 1948–66, the proportion remains below 20 per cent. Figure 6 shows the percentages in the form of a graph from which it will be seen that, although there are troughs and peaks, the trend is fairly constant until 1966, when there is a sharp rise which appears to be continuing.

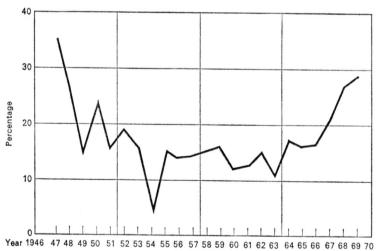

FIGURE 6 *Percentage of armed robberies in London in which firearms were used or carried*

171

Using the six-year averages, these trends are shown a little more clearly (see Table 44).

In Table 44, the figure for the period 1964–9 is slightly misleading

TABLE 43 *Percentage of armed robberies in London in which firearms were used or carried*

Year	Number of armed robberies	Number of firearms robberies	Percentage of armed robberies in which firearms were used or carried
1946	n/a	25	n/a
1947	132	46	34·8
1948	110	28	25·4
1949	83	13	15·6
1950	80	19	23·7
1951	63	10	15·8
1952	99	19	19·1
1953	105	17	16·1
1954	76	4	5·2
1955	84	13	15·4
1956	133	19	14·2
1957	136	20	14·7
1958	224	35	15·6
1959	312	51	16·3
1960	307	39	12·7
1961	407	53	13·0
1962	407	62	15·2
1963	380	43	11·3
1964	535	92	17·1
1965	702	114	16·2
1966	852	142	16·6
1967	791	165	20·8
1968	838	225	26·8
1969	950	272	28·6

and if this is shown for 1964–6 and for 1967–9, the sudden rise in the proportion of firearms used in the last three years becomes more apparent. Those averages are 16·6 per cent and 25·4 per cent respectively.

TABLE 44 *Firearms robberies in London expressed as a percentage of armed robberies–6-year averages*

Years	%
1946–51	23
1952–7	14
1958–63	14
1964–9	21

The proposition put forward is that the problem does not lie simply in the increasing use of firearms by criminals. It has been shown that there has been an increasing willingness to use some violence as a means of stealing, and that the degree of violence which the criminal is willing to use has also risen. Not only are criminals more willing to use violence, they appear to be more willing to resort to excessive violence. Amongst the general increase in the willingness to use weapons, the use of firearms has been a relatively constant proportion. Criminals have proved to us that firearms controls will not deny their small class of people access to firearms whenever they want them, but even if it were possible to deny them their guns, little would have been achieved if they simply turned to other weapons such as coshes, ammonia sprays and the like which, in fact, cause more injuries than firearms.

12 Accidents and Suicides

It is the use of firearms in crime which appears to be the major source of public concern at present, but concern has also been expressed, from time to time, about the involvement of firearms in fatal accidents and suicides. It has not been possible, in this present study, to make detailed analyses of fatal accident cases, or to conduct research into the very complicated problems connected with suicide. The evidence available is, therefore, largely restricted to information gathered from the Registrar General's Returns, and the study has been restricted to examination of these returns over a lengthy period, rather than to detailed year by year studies. No attempt has been made to study the variety of problems associated with these incidents in any depth, and the object has been only to examine the effects, if any, which firearms controls have had, or may have, on these problems.

Accidents

Any attempt to seek to establish a relationship between firearms controls and the incidence of fatal accidents caused by firearms is complicated by a number of factors, and a superficial examination of the statistics could easily lead to an erroneous conclusion. Table 45 gives figures, extracted from the Registrar General's Returns, for accidental deaths caused by firearms (Class E919) for the period 1890–1969, at ten-year intervals. The period selected covers the entire development of firearms controls.

In relating the figures in Table 45 to the introduction of controls, the periods in which the various measures were introduced must be noted. The Pistols Act 1903 was the first restriction imposed and, as described in Chapter 2, its effects must have been very limited. It may have reduced slightly the numbers of new pistols sold by reducing impulsive purchases, but its effect on the number of weapons in circulation must have been minimal. The Firearms Act 1920 did not come into operation until September of that year and its effect on the 1920 figure must therefore have been slight. For all practical purposes, the figures for 1920 and before can be related to a period when legislation had not restricted the numbers of firearms in circulation. The figures for 1890 and 1900, of course, relate to a period when no firearms controls existed. The controls introduced by the 1920 Act were strengthened in the 1937 Act but shotguns, which appear always to have been the type of firearm most frequently

TABLE 45   *Accidental deaths by firearms, 1890–1967*

Year	Number of accidental deaths by firearms	Population	Incidence of fatal firearms accidents
1890	91	29,001,000	1 in 318,692
1900	134	32,249,000	1 in 240,664
1910	71	35,796,000	1 in 504,169
1920	87	38,885,000	1 in 435,395
1930	86	39,806,000	1 in 462,860
1940	165	41,246,000	1 in 249,975
1950	99	43,830,000	1 in 442,727
1960	65	45,775,000	1 in 704,230
1969	41	48,826,000	1 in 1,190,878

concerned in accidents, remained completely uncontrolled until 1968. The restrictions imposed on shotguns in May 1968 may have reduced impulsive purchases of the cheaper shotguns, but it is doubtful if they significantly affected the number of shotguns in circulation during 1969.

On superficial examination, it might be concluded that the supposed reduction in the numbers of firearms in circulation between 1890 and 1969 has resulted in a very substantial decrease in the number of accidents. There are inconsistencies in this. The difference between 1890 and 1900 is marked, but there were no controls on firearms in either year. 1940 shows a substantial increase over both the preceding and following decades and it seems likely that this is due to wartime conditions when millions of men, a large proportion of them unaccustomed to firearms, were armed. Soldiers under training and such reserve units as the Home Guard may, at this early period of their existence, have been responsible for some of the increase.

Taking all these things into account, there has been a substantial reduction in the numbers of deaths from this cause. However, it is clear that factors other than the availability of firearms have influenced this. The significant advances in medical science mean that persons who, as a result of a serious injury, would have died in the early period, are now saved by surgery. The improvements in communications, particularly in the use of telephones and the efficient fleet of radio-controlled ambulances, mean that such cases receive medical attention much more quickly than they would in earlier years. The continuing reduction in the number of deaths between 1950 and 1969, when controls were more or less static, indicates that such factors may be significant.

Every accidental death caused by a firearm is, of course, a tragedy. Classification 5, case no. 3 (Chapter 9), which was finally regarded as an accident, gives some indication of the circumstances in which such deaths can occur, and the grief caused by such a case is not difficult to imagine. Yet, the question of fatal accidents with firearms must be kept in perspective. As a cause of death it ranks very low in the statistical tables. In 1969, road accidents accounted for 7,388 deaths or 1 per 6,608 of the population, against the less than one in a million for firearms accidents. Of course, there are many more motor vehicles than there are firearms, but even judged in relative numbers, firearms are less dangerous than motor vehicles. It has been shown in Chapter 16 that an accurate assessment of the total number of firearms in circulation is impossible, but even if the several million air weapons are excluded, the total is certainly not less than $1\frac{1}{2}$ million. The total number of firearms held on the authority of a certificate (shotgun or firearm certificate) is not less than 1,098,810, and this number underestimates the total in existence very substantially. Even accepting this total, the ratio of fatal accidents to firearms in 1969 was 1 accident per 26,800 firearms. According to the British Road Federation's Basic Road Statistics for 1969, there were 14,751,800 motor vehicles on the road and these accounted for 7,388 deaths, or one death per 1,996 vehicles. Thus it could be said that a motor vehicle is $13 \cdot 4$ times more dangerous than a firearm. Of course, such a comparison is not wholly valid. A motor vehicle tends to be actually in use for a greater part of its life than does a gun and to produce a true figure, it would be necessary to take account of this. However, it seems that, even if this were to be taken into account, a motor vehicle is much more likely to cause death than is a firearm.

Accidents are not, of course, the only cause of deaths involving firearms, but if all the deaths due to firearms are taken together the resulting figure is still small and, indeed, it can be shown that a person is more likely to choke on his food than to meet his death at the point of a gun (see Table 46).

TABLE 46 *Extracts from Registrar General's Returns, 1967—some causes of death*

Type of death	1960	1961	1962	1963	1964	1965	1966	1967
Accidental death by firearm	65	83	80	77	60	58	53	63
Suicide by firearm	177	186	192	156	159	194	173	193
Homicide by firearm	19	20	29	24	19	23	27	48
Total deaths by firearm	261	289	301	257	238	275	253	304
Deaths caused by accidental inhalation of food	403	450	488	473	544	573	552	499

It can be argued that the effects of firearms controls on the rate of fatal accidents cannot be judged because we do not know what the situation would have been if controls had not been introduced. Regrettably, the statistics are not broken down to show the different types of firearm, but a return submitted to parliament in 1893 (see Chapter 1) showed that, in 1890, 16 of the 91 deaths were due to pistols and revolvers. The figures supplied to the Bodkin Committee (see Chapter 4) indicate that shotguns featured in more accidents than any other type of weapon and, having regard to the large numbers of these firearms which are in circulation, it seems reasonable to assume that they have always accounted for the greater percentage of all firearms accidents. Controls on shotguns, instituted only in a relatively ineffective way in 1968, cannot have had any effect on the numbers of guns in circulation in 1969, and it can be seen that, despite this, the accident rate has been falling steadily.

The effect of controls on the rate of accidental deaths caused by firearms is virtually impossible to establish with certainty, and a great deal of research, beyond the scope of this study, would be needed to extract truly accurate information. What can be said is that, on the evidence available, it cannot be claimed that controls have been a significant factor. In considering the question of accidents involving shotguns, the Bodkin Committee said:

> When it is considered that this is the only type of weapon (apart from smoothbore pistols) which has been sold without restriction, that in rural districts it is a common and necessary weapon, and that accordingly the numbers in almost daily use by private persons far exceeds those of any other type of firearm, the figures in the table are not surprising and cannot be regarded as excessive . . . The very general use of sporting shotguns, often in circumstances in which accidents are very liable to occur, will inevitably result in casualties more or less serious.

If this comment was true in 1934, it is no less true in 1969, except that the rate of fatal accidents has fallen very substantially in the interim. Considering the numbers of firearms in use, the accident rate is, in fact, remarkably low and must reflect creditably on the vast majority of the individuals who own and use firearms.

Suicides

The use of firearms in suicides in this country has been declining steadily over the years, whilst the proportion of suicides in relation to the population has remained remarkably constant.

Table 47, compiled from the Registrar General's Returns, illustrates that the number of suicides who have turned to a firearm as the means of ending their lives has fallen from one in 12 in 1890, to one in 24 in 1967, yet the suicide rate has remained almost perfectly constant around the one in 10,000 mark. This tends to suggest that those not using firearms during the later years have simply turned to some other method of killing themselves. Examination over a shorter period of suicides by means of what the Registrar General calls, 'Analgesic and Soporific Substances' (pain-killing and sleep-inducing drugs) shows a substantial rise in suicidal deaths due to these substances (see Table 48).

The very marked rise in suicides from this cause must, however,

TABLE 47   *Suicides—England and Wales, 1890–1967*

Year	Total suicides	Firearm suicides number	ratio	Population	Suicide/ population ratio	Firearm suicide/ population ratio
1890	2,205	184	1/12	29,001,000	1/13,152	1/157,614
1900	2,896	216	1/13	32,249,000	1/11,135	1/149,300
1910	3,567	222	1/16	35,796,000	1/10,035	1/161,243
1920	3,759	258	1/14	37,885,000	1/10,078	1/146,841
1930	5,051	262	1/19	39,806,000	1/7,880	1/151,931
1940	4,517	283	1/15	41,246,000	1/9,131	1/145,745
1950	4,471	207	1/22	43,830,000	1/9,803	1/211,739
1960	5,113	177	1/28	45,775,000	1/8,952	1/258,615
1967	4,711	193	1/24	48,391,000	1/10,271	1/250,730

be compared to the constant rate of suicides in this country. The increasing use of these drugs in suicides has not resulted in a proportionate rise in the total number of suicides, indicating that these drugs are being used as a substitute for some other method. This tends to support the suggestion that the easy availability of one particular method of committing suicide is not one of the more significant factors in the overall suicide rate.

The comparative suicide rates over a substantial number of years does not give a complete picture of the problem. Improvements in medical and communications services may mean that some attempted suicides who, in the past, would have died, might now be saved (for the time being at least). In the case of an attempted suicide by an overdose of drugs, the subject might change his mind and be saved,

TABLE 48   *Suicides due to 'analgesic and soporific substances', 1931–60*

	1931	1940	1950	1960
Suicides by analgesic or soporific substances	21	128	421	839
Ratio to all suicides	1/240	1/35	1/10	1/6

whilst the person who shoots himself will have no opportunity to change his mind. This factor may not be as significant as it first appears if, as seems likely, a person intending suicide does not select a firearm as the method unless he really means to go through with it. Conversely, a proportion of those 'attempting' suicide with drugs who subsequently change their minds, may not have intended to kill themselves in the first place.

Clearly, an exhaustive study of the problem would be needed before one could establish precisely what the relatively constant suicide rate contrasted with the falling rate of the use of firearms in suicide might mean. What is clear is that the use of firearms in suicide has been falling over the years, but it seems likely that this can be attributed to the easy availability of other, more attractive methods, rather than to any effect which firearms controls might have had. The pattern of change shown in the table cannot be related to the pattern of change in controls in any significant way. It seems unlikely that a person intent on taking his own life will be deterred merely by the absence of one particular instrument. That a firearm is readily available in a particular case may well influence the choice of method used, and this suggestion is supported to some extent by the fact that in firearm suicides, males outnumber females by between 12 and 20 to 1, against the 1·7 to 1 ratio for all suicides. It does not seem likely, however, that the complete absence of firearms, even if this were possible, would materially affect the suicide rate.

Part III   Current Firearms Controls

13 Current Firearms Controls—The Law

The control of firearms in England and Wales is governed by the Firearms Act 1968, a consolidating measure, continuing the controls which have developed since 1903. The system of controls imposed on the individual varies according to the class of weapon involved. Broadly speaking, rifles, pistols and sawn-off shotguns are subject to a very strict firearm certificate procedure in which application to possess the weapon is made to the Chief Officer of Police: if the certificate is granted, full details of all weapons and ammunition are entered in the certificate. Sales of weapons must be notified to the police. An applicant for a firearm certificate must show that he has good reason for requiring the weapon and is subjected to the closest scrutiny.

Controls over shotguns are less stringent. An application for a shotgun certificate is also made to the Chief Officer of Police, but the applicant merely has to satisfy conditions about his character and antecedents. No record of weapons is maintained and no notification of sales need be given to the police. With the exception of a small number of the more powerful weapons which are subject to the firearm certificate procedure, air weapons are not subject to police control. Antique firearms are exempt from the provisions of the Act and so may be bought and sold without restriction. Fully automatic firearms such as machine guns and sub-machine guns, together with weapons designed to fire such things as tear gas, are subject to a special form of control administered by the Home Office in addition to the normal firearm certificate controls.

Trade in firearms is controlled by means of the registration of dealers who are subjected to very close scrutiny and are required to maintain high standards of security at their premises and keep full records of all dealings in firearms and ammunition to which the firearm certificate procedure applies, and in shotguns. The possession of firearms in the course of, or in connection with crime is heavily penalised, and possession without lawful excuse in public places, or whilst trespassing, is also subject to penalties. Persons who have received certain sentences are prohibited from possessing firearms for specified periods after their release from prison.

In many respects, the law on this subject is complicated and the following represents only an outline of the controls and is not intended as a definitive statement of the law on the subject; nor does it include any reference to the application of the law to Scotland or Northern Ireland.

Meaning of 'Firearm'. Broadly speaking, the Act applies to any firearm, defined at Section 57(1) as:

a lethal barrelled weapon of any description from which any shot, bullet or other missile can be discharged and includes:
  (a) any prohibited weapon, whether it is such a lethal weapon as aforesaid or not: and
  (b) any component part of any such lethal or prohibited weapon: and
  (c) any accessory to such weapon designed or adapted to diminish the noise or flash caused by firing the weapon.

This definition is worthy of close examination. Firstly, to fall within the definition, the article must be a weapon, fitted with a barrel and it must be lethal. In Bryonson *v.* Gamages Ltd (1907 XXI Cox 515), a person prosecuted under the Pistols Act for selling a spring-operated pistol had pleaded that the pistol did not come within the terms of the Act as it was neither a firearm nor a weapon, but a toy. The magistrates dismissed the case and the prosecutor appealed and, in the King's Bench Division, the Lord Chief Justice, Lord Alverstone, said, 'If he [the magistrate] finds this is a toy, his present decision ought to be affirmed, but if he finds that it was not a mere toy, but it was a "weapon" . . . he ought to convict.' Mr Justice Darling said:

I think it absolutely essential that, first of all, the magistrate should decide whether this thing is a weapon. Now, if it is a weapon from which a shot, or bullet, can be discharged then it is within the Act; but, of course, there are very many weapons from which shots and bullets cannot be discharged, such as a sword. Supposing we were dealing with the question of a sword, you might bring a thing which was in every sense a sword, and yet a man to whom it was shown might say: 'I decline to say that this thing is a weapon. A sword may be a weapon, and the most dangerous weapon, and this thing which you show me is capable of inflicting a wound and perhaps a dangerous wound and yet, having regard to what a sword is intended to do, I decline to regard this sword as a weapon.' So with this pistol. He may look at it, see what it will do, and come to the conclusion that it is a weapon, or that it is not a weapon. In order to do that I think he should carefully inform his mind as to what a weapon is, what a weapon is meant for in the way of offence and defence, and, having arrived at that, if he decides that it is a weapon, then it obviously discharges a bullet and would be within the Act; if not, it would not be.

The matter was taken a little further in the case of Read v. Donovan (1947 1 All ER 37), which was taken under the provisions of the 1947 Act when magistrates had held that a signalling pistol was not designed to kill or inflict injury and had dismissed a charge before them. The prosecutor appealed and the Lord Chief Justice, Lord Goddard, after referring to the fact that signalling apparatus was specifically exempted from the provisions of the Act in certain circumstances said:

> If the weapon is a lethal weapon (and a lethal weapon means a weapon capable of causing injury) and if it is barrelled, and if a shot, bullet or other missile can be discharged, it is a firearm. In this case it clearly is. The intention of the manufacturer is immaterial. The question is simply whether this is a weapon which is capable of inflicting harm, being a barrelled weapon and being one from which any shot, bullet or other missile can be discharged. It clearly is and this case must go back to the magistrates with an intimation that the offence is proved.

In Moore v. Gooderham (1960 3 All ER 675), the meaning of the word 'lethal' was explored still further. In this case a magistrate had held that an air pistol, though capable of causing injury, was not likely to cause death and so was outside the scope of the Act. On appeal, the Lord Chief Justice, Lord Parker, said:

> I think they were fully entitled to give effect to the word 'lethal' in the sense that the injury must be of a kind which may cause death. That is the ordinary meaning of the word, but it is to be observed that, in this connection, one is not considering whether a firearm is designed or intended to cause injury from

which death will result, but rather whether it is a weapon which, however misused may cause injury from which death will result.

The definition must, therefore, be taken as saying that the implement under consideration must:

1. Be a weapon, and whether or not a particular thing is a weapon is a question of fact in each case and cannot be decided merely on capability of causing injury.

2. If it is a weapon, it must be a lethal weapon, that is to say, it must be capable of causing an injury (even through misuse) which might result in death.

3. It must have a barrel and

4. It must be capable of discharging a shot, bullet or other missile.

By virtue of this part of the definition, mere toys are excluded from the controls, but there remain areas of uncertainty. Within the construction industry considerable use is made of 'nail guns', implements powered by blank cartridges and used for driving hardened steel pins into masonry or steel. In many of these devices the pin is located in a short barrel which is pressed against the masonry. By operating a trigger, a blank cartridge is fired and the nail is projected at considerable velocity. In most, a safety device prevents the nail being discharged unless it is pressed firmly against some solid object. These devices are, by practice, not subjected to the Firearms Act controls, the distinction apparently being made being that the instrument is not a weapon, but an industrial tool. However, with minor adaptations, such instruments could, in many cases be made to fire without being pressed against a solid object and they are certainly capable of discharging a missile which is lethal. It is possible to distinguish between nail guns and signalling guns by saying that the latter are specifically mentioned in the Act (for example in Section 13(1)) and it is also possible to suggest that whilst used as tools, these 'nail guns' are outside the Act, but if they were to be used as weapons, they would fall within it. Bearing in mind the latter part of the judgment in Read v. Donovan, these become questionable distinctions, made even less tenable when considered in conjunction with the decision in Cafferata v. Wilson.

Be that as it may, in broad terms, any weapon which is capable of causing injury, which has a barrel, and from which any shot, bullet or other missile can be discharged, falls within the controls of the Firearms Act to a greater or lesser degree, and the three qualifications on the basic definition add to the strength of the controls. The qualification relating to prohibited weapons will be considered separately in conjunction with the degree of control exercised over them.

The inclusion of the phrase, 'any component part of such lethal or prohibited weapon' within the definition means that when such a component is held separately from the weapon, it is considered to be a firearm in its own right. Whilst the component is part of the weapon, it does not require separate mention because the certificate for the weapon includes all its component parts (except a flash eliminator or sound moderator) (Watson *v.* Herman (1952 2 All ER 70)). If, however, a person held a rifle on a firearm certificate and wished to acquire a spare barrel, then the barrel would have to be the subject of a separate entry in the firearm certificate. By practice, and by any reasonable interpretation, the term 'component part' refers to essential components and not to such items as screws or small accessories. One other effect of this part of the definition was illustrated in the case of Cafferata *v.* Wilson (1936 53 TLR 34) which was followed in the case of R. *v.* Freeman (1970 1 WLR 788). In both cases a person was found in possession of a blank cartridge revolver which, although at the time was incapable of discharging a missile, was capable of being readily converted. In each case, the only operation necessary to achieve the conversion was the drilling out of the barrels and cylinder. It was held that such weapons, even though not capable of discharging a missile at the time, contained many of the components parts of a firearm and were thus within the definition. The effect of these decisions has been that blank cartridge weapons which are not normally capable of discharging a missile, will be considered to be firearms subject to control, if they can readily be converted into useable weapons.

The effect of paragraph (c) in the definition is to distinguish from other components and accessories, those accessories which are designed or adapted to diminish the noise or flash caused by firing the weapon. Thus, if a person wishes to have a 'sound moderator', or silencer, fitted to his weapon, this has to be specifically authorised in the firearm certificate.

This broad definition of a firearm brings within the terms of the Act all those weapons which would commonly be considered to be firearms, together with a number of weapons which might, at first glance, be thought not to be firearms. The degree of control exercised over each depends upon which of five categories the weapon falls under.

Section 1 firearms. Every firearm (as defined above) which is not specifically exempted falls under the terms of Section 1 of the Act and is subject to the firearm certificate procedure. By sub-section (3), shotguns with a barrel length exceeding 24 in. are excluded, together with air weapons which are not of a type declared to be specially dangerous. Section 58 exempts antique firearms under certain circumstances. Broadly speaking, Section 1 can be said to apply to pistols, rifles, short-barrelled shotguns, 'specially dangerous' air weapons, and any other weapon not falling into one of the exempted categories discussed later. Strict controls are imposed on this class of weapon. With certain specific exemptions, a person wishing to acquire a firearm or ammunition to which Section 1 applies must first make application (in the prescribed form) to the Chief Officer of Police for the area in which he normally resides for the grant of a firearm certificate. The effect of Section 27 of the Act is that the Chief Officer is prohibited from granting a certificate to any person whom he has reason to believe to be:

(a) prohibited by the Act from possessing firearms (persons who have received certain sentences—see p. 198),

(b) of intemperate habits or unsound mind,

(c) for any reason unfitted to be entrusted with a firearm.

If these qualifications are met, the Chief Officer SHALL grant the certificate if he is satisfied that the applicant:

(a) has good reason for requiring the firearm or ammunition,

AND

(b) can be permitted to have it in his possession without danger to the public safety or to the peace.

The effect of this Section is to give Chief Officers a very wide area of discretion in the granting of certificates, although it is intended that this discretion shall be limited by the applicant's right of appeal to a Court of Quarter Sessions (Section 44 and the Third Schedule).

The firearm certificate, when granted, will specify the weapon which is authorised and the amounts of ammunition which may be acquired or possessed. When the holder acquires a weapon, the person transferring it to him is required to enter details on the firearm certificate and to give notice to the Chief Officer of Police who issued the certificate, within 48 hours (Section 42). If the holder subsequently wishes to acquire further weapons, he is required to apply to the Chief Officer for a variation of his certificate. By Section 27(2) and by Rule 11 of the Firearms Rules 1969, the Chief Officer may impose conditions on the certificate. Four conditions must be imposed on every certificate:

(i) The holder is required to sign the certificate, in ink, on receipt.

(ii) The firearms and ammunition are to be kept in a safe place when not in use.

(iii) The holder is required to report to the police any theft or loss of the firearms.

(iv) The holder is required to notify any change of address to the police.

In addition, Chief Officers usually impose further conditions, for example, restricting the use of the weapons to 'approved ranges' or to one specific piece of land, or by requiring that weapons kept as collector's items shall not be used or fired.

Thus, a firearm certificate relates both to a person and to specific weapons and the procedure is designed to control the movement of weapons from person to person and to facilitate the keeping of police records of these movements.

Shotguns. A shotgun is defined by Section 1(3)(a) as a smooth-bore gun with a barrel not less than 24 in. in length, not being an air gun. Thus, where a shotgun has barrels less than 24 in. in length, it is treated as a firearm to which Section 1 applies and the firearm certificate procedure is applicable. Subject to a number of exemptions (see p. 193) no one may possess a shotgun unless he is the holder of a shotgun certificate. This document differs in many ways from the firearm certificate. Application must be made to the Chief Officer of Police for the area in which the applicant normally resides, and must be in the prescribed form (Section 26(1)). However, Section 28(1) provides that the shotgun certificate shall be granted unless the Chief Officer has reason to believe that the applicant:

(a) is prohibited by the Act from possessing a shotgun, OR

(b) cannot be permitted to possess a shotgun without danger to the public safety or to the peace.

There is here no requirement for the applicant to have 'good reason' for requiring the shotgun and the effect of the Section is that anyone of good character is entitled to the grant of a shotgun certificate. A further contrast with the firearm certificate procedure is that a shotgun certificate refers only to a person and permits him to hold any number of weapons without further formalities, whereas the firearm certificate refers both to the person and to specific weapons, authorising the possession only of those weapons detailed in the certificate. In the case of shotgun certificates, the power of the Chief Constable to impose conditions is restricted to those specified in Rule 2 of the Firearms Rules 1969, and no others. These conditions are:

(i) The holder is required to sign the certificate in ink on receipt.

(ii) Any theft or loss of any shotgun must be reported to the police at once.

There is no requirement to notify a change of address, or any requirement about safe custody, and the Chief Officer is not able to restrict the use of the weapon.

Air weapons. Under the Firearms (Dangerous Air Weapons) Rules 1969, certain air weapons are declared to be 'specially dangerous' and are made subject to the firearm certificate procedure. This applies to any air weapon capable of discharging a missile with a muzzle energy in excess of, in the case of an air pistol, 6 ft-lbs; or in the case of any other air weapon, 12 ft-lbs. The effect of this is to make the more powerful air weapons subject to Section I of the Act whilst the majority of weapons in common use in this country, which do not produce the energies referred to, are exempt. Air weapons which are not classified as 'specially dangerous' are not subject to any restrictions except those which are applicable to all firearms and those which are applicable to young persons.

Antiques. Section 58(2) of the Act provides that nothing in the Act relating to firearms shall apply to an antique firearm which is sold, transferred, purchased, acquired or possessed as a curiosity or ornament. The term antique firearm has not been defined in the Act, nor has it been the subject of a judicial interpretation. There exist many weapons which are clearly antiques by any definition, but there are many others whose status is by no means clear, and the interpretations given to the term by Chief Officers vary. Many follow the guidance of the Commissioner of Police for the Metropolis who issued a statement published in various magazines (for example, *Guns Review*, March 1968) to the effect that a breach-loading weapon capable of use with metallic cartridges would not be regarded as an antique. There is a contrary view which holds that any weapon which is one hundred years old or more should be so regarded (see, for example, *The Justice of the Peace*, April 1969) and the question is not capable of resolution unless a statutory definition is included in future legislation, or until the courts produce a binding precedent. It should be noted that antique firearms are exempted from the provisions of the Act only if they are possessed as a 'curiosity or ornament'. An antique firearm which was possessed otherwise would cease to be exempt and would fall into its appropriate category under the Act (Section I firearm or shotgun), thus, the muzzle-loading rifles used for target practice by some enthusiasts are subject to the firearm certificate procedure despite the fact that they would otherwise qualify as antiques.

Prohibited weapons. A prohibited weapon and prohibited ammunition are defined by Section 5 as:

(i) any firearm which is so designed or adapted that, if pressure is applied to the trigger, missiles continue to be discharged until pressure is removed from the trigger or the magazine containing the missiles is empty;

(ii) any weapon of whatever description, designed or adapted for the discharge of any noxious liquid, gas or other thing; and

(iii) any ammunition containing, or designed or adapted to contain any such noxious thing.

All prohibited weapons are, by virtue of the definition in Section 57, firearms to which Section 1 applies. However, additional controls are placed over these weapons by requiring that before anyone possesses or deals in such weapons he must obtain an authority from the Home Office (the responsibility was transferred from the Defence Council by the Transfer of Functions (Prohibited Weapons) Order 1968). Such authority is only granted after searching inquiries made in consultation with the police and there is no avenue of appeal against a refusal by the Home Secretary to grant such authority. Once the authority has been granted, however, the appropriate Chief Constable is not able to refuse a firearm certificate if the person concerned requires one. The definition of prohibited weapons includes machine guns and other fully automatic weapons, together

191

with weapons for discharging tear gas or tranquillizer-darts, but part (ii) above brings within its ambit various things which might otherwise fall outside the scope of the Act. This refers to any weapon of whatever description and not simply to a firearm. Thus, the aerosol container of tear gas is classified as a prohibited weapon and therefore as a firearm.

Ammunition.   Ammunition is defined by Section 57(2) as: 'ammunition for any firearm and includes grenades, bombs and other like missiles, whether capable of use with a firearm or not, and also includes prohibited ammunition.' Section 1(4) subjects to the full firearm certificate procedure any ammunition for a firearm except:

(i)   cartridges containing five or more shots, none of which exceeds .36 in. in diameter (effectively, normal sporting ammunition for a shotgun);

(ii)   ammunition for an air gun, air rifle or air pistol; and

(iii)   blank cartridges not more than 1 in. in diameter measured immediately in front of the rim or cannelure of the base of the cartridge.

Thus, ammunition which is exempted from Section 1 is subject to no controls except those which prohibit certain persons from acquiring any ammunition by virtue of their previous convictions or age. Any ammunition not specifically exempted from the Section can only be acquired (subject to limited exceptions) on the authority of a firearm certificate which will specify the calibre and quantities of ammunition which may be acquired.

Registered firearms dealers.   By Section 3, it is an offence for anyone to manufacture or deal in firearms to which Section I applies, or shotguns, by way of trade or business unless he is registered with the police as a firearms dealer. A person wishing to be registered must make application in the prescribed form to the Chief Officer of Police for the area in which he proposes to conduct his business and the Chief Officer may refuse to register him if:

(i)   The applicant is prohibited from being registered by any Court Order.

(ii)   The Chief Officer is satisfied that he cannot be permitted to carry on his business without danger to the public safety or to the peace; or

(iii)   the premises are such that there is danger to the public safety or to the peace.

This discretion is subject to a right of appeal to Quarter Sessions against a refusal to register an applicant. The registration can be made subject to conditions imposed by the Chief Officer, and conditions relating to the security of premises are frequently inserted.

A registered firearms dealer is required by Section 40 to maintain a register of transactions and to record all dealing in Section I firearms and ammunition, and in shotguns. This register must be made available for police inspection and the dealer is required to permit the police to inspect all stock in hand. The gun trade, and in particular the Birmingham gun trade, often consists of numerous outworkers, many of whom specialise in making just a single component. Under certain circumstances, such outworkers can be exempted from the requirement to maintain a register of transactions provided that no complete weapons are likely to come into their possession during the course of the business.

A registered firearms dealer, or his servants, are exempted from the requirement to possess a firearm or shotgun certificate in respect of those weapons and ammunitition handled in the normal course of their business.

Other exemptions. Various exemptions made under the Act permit the possession of firearms or ammunition without the authority of a certificate. Except in two cases, these exemptions permit only the possession of the firearm and ammunition and not the acquisition of it. This is clarified by Section 8(2) which authorises a person legitimately in possession of a firearm to part with it to one of the exempted persons, provided that he does not do so by way of sale, hire or gift. In other words, the exemptions allow for possession without ownership on a temporary basis and in carefully defined circumstances. The exemptions are:

(a) *Police permits (Section 7).* The holder of a permit issued by the Chief Officer of Police may have in his possession firearms and ammunition strictly in accordance with the terms of the permit. This document is frequently referred to as a temporary permit. It does not authorise the purchase or acquisition of firearms, but is most usually granted to allow a person time to dispose of a firearm which has come into his possession. Such a permit might be granted, for instance, when the holder of a certificate dies and the executors wish to keep the weapon for a short time until they can arrange for suitable disposal; or if a firearm certificate is not to be renewed, a permit valid for a month or two might be issued to allow the holder to sell his weapons.

(b) *Carriers, auctioneers etc. (Section 9)*. Persons carrying on a business as carriers, warehousemen or auctioneers may have firearms or ammunition in their possession in the normal course of their business. Thus, the postman who delivers a parcel containing a firearm, or the railwayman who delivers a consignment of ammunition may have these things in their possession without the need for a firearm certificate or shotgun certificate. They are also relieved of the responsibility for ensuring that the the person to whom they deliver their goods is authorised to possess firearms. An auctioneer may possess a firearm in the ordinary course of his business without holding a certificate, but he may not sell firearms unless he is registered as a firearms dealer or has obtained from the Chief Officer of Police a permit authorising the sale. In both cases he is, of course, required to ensure that the person to whom he sells the weapon is authorised to possess them.

(c) *Slaughtermen etc. (Section 10)*. A licensed slaughterman and the proprietor of a slaughterhouse is authorised to have possession of a 'slaughtering instrument' and ammunition for it in connection with their business. The exemption refers to possession only and the acquisition of slaughtering instruments requires a firearm certificate.

(d) *Sporting use (Section 11)*.

(i) A person carrying a firearm or ammunition belonging to another person who is the holder of a certificate, may have them in his possession only under the instructions of, and for the use of the holder of a certificate, for sporting purposes.

(ii) A person may have a firearm in his possession for the purpose of starting races at an athletics meeting. This exemption does not apply to ammunition as blank cartridges will invariably be used and these do not require a firearm certificate.

(iii) A member of a rifle club, miniature rifle club or cadet corps approved by the Secretary of State may, without holding a certificate, have in his possession a firearm and ammunition when engaged as a member of the club or corps in, or in connection with drill or target practice. This exemption allows approved rifle clubs to provide weapons and allow their members to use them in connection with the club's activities.

(iv) A person conducting or carrying on a miniature rifle range (whether for a rifle club or otherwise) or shooting gallery at which no firearms are used other than air weapons or miniature rifles not exceeding .23 in. calibre may, without holding a certificate, have in his possession or purchase or acquire such miniature rifles and ammunition suitable therefor; and any person may, without holding a certificate, use any such rifle and ammunition at such range or gallery. Whilst this exemption appears to be very broad, its application is limited by practice. The fairground shooting gallery in which .22 rifles are used is exempt from the requirements of the Act, but the Showman's Guild exercise a substantial degree of control over them. Smallbore rifle clubs are similarly exempt and frequently acquire their ammunition in bulk and sell it to members for immediate use on the range without any of the transactions being recorded in a firearm certificate.

(v) A person may, without holding a shotgun certificate, borrow a shotgun from the occupier of private premises and use it on those premises in the occupier's presence. This exemption is intended to cater, in very restricted terms, for the guest at a shoot.

(vi) A person may, without holding a shotgun certificate, use a shotgun at a time and place approved for shooting at artificial targets by the Chief Officer of Police for the area in which that place is situated.

(e) *Theatrical use (Section 12)*. A person taking part in a performance or rehearsal for a play, film or similar event, may, without holding a certificate, have a firearm in his possession during and for the purposes of the performance or rehearsal. Where appropriate, this can be extended to cover prohibited weapons by the grant of a Home Office permit to the person in charge, permitting him to allow other persons to be in possession of the prohibited weapons.

(f) *Equipment for ships and aircraft (Section 13)*. A person may, without holding a certificate:

(i) Have in his possession a firearm on board ship, or signalling apparatus or ammunition on board an aircraft or at an aerodrome, as part of the equipment of the ship, aircraft or aerodrome.

(ii) Remove signalling apparatus from one aircraft to another, or to a place of storage at the aerodrome.

(iii) If he has obtained a permit, remove the items specified above to some place mentioned in the permit.

(g) *Visitors (Sections 14 and 15)*. A person who has been in Great

Britain for not more than thirty days in the preceding twelve months may have in his possession, or purchase or acquire a shotgun without holding a certificate. The holder of a Northern Ireland firearm certificate authorising possession of a shotgun is exempt from the requirement to obtain a shotgun certificate.

(h) *Proof houses (Section 58(1))*. This provides that nothing in the Act shall apply to the Statutory bodies which operate the Proof Houses at Birmingham and London so as to interfere in any way with the operation of the Companies, or to anyone taking firearms to or from a Proof House.

(i) *Crown servants (Section 54(1))*. Persons in the service of Her Majesty (including police) are exempt from those provisions of the Act which restrict possession of firearms, but not from those which restrict purchase or acquisition. This means that they can, in connection with their duties, carry and use firearms, but may not purchase them without a certificate unless specially authorised.

The provisions of the Act restricting the possession of firearms by young persons, contained in Sections 22, 23 and 24, are complicated and confusing and are, perhaps, best considered in relation to the type of weapon and ammunition.

1 *Section I firearms and ammunition*
   (a) A person under 17 may not purchase or hire firearms or ammunition.
   (b) A person under 14 may not have a firearm or ammunition in his possession except in the following circumstances when he is exempt from the requirements to hold a firearm certificate:
      (i) When carrying the firearm or ammunition for the use of another person who holds a certificate (Section 11(1)).
      (ii) As a member of an approved rifle club or cadet corps in connection with drill or target practice (Section 11(3)).
      (iii) When using a .22 rifle on an approved range or at a shooting gallery (Section 11(4)).
   It follows, therefore, that a person under 14 years of age cannot be granted a firearm certificate because the only occasions when he can have a Section I firearm or ammunition in his possession are in circumstances when he will not need a certificate. A person between the ages of 14 and 17 may be granted a certificate to accept a firearm as a gift, or to borrow a firearm held on someone else's certificate.

His ammunition will have to be bought for him by someone who is over the age of 17. It is an offence for anyone to sell, or let on hire, a Section I firearm or ammunition to a person under the age of 17 and it is an offence to make a gift of or lend a Section I firearm to a person under 14. It is also an offence to part with possession of a Section I firearm or ammunition to a person under 14, except in the sets of circumstances outlined above.

2 Shotguns and shotgun ammunition

(a) A person under the age of 17 may not purchase or hire a shotgun or shotgun ammunition.

(b) A person under the age of 15 may not have an assembled shotgun with him except:

(i) When under the supervision of a person who is over the age of 21, OR

(ii) When the shotgun is in a securely fastened gun cover so that it cannot be fired.

There is no mention of ammunition in these restrictions. It is an offence for a person to sell or let on hire a shotgun or ammunition to a person under the age of 17 and it is an offence to make a gift of a shotgun or ammunition to a person under the age of 15. Thus, a person under 15 may borrow a shotgun and use it under supervision and a person between the ages of 15 and 17 may accept a shotgun and ammunition as a gift, or borrow it, but may not purchase his own. A person over 15 is not required to be supervised when he has a shotgun. A shotgun certificate is, of course, needed in all cases, unless one of the exemptions mentioned above applies.

3 Air weapons and ammunition

(a) A person under the age of 17 may not purchase or hire air weapons or ammunition.

(b) A person under 17 commits an offence if he has an air weapon with him in a public place except:

(i) If he has an air gun or air rifle which is in a securely fastened gun cover so that it cannot be fired. The exemption does not include an air pistol and a person under 17 commits an offence if he has an air pistol with him in a public place, no matter how it is covered or carried.

(ii) When he is engaged as a member of an approved rifle club or cadet corps in connection with drill or target practice.

(iii) When using the weapon at a shooting gallery (for example on a fairground).

(c) A person under the age of 14 may not have an air weapon with him except:

(i) When he is on private premises and under the supervision of a person over the age of 21 (but both juvenile and adult commit an offence if he fires a missile beyond the premises).

(ii) When engaged as a member of an approved rifle club or cadet corps in drill or target practice.

(iii) When using the weapon at a shooting gallery.

An offence is committed by any person who sells or lets on hire an air weapon or ammunition to a person under the age of 17 or who makes a gift of an air weapon or ammunition to a person under the age of 14 or who parts with possession of an air weapon or ammunition to a person under 14, except in the circumstances where he is permitted to have one under the exemptions outlined above.

The complications and anomalies relating to the possession of various types of firearms by young persons arise from the fact that the 1968 Act is a consolidating measure which brought together the provisions of various previous Acts. Some of the results of this legislation are, to say the least, odd. For example, a person of 15 years can have an uncovered shotgun with him in a public place, but not an uncovered air weapon. If a person under 14 is using an air weapon under supervision on private premises, and he fires a missile beyond the premises, both he and the supervising adult commit an offence; if the weapon is a shotgun, no offence is committed. A person under 14 may not have ammunition for air weapons except in the special circumstances outlined, but he may, apparently, have shotgun cartridges, although the person who gave them to him may have committed an offence. These complications are such that it is doubtful if any young person, or parent, can be expected to understand them.

Convicted persons who have received certain punishments are prohibited from possessing firearms or ammunition (the term being used in its broadest sense) for varying periods, unless they successfully apply to a Court of Quarter Sessions to have the prohibition removed.

(i) A person who has been sentenced to preventive detention, or to corrective training or imprisonment for three years or more is prohibited from possessing firearms or ammunition at any time.

(ii) A person sentenced to Borstal training, to corrective training for less than three years or to imprisonment for a period between three months and three years, or to detention in a detention centre for a period of three months or more, is prohibited from possessing a firearm or ammunition for five years after the date of his release.

(iii) A child or young person sentenced to be detained during Her Majesty's pleasure, or for a long period on conviction for a serious crime and subsequently released on licence; a person who is subject to a recognisance to keep the peace, a condition of which is that he shall not possess, use or carry a firearm, or a person subject to a probation order with a similar condition; may not during the currency of the licence or order, have a firearm or ammunition in his possession.

By Section 5, it is an offence for any person to transfer a firearm or ammunition to a person whom he knows, or has reasonable cause to believe to be prohibited from possessing firearms or ammunition by this Section.

It might be thought that possession of a firearm by a person who had previously served a term of imprisonment was to be considered one of the more serious offences under the Act. However, the Sixth Schedule indicates that, if parliament took that view, it did not express it. All the offences are triable either summarily or on indictment and the maximum penalties are six months' imprisonment or a fine of £200 summarily and three years' imprisonment or a fine on indictment. These penalties are precisely the same as those provided for the possession of a firearm without a certificate by any person, but in the case of an offence under Section 1 (possession by anyone without certificate), an aggravated penalty of five years' imprisonment can be imposed on indictment if the offence was in respect of a sawn-off shotgun. This aggravated penalty does not apply to a charge relating to possession by a convicted person. Whilst, in practice, the sentence imposed on an otherwise respectable citizen who possessed a firearm without a certificate, is likely to be less than that imposed on a previously convicted person, parliament has certainly not given any indication of a distinction in gravity between the two classes of offender.

A relatively small portion of the Act deals with the possession or use of firearms in connection with crime. The various provisions have been introduced progressively into the legislation over the years and have been consolidated in the 1968 Act.

The possession of any firearm or ammunition with intent to endanger life or cause serious injury to property by means of the

199

firearm or ammunition, or to enable another person by means thereof to endanger life or cause serious injury to property is punishable, on indictment only, by up to fourteen years' imprisonment or an unlimited fine whether injury or damage resulted or not (Section 16). Such an offence may be difficult to prove if the offender is interrupted before the act is completed, because of the problems of establishing intent where this is not demonstrated by the resulting actions.

Section 17 encompasses the use of firearms to resist arrest, or the possession of firearms at the time of committing, or being arrested for one of a number of offences listed in Schedule 1, which include most of the criminal attacks on persons or property. This Section refers to any firearm or imitation firearm and the latter is defined as, 'Anything which has the appearance of a firearm (other than a weapon designed for the discharge of a noxious liquid, gas or other thing) whether or not it is capable of discharging any shot, bullet or other missile'. A person commits an offence if, with intent to resist or prevent the lawful arrest of himself or another person, he makes, or attempts to make, any use whatsoever of a firearm or imitation firearm. The Section is framed in very broad terms and provides for a penalty on indictment of up to fourteen years' imprisonment or a fine. Sub-section 2 of Section 17 does not require that there should be any use, or attempted use of the weapon, but penalises the mere possession of a firearm or imitation firearm at the time of committing or being arrested for one of the specified offences, unless the offender shows that he had the firearm in his possession for a lawful object, and the wording clearly indicates that the burden of proof lies squarely on the defendant. Conviction of this offence carries a penalty on indictment of up to seven years' imprisonment or a fine.

In an obvious effort to facilitate the prevention of crimes involving firearms, Section 18 penalises the person who has with him a firearm or imitation firearm with intent to commit an indictable offence, or to resist arrest or prevent the arrest of another, in either case while he has the firearm or imitation firearm with him. This Section is much wider in application than Section 17 and is clearly intended as a preventive measure, enabling action to be taken before the event rather than merely providing an additional penalty for the commission of an offence with a firearm. The burden of proof may, in many cases, be a difficult one to discharge despite the provisions of sub-section 2 which states that proof that a person had a firearm or imitation firearm with him and that he intended to commit an indictable offence, or intended to resist or prevent arrest, is evidence that he intended to have the firearm with him while doing so. The difficulty lies in proving the intention to commit an offence until events have progressed to such a stage that at least an attempt has been made.

Whilst the preceding three Sections are obviously intended to help cope with the dangerous criminal, the two following Sections are, perhaps, designed more to cope with the irresponsible or the hooligan. Section 19 controls the carrying of firearms in public places and provides that a person commits an offence if, without lawful authority or reasonable excuse (the proof whereof lies on the accused), he has with him in a public place:

(a) a loaded shotgun or
(b) a loaded air weapon or
(c) any other firearm, whether loaded or not, together with ammunition suitable for use in that firearm.

This Section would, of course, apply equally to the holder of a firearm certificate as to the person illegally in possession of a firearm. The holder of a certificate going to or from a place where he could properly use a firearm, would have reasonable excuse for having it with him in a public place, though he might, for example, find difficulty in justifying having a loaded shotgun with him if he were some distance from the place where he normally shoots.

Section 20 deals with trespassing with firearms and provides that a person commits an offence if, while he has a firearm with him, he

(i) enters or is in any building or part of a building or
(ii) enters or is on any land,

in each case, as a trespasser and without reasonable excuse. Offences under Section 19 and 20(1) are triable either summarily or on indictment and carry penalties of up to six months' imprisonment or a £200 fine summarily and five years' imprisonment and an unlimited fine on indictment. Section 20(2) is triable summarily only and carries three months' imprisonment and a fine of up to £100.

Conversions of firearms in certain cases are prohibited by Section 4. It is an offence to shorten the barrels of a shotgun to a length less than 24 in. under any circumstances except the replacing of barrels by sleeving (a relatively recent method of renewing shotgun barrels which involves cutting them off near to the breach and fitting new tubes to the old breech). This prohibition extends to dealers. Possession of an illegally shortened shotgun renders the offender liable to an aggravated penalty of up to five years imprisonment on indictment. It is also an offence for anyone other than a registered dealer to convert into a firearm anything which, though having the appearance of a firearm, was incapable of being fired.

Pawnbrokers are prohibited from taking in pawn any firearm to which Section I applies, or any shotgun (Section 3(6)). It is an offence for any person to sell, or transfer any firearm or ammunition to, or to repair, prove or test, any firearm or ammunition for another person whom he knows or has reasonable cause to believe to be drunk or of unsound mind. The word firearm is here used in its broadest sense.

Relatively wide powers are conferred on the police by Sections 46–50. In addition to authorising the issue of warrants to search in certain circumstances, the Act also authorises the police, without warrant, to stop and search individuals and vehicles, to require the handing over of weapons for examination and, in fairly wide areas, to arrest without warrant. The courts, in addition to their powers to imprison or fine, are given power to confiscate weapons and to cancel firearm or shotgun certificates, or to cancel the registration of a firearms dealer.

The fees payable to the police under the Act were first set out in 1920 when they were 5s for the grant of a certificate and 2s 6d for a renewal. Registration of a firearms dealer was subject to a fee of £1. In 1937 these were varied slightly by making a charge of 2s 6d for any variation to a firearm certificate and by making the fees for registered dealers £5 on registration and £1 for a renewal. When shotgun certificates were introduced in 1967, they were subject to the same fees as the firearm certificate. In 1968, however, the fees were reviewed and the new fees set were £2 10s for the grant of a firearm certificate and £1 5s for any variation or renewal. The grant of a shotgun certificate, or a renewal cost 15s, registration as a dealer cost £20 and renewal of the registration cost £4. Further increases came into effect on 1 January 1971 when the fee for the grant of a firearm certificate was raised to £3 10s and that for renewal or variation to £2 10s. Grant or renewal of a shotgun certificate was also subject to a fee of £1. The increases in fees are apparently based on the actual cost to the police of administering the system, but there is nothing to indicate that this was the basis on which the fees were first calculated.

14 Current Firearms Controls—The Practice

A mere recital of the current law on firearms controls does not, of itself, give a clear indication of what these controls involve in terms of police effort, or of the inconvenience, if any, to legitimate users of firearms. In this chapter, the individual processes involved in applying the law are discussed in detail so as to give an indication of the work load involved. Problems concerning the numbers of certificates in existence, and the numbers of variations and renewals, together with estimates of the amount of time taken in the various processes are examined in Chapter 15. The practice differs in detail from area to area and the following résumé does not represent the practice in any particular force; rather it is a composite account intended to represent a procedure which, with slight modifications, is more or less representative of the general practice. Possibly the most convenient method of describing the mechanics of the system is to follow the various types of application through this composite procedure.

Firearm Certificates—Application for Grant

A person who wishes to acquire any firearm or ammunition to which Section 1 of the Act applies will find himself directed to his local police station where he will be required to complete a 'firearms form 1'. This form consists of four sides of A4 paper ($11\frac{3}{4}$ in. × $8\frac{1}{4}$ in.), one side of which contains fifteen notes explaining some of the provisions of the Act and giving instructions for completing the form. Despite the instructions, virtually every applicant requires assistance in completing the form. Personal details required include full name, address, height, date of birth, any previous names used (including the maiden name of a married woman), business address, nationality, occupation and all residence during the previous five years. The applicant is required to give details of the weapons required—quantity, calibre and type, but he is not (or should not be) required to specify an individual weapon at this stage. As an example, the applicant may wish to acquire 'one .22 rifle'. It is also necessary to specify the amount and calibre of ammunition it is desired to possess at any one time, and the amount to be purchased at any time. Clearly, the former should be greater than the latter. If a person wishes to buy .22 ammunition in boxes of 500 rounds, the amount to be possessed will normally be sufficient to allow the purchase of a further box before his stock is exhausted, and could be 600 or 750 rounds.

The form requires details of any mental disorders or defects from which the applicant has suffered, together with details of any convictions for offences other than minor motoring offences. It also requires the applicant to specify:

(a) The reasons for requiring the firearms and ammunition.

(b) Where it is proposed to use the weapon.

(c) Where the firearm and ammunition will be kept when not in use and what arrangements have been made for safe custody.

The applicant is required to sign the application form and one of the notes draws his attention to the fact that the making of a false statement on the form renders him liable to a penalty of six months' imprisonment or a fine of £200 or both.

Having completed the form, the applicant will be interviewed by the officer who will be continuing the enquiry. In a number of forces it is usual for this officer to be of or above the rank of inspector, whilst in other forces (particularly in rural areas), the local constable will deal with the matter. It is usual for the enquiring officer to complete a further form showing the result of his enquiries and this may well require elaboration of the information supplied on the application form. In particular, the officer will wish to discuss the applicant's background, his knowledge of firearms, the places where he proposes to use the weapon and the facilities for secure storage. He may well wish to inspect the latter. It is clear that a number of people are dissuaded from pursuing their applications at this stage, particularly if their application appears to be hopeless, either because of previous convictions, perhaps amounting to a prohibition under the Act, or if the enquiring officer feels satisfied that the applicant cannot advance a sufficiently 'good reason'. Whilst it is not possible to give a reasonable estimate of the numbers who are dissuaded at this stage, the total might not be inconsiderable.

Following his interview with the applicant, the enquiring officer will seek to verify the entries on the form and to supply his chief officer with such information as will allow a decision to be made about the grant or refusal of the application within the framework of the Firearms Act. The amount of work involved at this stage varies tremendously. For example, the applicant might be known personally by the enquiring officer and may wish to acquire a target rifle for use with a local club. In such a case a telephone call to the secretary of the local club, to verify that the applicant is a full member, might be all that is required. Alternatively, a person who is not known to any local officer might wish to acquire a powerful rifle for deer stalking in Scotland and this will necessitate a number of enquiries.

Unless the applicant is known personally, enquiries will be made about his background, possibly from other police officers or by discreet enquiries in the locality. If the applicant has lived in another police area in the recent past, enquiries will be made from the police in that area, either by telephone or by letter. In some forces the enquiring officer will check on any convictions which the applicant may have, whilst in other forces this will be done at force headquarters. Usually, the enquiring officer will at least check on any local convictions. These enquiries are directed to satisfying the requirements of the Act; that the applicant is not prohibited from possessing firearms by virtue of convictions; that he is not of intemperate habits or unsound mind and that he is not for any reason unfitted to be entrusted with a firearm. This will also have a bearing on one of the matters within the Chief Constable's discretion—that the applicant can be permitted to have a firearm without danger to the public safety or to the peace.

Next, the enquiring officer must address himself to the problem of satisfying the chief officer on the question of whether the applicant has 'good reason' for requiring the firearm, and it is at this stage that the wide differences in police effort are involved. Many applicants require weapons for target shooting and it will normally be necessary to establish that the applicant is a full member of an approved club. All clubs affiliated to the national organisations require new members to complete a three month probationary period during which support will not be given to any application for a firearm certificate. During this period, the new member is permitted to use weapons supplied by the club and this allows him to decide whether or not he intends to pursue the sport. It also gives the club officials time to consider the application carefully. The system appears to work extremely well. The enquiring officer will also have to satisfy himself that the weapon applied for is appropriate for the purpose. Club ranges are inspected by the military authorities who issue range safety certificates which specify the type of weapon to be used. A range might be approved for .22 rifles only, for .22 rifles and pistols only, or for rifles and pistols of all calibres. Occasionally, a person who is not a member of a club might apply for a certificate to use weapons on a private range. Whilst such applications could be granted, they are invariably treated with great reserve and are likely to fail.

If an applicant wishes to use a rifle for shooting game or vermin, the police first satisfy themselves that he has authority to shoot over the land in question. Frequently such an application will come from the farmer or landowner, but if the applicant is a shooting tenant, or is shooting only by leave of the owner, the enquiring officer will check with the landowner that permission has been given. It also appears to be standard practice for the enquiring officer to verify that a weapon of the type applied for can be used with reasonable safety on the land mentioned (although the qualification of some officers to make such judgments might well be questioned). Such verification will usually necessitate a visit to the land to check on the physical layout, the presence of roads or footpaths, houses or other buildings; and may also involve a visit to the offices of the local authority to check on rights of way. In some cases, particularly in rural areas, the enquiring officer may already be sufficiently familiar with the land and might be able to satisfy himself on all these points without leaving his desk. When the land in question is in another area, a letter is usually sent asking the local police to conduct the enquiries.

Applicants not falling into either of these two categories will be required to establish their good reasons with equal clarity. The slaughterman requiring a humane killer will have to show that he is currently licensed and employed in that capacity. A person wishing to acquire a firearm as a collector's item is likely to meet with searching enquiries, particularly on a first grant. Many such persons may already have a collection of antique weapons and this may help establish his bona fides—in any event, he is likely to be the subject of considerable enquiries in the first instance. Every applicant is certain to be called upon to establish a good reason for requiring the firearm in very clear and precise terms, and this will be subjected to close scrutiny.

When he has completed his enquiry, the officer will submit his report, together with the application form. In smaller forces, particularly in cities, this might go direct to headquarters, but normally it will be submitted through the officer in charge of the territorial division, who will consider the application and add his recommendations before submitting it to headquarters. In some cases, the divisional officer may return the papers for further enquiries to be made. When the application arrives at headquarters, a clerk in the firearms department will enter some details in his records and then submit the papers, with his observations, for consideration by the Chief Officer. A report prepared by a committee which studied the procedure in one large force[1] indicates that, at this stage, approximately 20 per cent of all applications are returned to the enquiring officer before a final decision is made. Generally, there is a reluctance to make a firm decision to refuse an application at this point. It appears usual for questionable applications to be returned with comments and instructions for the enquiring officer so that he can see the applicant again and give him the opportunity of either withdrawing his application or making further representations on the points raised. The report indicated that approximately 9 per cent of all applications are withdrawn as a result of this procedure. The system appears to have much to commend it, but there is little doubt that a number of applicants withdraw rather than face the extra inconvenience, or appear to be in dispute with the police.

If no queries arise, or if an applicant persists with his application, the chief officer must make a final decision about the grant or refusal, and this must be considered in the light of the Act. The application must be refused if:

1. The applicant is prohibited by the Act from possessing fire-arms—this is a specific ground which will be made clear from the applicant's record of convictions. Very few applications are refused on this ground and it is safe to presume that any such person who applied for a certificate would be told at an early stage that it could not be granted and he would have no choice but to withdraw.

2. The applicant is of intemperate habits or unsound mind. A small number of applications appear to have been refused on this ground, but as this must be interconnected with numbers 3 and 5, it is not possible to be specific. A person with a number of convictions for drunkenness, or who has a known history of mental disorder is almost certain to be refused the grant of a certificate, and few such applications will reach the chief officer. There must, however, be questionable cases such as the man who is known to drink heavily, but has never been convicted of an offence connected with drunken-

ness; or the person whose mental state is thought to be questionable, but who has never received treatment. Bearing in mind the right of appeal, it appears that Chief Officers demand evidence based on facts which would stand up in court before they are prepared to either grant or refuse a certificate.

3. The applicant is for any reason unfitted to be entrusted with a firearm. Once again this requirement overlaps with others (numbers 2 and 5) and it is not possible to specify which of the requirements is being invoked in a particular case. Persons with convictions (particularly for violence) which do not amount to a prohibition under the Act are likely to be refused the grant of a certificate, and these may well fall under this heading.

If the first three conditions are fulfilled, the Chief Officer should grant the certificate if he is satisfied:

4. That the applicant has good reason for requiring the firearm. It is this requirement that causes the difficulty and disputes in many cases. Practice built up over the years, coupled with advice from the Home Office, appears to have created a relatively consistent set of policies, but there remain variations from force to force. Active membership of an approved rifle club is normally considered to be good reason for acquiring a rifle or pistol of suitable design, at least as far as the first weapon is concerned. The use of a rifle for sporting purposes is usually considered proper if the land is reported to be safe for the use of that class of weapon. It seems to have been accepted that the .22 rimfire rifle is the most suitable weapon for shooting small game (although this is a questionable proposition in some cases), but deer shooting clearly demands a rifle of larger calibre. Collecting firearms is likely to be accepted as a good reason only after the applicant has been subjected to rigorous checks. Commercial or professional use, as for instance the slaughterman with the humane killer; or the use of signalling equipment by boat owners and the like, are well-established 'good reasons'.

The use of pistols for hunting game is well established in some countries, but appears to be unacceptable in this country, although with the exception of shooting deer, there is no reason in law why such an application could not be granted, provided the Chief Officer was satisfied that all the requirements had been met. Certificates relating to pistols for self-defence or protection of the household are virtually never granted and this is in accordance with Home Office advice. There is no reason in law why such an application could not be granted and many such applications were granted during the early years of control. By purely executive decisions at the Home Office and by Chief Officers, which appear to have been supported at Quarter Sessions whenever such cases have gone on appeal, these grounds are now considered not to provide a good reason for requiring a firearm. The effect of the Common Law right to keep arms on this executive decision is discussed in Chapter 7. By and large it can be said that the only grounds on which certificates for pistols are granted is either for target shooting to members of approved clubs or, less frequently, to collectors. A new grant in respect of a pistol as a trophy or item of sentimental value is extremely rare.

5. The final point upon which the Chief Officer has to be satisfied is that the applicant can be permitted to have the firearm or ammunition without danger to the public safety or to the peace. Clearly, this requirement is bound up with those under numbers 2 and 3, and it is difficult to distinguish cases which have been refused on this ground alone. It might well be applied if an applicant were a member of an extreme organisation likely to resort to violence and could so be said to be a danger to the peace. It seems also to be the ground upon which Chief Officers frequently insist on inspection of the land over which a sporting firearm is to be used, and some applications are refused on the ground that the land in question is not suitable.

If the decision of the Chief Officer is to grant the certificate, it will be subject to the four conditions which must be imposed on every certificate and which are detailed in Chapter 13. It now appears to be the general practice to impose further restrictions on virtually every certificate. If weapons are for target practice, a condition will usually specify that the weapons are to be used only on ranges currently approved for that class of weapon. If for sporting purposes, a condition may restrict the use of a weapon to a specified area of land. A certificate issued to a collector is likely to be subject to a condition that the weapons shall not be fired.

Some forces accept the appropriate fee at the time that the application is made, whilst others do not accept it until the decision to grant has been made, when the applicant is asked to send the fee by post. When the fee has been received, a certificate is made out and submitted for signature, a file is created at headquarters in which all the relevant documents will be stored, and an entry is made in a nominal index. A method of retrieval is incorporated into the system. The systems of filing and indexing records vary tremendously from force to force. The completed certificate is sent to the applicant who is then authorised to acquire his firearm. When he does this, the person who transfers the weapon to him is required to enter full details in the certificate and to send written notice to the Chief Officer of Police who issued the certificate. It appears to be the normal practice for all such notices to be sent to the local police and for an officer to call on the certificate holder to check the weapon and to ensure that details have been correctly entered in the certificate and on the notice. The notice is then returned to headquarters where, in many cases, an entry is made in a weapons index in which all weapons held on certificate in the area are filed by calibre, make, type and serial number. Such an index is not maintained by some forces, whilst others maintain only a limited index (for example, one force maintains an index of pistols only).

If the certificate is to be refused, it is usual to call for further enquiries to ensure that the Chief Officer is on firm ground in case an appeal should be launched. In the case of a refusal, the applicant is notified in writing and is advised of his right to appeal to Quarter Sessions. Should a notice of appeal be received, a file is prepared for the advice of the force solicitor and, if pursued, the appeal will normally require the attendance of the Chief Officer and the enquiring officer at the hearing. Appeals, however, are extremely rare.

The amount of police time taken up by the grant of a new certificate varies tremendously. A straightforward application like the example quoted of the member of a rifle club known to the enquiring officer could occupy less than one hour in total, whilst other applications could take much longer. By far the greatest amount of time is taken up by a relatively small number of questionable applications. Every aspect of such cases is very carefully examined and the papers are likely to be returned to the enquiring officer for even the most minor query to be clarified. An application which is finally refused is likely to have taken up three or four times as much police effort as any straightforward application.

Firearm Certificates—Variations

Having acquired his first firearm, the holder of a certificate may, at some time, feel the need to have his certificate varied. It may be that the weapon originally acquired has been found to be not quite what was required and the holder may wish to exchange it for another weapon of similar calibre. Alternatively a need may be felt for an additional weapon. A rifle suitable for target shooting will not be suitable for shooting small game, and the .22 rifle used on small game could not be used for deer. The smallbore target shooter with either rifle or pistol may wish to take up fullbore shooting as well. Whatever the reason for wishing to acquire an additional or replacement weapon, it will be necessary for the holder to seek a variation of his certificate.

Once more he must visit the local police station and complete the same firearms form 1, giving all the same details plus his reasons for requesting the variations. Again, most applicants require assistance in completing the form. On this occasion the enquiring officer is able to confine his enquiries to the reasons for requiring the additional weapons, background enquiries already having been made for the grant. The enquiries into the reason will, however, follow similar lines to those for a grant and consequently will be just as variable in their demands on police time. The application will subsequently follow a similar course to headquarters, but in his consideration of the application, the Chief Officer need generally only give consideration to the question of the reasons for requiring the additional weapon.

In recent years, Chief Officers have shown an increasing tendency to restrict the number of weapons held on a certificate very strictly, and many of them commented on this fact in their reports for 1969. This has been the cause of a number of complaints (for instance a memorandum sent to the Home Office by the National Smallbore Rifle Association and subsequently published in the *Rifleman*, Spring 1969), particularly in respect of pistol shooters of national or international standing who require different weapons for each type of match.

If the application to vary the certificate is successful, the applicant will be required to pay the fee, his file at headquarters will be updated and the varied certificate will be returned to him. When he acquires the additional weapon, the vendor must again enter full details in his certificate and send a notice of sale to the police. The notice, certificate and weapon are again checked by the local police and, when the notice is returned to headquarters, the weapons index, if maintained, will be brought up to date. If the application to vary is to be refused, it is likely to be the subject of further enquiries to ensure that the Chief Officer is on firm ground. In the event of a refusal, the applicant is notified in writing and is informed of his right of appeal.

Firearm Certificates—Renewal

A firearm certificate is valid for three years and about one month before the date upon which renewal is due, the papers will be retrieved from the headquarters filing system and sent to the local station via divisional headquarters. An enquiring officer then calls on the holder at his home, or sees him by appointment at the police station. This can involve considerable time-wasting if the officer has difficulty in contacting the applicant, and it may involve several visits to his home. The holder is required to complete the lengthy firearms form 1 in respect of the renewal, and it appears to be standard practice for the enquiring officer to check the weapons against the certificate to ensure that none has been disposed of. In many cases the security of the storage facilities is also checked. When the form has been completed, the officer will check that there has been no change of circumstances during the past three years and he will ensure that the 'good reasons' originally advanced are still valid. This may involve checking that the applicant is still a current member of a rifle club, or that he still has authority to shoot over the land mentioned in the original application. There will also be a check on any convictions during the past three years.

The enquiring officer's report, together with the firearm certificate and application form will be submitted to headquarters through the divisional officer who will add his recommendations. In considering the application, the Chief Officer will be mainly concerned with any changes of circumstances which might affect the applicant's standing, and with satisfying himself that the 'good reason' still exists. It appears that the tightening of policy on firearms in recent years has also affected renewals—a point made by a number of Chief Officers in their annual reports. If consumption of ammunition, as recorded in the certificate, indicates that little use is being made of the weapon, the applicant is likely to be invited to consider disposing of it and may experience considerable difficulty in getting the certificate renewed. If the weapon is held as a trophy, or for sentimental reasons, the certificate holder is likely to find considerable resistance to the renewal of his certificate, even though he may have held it for many years.

If the certificate is to be renewed, the applicant will be informed and required to pay the fee. The new renewal date is entered on the certificate and headquarters records are updated. If the renewal is to be refused, it is likely that further enquiries will be called for. In the event of a refusal, a notice is sent to the holder and he is informed of his right of appeal. It is usual to issue a 'temporary permit' under Section 7, to allow the holder time to dispose of the weapon concerned.

Shotgun Certificates—Applications for Grant

There is rather more variation in practice in the procedures for shotgun certificates, but the following is reasonably representative. The applicant will be required to obtain an application form and complete it. The personal details required are similar to those required on an application for a firearm certificate, but there are, of course, no references to the weapons or ammunition, nor to the reasons for requiring the weapon. If the applicant is not the holder of a firearm certificate he must have his application countersigned by a person who is:

(a) A British subject;

(b) A member of parliament, justice of the peace, minister of religion, doctor, lawyer, bank officer or person of similar standing and

(c) has known the applicant personally for at least two years.

In the case of a visitor to this country or a person who has been living out of the country for the previous two years, this condition is varied to require the countersignature of a person of like standing who knows the applicant personally. If the applicant is already the holder of a firearm certificate, the requirement for a countersignature is dispensed with.

The completed form is handed in at the local police station and in some cases the fee is accepted at that time, whilst in others it is requested from headquarters after the application has been approved. On receipt of the form at the local station, an officer will check on local convictions and on the known character of the applicant. In most cases, this local check will take very little time, but if the application is a questionable one, the enquiries made will probably take three or four times as long to complete. If the applicant has resided in another police area during the preceding five years, enquiries will be made from the police of that area.

The application is submitted, with a covering report, to the divisional officer who will add his observations before forwarding the papers to headquarters. At headquarters, a full check will be made on previous convictions before the papers are placed before the

213

Chief Constable, or an Assistant Chief Constable. Only two questions arise for consideration by the Chief Officer:

1. Is the applicant prohibited by the Act from possessing shotguns? This is a specific issue easily settled by reference to previous convictions.

2. Can the applicant be permitted to possess a shotgun without danger to the public safety or to the peace?

This allows a fairly wide area of discretion and examination of the refusals made in a number of forces indicates that the following have been taken to fall into this category: history of mental disorders; convictions not amounting to a prohibition, particularly convictions for violence; a known history of violence, even if this has not resulted in any number of convictions; a history of drunkenness, usually based on convictions; known drug-taking.

If the application is successful and the applicant has not already paid the fee, he will be asked to do so. When the fee is received, a certificate will be made out, signed by or on behalf of the Chief Officer and sent to the applicant. A clerk at headquarters will create a file in which all the papers will be stored, and make an entry in a nominal index. A system of retrieval for renewals will also be created. When the applicant has received his certificate, he is free to acquire shotguns as and when required. An application which is likely to be refused will probably be the subject of further enquiries to ensure that the grounds are reasonable. In the event of a refusal, the applicant will be informed in writing and will be told of his right of appeal.

Shotgun Certificates—Renewal

The renewal of a shotgun certificate is much simpler than the renewal of a firearm certificate. A typical procedure would be that about one month before the renewal date, a renewal application is sent to the holder by post and he is invited to complete it and return it with the appropriate fee direct to headquarters. At the same time a note is sent to the local station, informing them of the renewal and seeking any further information which may come to light about the applicant. When both documents are returned to headquarters, a further check will be made on any convictions during the past three years. If all is correct, the certificate is submitted for renewal and headquarters records are brought up to date before the certificate is returned to the holder. If, for any reason, the certificate is not to be renewed, the grounds for refusal are likely to be thoroughly checked before a decision is made. If there is a refusal, the holder is informed in writing and is told of his right to appeal. Failure of the holder to reply to the renewal notice is usually dealt with by a reminder posted to him. Thereafter, some forces follow this up with personal enquiries, whilst others treat the certificate as cancelled. In most forces, a continuous check on convictions is maintained in respect of shotgun and firearm certificate holders, and any conviction which requires the revocation of a certificate will normally be acted upon at once.

Registered Firearms Dealers—New Registration

The registration of a new firearms dealer tends to be a relatively lengthy process and is subject to many variables, particularly in relation to the size of the proposed business. First, an applicant will be required to complete the appropriate parts of an application form providing personal details and information about the proposed business. An officer will then make enquiries about the applicant and about any other person who may be associated with the proposed business. These enquiries will be directed to showing that the applicant will be a bona fide dealer by way of trade or business; that he is not prohibited from being registered by a court order, and that he can be permitted to carry on such a business without danger to the public safety or to the peace.

To satisfy these requirements it will be necessary for the enquiries into the background of anyone associated with the business to be at least as searching as those made before the grant of a firearm certificate. The enquiring officer will also want to know about the proposed business, but there is no requirement that dealings should be on a large scale—a number of dealers do not operate from a retail shop, and their dealings may be very limited. If the applicant has satisfied the enquiries about himself and the nature of his business, the premises which he proposes to use will be subjected to the closest scrutiny and this is normally undertaken by a full-time crime prevention officer. An inspection of the premises will be made and, in addition to satisfying himself about the security of the premises as a whole, the crime prevention officer will probably make specific recommendations about the storage of weapons. For example, he may suggest lockable racks for long arms and recommend that the bolts or other parts of the actions of rifles, together with handguns, should be stored in a safe. Such suggestions are likely to be made a condition of any registration which is made.

When these enquiries are complete, the application, together with the reports of the enquiring officer and the crime prevention officer, will be sent to the divisional officer who will add his comments before passing the papers to headquarters. At headquarters additional checks on convictions are usually made before the file is submitted for consideration. Although the grounds upon which a Chief Officer can refuse such an application appear at first glance to be more restricted than those relating to firearm certificates, this in practice is not so. First, the Chief Officer has to be satisfied that the proposed business is bona fide; second, that the applicant is not prohibited from being registered; and third, that he can be permitted to carry on such a business without danger to the public safety or to the peace. It is this last ground which provides the widest discretion. Failure to provide reasonable security precautions, convictions not amounting to a prohibition, known mental illness, drunkenness or drug-taking, although not specifically provided for, fall within this broad area of discretion.

If the application is granted, the applicant will be asked to pay the fee and then his name will be entered in the police register of firearms dealers. A certificate of registration will be sent to him, and a file will be opened at headquarters. The registration is likely to be subject to conditions relating to security and to require the dealer to permit inspection of the security of the premises at reasonable times. This will be in addition to the power of entry granted to the police by the Act for the purpose of checking his register of transactions and stocks of weapons. All this having been completed, the dealer may start his business. He will be required to maintain a register of all transactions in Section I firearms and ammunition and shotguns, but subject to this, and to his compliance with such matters as the requirements to notify sales to certificate holders, he will be able to deal freely in firearms.

Registered Firearms Dealers—Renewal of Registration

All registrations are renewable annually and are due on 1 June each year. The relevant file will be retrieved from the headquarters records well in advance and sent to the local station where the enquiry is normally undertaken by an officer of the rank of inspector. The usual check will be made of the background of the applicant, although in the case of a registered dealer it is most unlikely that any convictions during the preceding year will not have been brought to notice at once. The officer will visit the premises and check that the security arrangements are still as recommended by the crime prevention officer and that any conditions imposed on the registration are being complied with. Then the officer will be required to check the register of transactions.

The scope of a dealer's business can vary from the large manufacturer with tens of thousands of transactions through large retailers with perhaps well over a thousand transactions, to the small dealer with no more than a dozen or so transactions in the year. The form of register of transactions is specified in the Firearms Rules, 1969, Schedule 9, and it might well have been designed to prevent ease of checking. It requires separate parts of the register to be kept for the manufacture, acquisition and sales of firearms, plus a fourth part to contain the annual stocktaking. Comprehensive cross-checking to ensure, for example, that all the weapons which have been acquired are either in stock or are the subject of an entry in the sales section is virtually impossible unless the register is rewritten in a double entry form. In one case in the writer's experience, a thorough and comprehensive check on the dealings of one man suspected of irregularities over a few years, including the taking of stock and checking all acquisitions against stock and sales, occupied two officers for three days, with two other officers assisting at the stocktaking—and this was a person in business in a small way only. There is clearly a need for a simple double-entry system in the register of transactions and, possibly, for allowing the use of mechanical recording by manufacturers and large scale dealers.

In most cases, the enquiring officer will limit his checks of the register to random cross-checks of one part against another or against stock. If all this is satisfactory, the dealer will complete an application form which will be submitted with the enquiring officer's report, through the divisional officer, to force headquarters. At headquarters the application will be dealt with in exactly the same manner as a new registration.

The foregoing represents a relatively brief explanation of the mechanics of some of the processes under the Act. Others, such as cancellations, revocations and transfers between forces, have not been touched upon. The description given should be sufficient to give an indication of the type of work and effort involved in dealing

P

15 Current Firearms Controls—Policies, Effort and Effects

The detailed description of police procedure in granting firearm and shotgun certificates, etc. given in Chapter 14 indicates the amount of police effort entailed in individual applications. To establish the amount of effort this might entail in any year for England and Wales, it is necessary to arrive at a total figure for each form of activity. Such totals can only provide an approximate figure. The number of certificates varies from day to day, and the number of weapons held on any one firearm certificate can vary from one day to the next. Similarly, as described in Chapter 14, the time taken over any one process will vary substantially from case to case.

The total number of firearm and shotgun certificates in existence on 31 December 1969 is shown in Table 49. The totals are broken down by police force areas and Map I indicates the location of each area. The number of certificates has been related to the type of area and to the population, and it will be seen that the number of certificate holders in rural areas is much greater than that in cities. It has been suggested in Chapter 11 that the figures for robberies involving a firearm provide a reasonable index of the criminal use of firearms, and that the Home Office figure of indictable offences involving a firearm is much less reliable. Table 50 shows both these figures, together with the number of households per certificate holder, for each force area. It will be seen from this that the rate of armed crime is in no way connected with the density of firearms in the community. Indeed, if anything, the reverse appears to be true. The legitimate use of firearms is largely a rural pursuit, and crime is largely a city pursuit.

The total number of firearm certificates in existence in England and Wales on 31 December 1969 was 209,946. A Home Office survey carried out early in 1969 indicates that the total for 31 December 1968 was 216,611, showing a reduction of 6,665 certificates (3 per cent) in one year. This downward trend in firearm certificate holders appears to have been going on for some time, at least in some police areas. In a parliamentary reply in 1938, the then Home Secretary indicated that the number of firearm certificates in the Metropolitan

TABLE 49   *Distribution of holders of shotgun and firearm certificates in England and Wales*

1	2	3	4	5	6	7	8	9	10
Force area	Predominant character of area	Population	Approximate number of households	Number of firearm certs. on 31.12.69	Number of households per firearm certificate	Number of shotgun certs. on 31.12.69	Number of households per shotgun certificate	Total of certificates allowing for overlap	Number of households per cert. holder
1 Bedford & Luton	Urban/Rural	417,650	146,031	1,731	84	7,539	19	8,216	18
2 Birmingham	City	1,086,400	379,986	786	483	2,834	134	3,141	120
3 Bradford	City	294,440	102,951	293	351	789	130	903	114
4 Bristol	City	427,780	149,573	861	173	1,643	91	1,980	75
5 Cheshire	Urban/Rural	1,531,412	535,458	6,714	79	16,379	32	19,004	28
6 Cumbria	Rural	361,483	126,392	6,000	21	9,690	13	12,036	10
7 Derby County & Borough	Urban/Rural	1,010,180	353,209	3,984	89	12,074	29	13,631	26
8 Devon & Cornwall	Rural	1,204,614	421,193	13,828	30	39,964	10	45,370	9
9 Dorset & Bournemouth	Rural	487,296	170,383	3,616	47	10,349	16	11,762	14
10 Durham	Urban/Rural	1,515,193	529,787	4,043	131	8,338	63	9,918	53
11 Dyfed Powys	Rural	433,010	151,402	5,491	27	22,916	7	25,062	6
12 Essex	Rural/Urban	1,246,450	435,821	5,426	80	23,204	19	25,325	17
13 Gloucestershire	Rural	633,240	221,412	4,919	45	14,086	16	16,009	14
14 Gwent	Rural/Urban	462,990	161,884	1,026	158	7,619	21	8,020	20
15 Gwynedd	Rural	563,036	196,865	3,935	50	15,007	13	16,545	12
16 Hampshire	Rural/Urban	1,486,324	519,693	9,052	57	23,750	22	27,289	19
17 Hertfordshire	Rural/Urban	742,376	259,572	2,616	99	10,339	25	11,361	23
18 Hull	City	295,500	103,321	509	202	1,028	100	1,227	84
19 Kent	Urban/Rural	1,345,878	470,586	7,000	67	26,000	18	28,737	16
20 Lancashire	Urban/Rural	3,652,774	1,277,193	8,389	152	25,136	51	28,416	45
21 Leeds	City	508,000	177,622	539	329	1,082	164	1,292	137
22 Leicester & Rutland	Rural	762,470	266,597	3,066	87	12,571	21	13,769	19
23 Lincolnshire	Rural	744,290	260,241	7,887	33	26,238	10	29,321	9
24 Liverpool & Bootle	City	828,500	289,685	615	471	988	293	1,228	235
25 London—City	City	5,000	1,748	47	37	24	73	52	96
26 London—Metropolitan	City	8,246,360	2,883,342	14,663	196	33,165	87	38,898	74
27 Manchester & Salford	City	756,230	264,416	477	554	940	281	1,127	234
28 Mid-Anglia	Rural	477,720	167,034	4,546	37	16,393	10	18,170	9
29 Norfolk	Rural	602,810	210,772	5,339	39	25,134	8	27,221	8
30 Northampton & County	Rural	433,880	151,706	3,010	50	9,031	17	10,207	15
31 Northumberland	Rural/Urban	818,136	286,061	5,678	50	7,800	36	10,020	28

1 Force area	2 Predominant character of area	3 Population	4 Approximate number of households	5 Number of firearm certs. on 31.12.69	6 Number of households per firearm certificate	7 Number of shotgun certs. on 31.12.69	8 Number of households per shotgun certificate	9 Total of certificates allowing for overlap	10 Number of households per cent. holder
32 Nottinghamshire	Urban/Rural	962,450	336,520	3,061	109	11,227	30	12,423	27
33 Sheffield/Rotherham	City	622,830	217,751	804	271	1,885	115	2,199	99
34 Somerset and Bath	Rural/Urban	657,830	230,010	5,791	40	18,626	12	20,890	11
35 South Wales	Urban/Rural	1,262,080	441,286	2,108	209	13,814	31	14,638	30
36 Staffordshire	Urban/Rural	1,306,940	456,972	3,565	128	13,638	33	15,031	30
37 Suffolk	Rural	499,060	174,706	5,088	34	21,397	8	23,386	7
38 Surrey	Rural/Urban	714,410	249,793	4,382	57	13,137	19	14,850	17
39 Sussex	Rural/Urban	1,173,730	410,395	6,750	60	22,240	18	24,879	16
40 Teesside	City	392,900	137,377	664	200	1,009	136	1,268	108
41 Thames Valley	Rural/Urban	1,642,919	574,447	10,665	54	29,037	20	33,207	17
42 Warwick & Coventry	Urban/Rural	1,026,320	358,853	3,325	107	13,460	26	14,760	24
43 West Mercia	Rural/Urban	979,580	342,510	7,251	47	30,951	11	33,786	10
44 West Midlands	Urban	969,350	338,933	1,227	276	3,198	105	3,677	92
45 West Yorkshire	Urban/Rural	2,270,850	794,003	7,088	112	25,757	30	28,528	28
46 Wiltshire	Rural	490,250	171,416	3,345	51	11,085	15	12,392	14
47 York & N.E. Yorks	Rural	681,350	238,234	8,746	27	22,110	11	25,529	9
ENGLAND & WALES		48,826,000	17,072,027	209,946	81	664,621	25	746,710	23

Notes to Table 49

1 The population figures in column 3 have been taken from the *Police and Constabulary Almanac* for 1970, except in relation to the total population of England and Wales, and that of Birmingham, which were taken from the Registrar General's Statistics.

2 The approximate number of households shown in column 4 has been based on the Registrar General's calculation that there are, on average, 2·86 persons to each household. This figure is very similar to that of the number of males over the age of 17 and so the column can be taken to indicate the relative size of that population group. With very few exceptions, firearm and shotgun certificates are held by males over 17.

3 Details of the numbers of firearm and shotgun certificates in existence have either been extracted from the Annual Report of the Chief Constable for 1969, or obtained by direct enquiry from the force. In a small number of cases, the figures appear to have been rounded off.

4 The overlap of shotgun and firearm certificates has not previously been established, but clearly many people hold both. A count was made, in one rural force area, which showed that out of over 1,000 firearm certificate holders whose names began with the letters A to H, 60·9 per cent also held a shotgun certificate. This would amount to 17 per cent of all shotgun certificates. This formula was used to estimate the overlap for all forces except the City of London (which was counted). The result, with an overlap based on a rural force, may be an underestimate of the total number of certificate holders.

TABLE 50 *Number of legitimately held firearms compared with numbers of offences*

Force	Type of area	Number of households per cert. holder	Number of robberies involving firearms	Number of indictable offences involving firearms
1 Bedford & Luton	Urban/Rural	18	5	41
2 Birmingham	City	120	5	58
3 Bradford	City	114	2	20
4 Bristol	City	75	1	11
5 Cheshire	Urban/Rural	28	3	102
6 Cumbria	Rural	10	0	15
7 Derby County & Borough	Urban/Rural	26	5	81
8 Devon & Cornwall	Rural	9	3	53
9 Dorset & Bournemouth	Rural	14	1	15
10 Durham	Urban/Rural	53	3	75
11 Dyfed Powys	Rural	6	1	29
12 Essex	Rural/Urban	17	15	121
13 Gloucestershire	Rural	14	2	48
14 Gwent	Rural/Urban	20	1	22
15 Gwynedd	Rural	12	1	70
16 Hampshire	Rural/Urban	19	3	82
17 Hertfordshire	Rural/Urban	23	6	81
18 Hull	City	84	0	0
19 Kent	Urban/Rural	16	4	86
20 Lancashire	Urban/Rural	45	9	162
21 Leeds	City	137	1	20
22 Leicester & Rutland	Rural	19	5	68
23 Lincolnshire	Rural	9	0	55
24 Liverpool & Bootle	City	235	19	32
25 London—City	City	96	5	8
26 London—Metropolitan	City	74	345	847

(*continued*)

TABLE 50—*continued*

Force	Type of area	Number of households per cert. holder	Number of robberies involving firearms	Number of indictable offences firearms
27 Manchester & Salford	City	234	3	71
28 Mid-Anglia	Rural	9	0	38
29 Norfolk	Rural	8	2	47
30 Northampton & County	Rural	15	0	35
31 Northumberland	Rural/Urban	28	0	44
32 Nottinghamshire	Urban/Rural	27	0	57
33 Sheffield/Rotherham	City	99	2	9
34 Somerset & Bath	Rural/Urban	11	1	40
35 South Wales	Urban/Rural	30	2	38
36 Staffordshire	Urban/Rural	30	3	69
37 Suffolk	Rural	7	2	34
38 Surrey	Rural/Urban	17	3	48
39 Sussex	Rural/Urban	16	2	61
40 Teesside	City	108	0	0
41 Thames Valley	Rural/Urban	17	9	106
42 Warwick & Coventry	Urban/Rural	24	2	44
43 West Mercia	Rural/Urban	10	1	23
44 West Midlands	Urban	92	2	67
45 West Yorkshire	Urban/Rural	28	4	203
46 Wiltshire	Rural	14	—	26
47 York & N.E. Yorks	Rural	9	1	34
ENGLAND & WALES	—	23	484	3,298

Notes

1. Map 1 indicates the location of each force area.
2. The number of households per certificate-holder is extracted from Table 49: see note 2 to that table.
3. The numbers of robberies and indictable offences in each force area are those for 1969 and have been supplied by the Home Office Statistical Division.

Police District was 26,120. According to the Commissioner's report, the figure for 1969 was 14,663. The trend does not appear to be constant from force to force. Comparison of the 1968 and 1969 figures in various annual reports reveals what appear to be substantial differences between similar force areas. Whilst the average

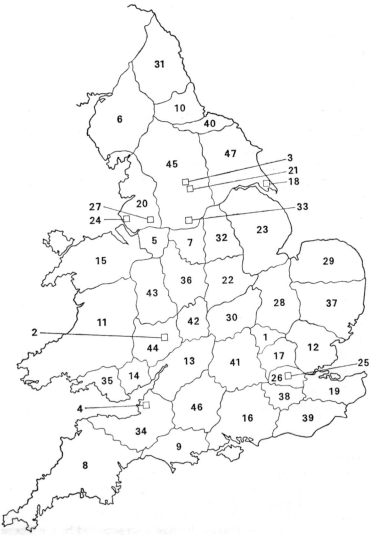

MAP 1   *Police force areas in England and Wales*

224

reduction in certificate holders was 3 per cent, one force showed a drop of 5·9 per cent whilst another similar area showed an increase of 3 per cent. The number of forces showing an increase was, however, very small, and the majority showed a substantial decrease over the year.

The cause of the decrease is, perhaps, indicated by the following quotations from Chief Constable's Annual Reports:

1. From a report for 1969: 'The tighter control over the issue and renewal of firearm certificates, instituted in 1967, is being continued'.

2. From a 1968 report:

These reductions are mainly attributable to the policy which was initiated during 1967. Certificates are not granted or renewed for small arms unless the weapons have been specially adapted for target practice and the applicants are members of approved clubs. Whenever the holder of a certificate which did not conform to this policy applied for renewal during the year, the applicant was invited to dispose of the weapons. In the majority of cases, the invitation was accepted without question but there were a few persons who found the policy difficult to accept.

The same Chief Constable's report for 1969, after giving details of a further reduction in the numbers of firearm certificates amounting to 5 per cent, said:

This further reduction in certificate holders and firearms in circulation is in accordance with the policy which has operated for over two years whereby, in the public interest, certificates are only issued or renewed in those cases where the applicants have a very real need to possess firearms. It is appreciated that where persons have been in possession of firearms for a number of years it is very difficult for them to accept a request from the police to dispose of their weapons and an intimation that their certificates are unlikely to be renewed. In this connection, however, it cannot be too strongly emphasised that the continuing upsurge in the use of firearms for criminal purposes makes it essential to apply a very stringent policy.

3. The 1969 report of a force with a 3·7 per cent reduction in certificate holders:

225

Work in connection with these certificates involves a great deal of time consuming enquiries by officers in divisions, but there is little doubt that the strict control over firearms in this country is one of the major factors in the relative infrequency of the use of firearms in connection with crime.

4. 1969 report: 'Every application for the grant or renewal of a firearm certificate is scrutinised most carefully as I am anxious that the number of firearms in possession of members of the public should be kept to a minimum.'

5. 1969 report: 'Comparison with 1968 shows a marked decrease in the number of firearm certificates held, granted and renewed in 1969 and a decrease in the number of certificates of registration as firearms dealers. It is considered that the increase in fees operative from 1st January 1969, an increase in fact of 400%, and the tighter control on the grant and renewal of firearm certificates have been the major factors in this trend.'

It appears from the figures, and from these remarks, that the reduction in the number of firearm certificate holders is largely a result of increasingly strict policies applied by most Chief Officers, and that the degree of strictness varies considerably. There is no evidence to suggest that it is due to any falling off in the demand for firearms by legitimate users. That this stricter policy dates from 1967 appears to be well established and it appears to have been imposed in the belief that stricter controls on the holders of firearm certificates would make some significant contribution to the control of armed crime.

The position in relation to shotgun certificates is quite different. The absence of a requirement to provide a good reason for requiring a shotgun means that the opportunities for refusal are limited to matters relating to the fitness of the applicant to be entrusted with a shotgun. The 1968 total of certificates was 604,875, and that for 1969 was 664,621—an increase of 59,746 or 9·8 per cent. The increase has been shown in virtually every force and varies from 14 per cent to 5 per cent. The requirement for a shotgun certificate dates from 1 May 1968 and the figures indicate that the peak of the demand has not yet been reached. It seems likely that the increase will continue.

The amount of police time devoted to various aspects of firearms controls is extremely difficult to compute with any accuracy. The large variations between individual cases, the constantly changing number of certificates in existence, and changes in policy from time to time, all contribute to making the total a constantly changing figure. A detailed analysis of the time involved in each operation, and the number of operations in every force for one year, would be time-consuming and, by the time it had been completed, it would be out of date. A completely accurate figure is therefore impractical and, for this purpose, unnecessary. To arrive at a broad indication of the amount of time involved, each stage of the various operations was listed and representatives from four different forces were asked to give their estimate of the average time taken on each operation by all those concerned, from the civilian clerk to the Chief Constable, and taking into account both the simple and the difficult cases. The persons concerned had considerable experience in the administration of the controls and the resulting figures were surprisingly constant. A mean of the four figures will therefore give a fair indication of the average amount of time taken. This is not to say that each certificate takes the time indicated, nor even that the majority of them do so. A small number of difficult cases take up a disproportionate amount of time for the reasons indicated in Chapter 14. The majority of cases take less time than that shown as an average.

Detailed figures for the numbers of new grants, variations, renewals, etc., are not available in respect of every force. A national total has been arrived at by relating the numbers of each type of operation to the total number of certificates in existence for the forces where the information is available. The average of these figures has been related to the national total of certificates to produce an approximate figure in respect of each operation. Tables 51, 52 and 53, therefore, represent only an indication of the number of operations and the amount of time involved. Taking account only of the processes listed in Table 51, the total time spent on these operations in England and Wales is approximately 199,717 man-hours.

Taking account only of the processes listed in Table 53, the total time taken in administering the shotgun certificate procedure is about 232,590 man-hours.

In Tables 51, 52 and 53, no account has been taken of such matters as transfers of certificates between forces, checking notices of sales relating to Section 1 firearms, replacing certificates which have been damaged, answering queries and other routine administrative matters. Leaving all these aside, the tables indicate that something of the order of 440,858 man-hours, or 55,107 man-days, are

TABLE 51   *Firearm certificates—time spent on administration*

	New grant	Varia- tion	Renewal	Refusal	Appeal
Number of forces in sample	28	7	17	15	5
Average % of total cert.	7·67	10	23·3	0·478	0·006
Est. national total	16,102	20,994	48,917	1,003	13
Average time per process (hrs.)	$2\frac{1}{2}$	2	$2\frac{1}{4}$	7	30
Total time taken—M/hr	40,255	41,988	110,063	7,021	390

taken up with this work. Much of the administrative work is done, in most forces, by civilians; the most time-consuming part of the effort, the enquiries, are undertaken by police officers, frequently of inspector rank. An examination of the times spent on various tasks indicates that two thirds of the time involved is that of police officers, and only one third that of civilian clerks. This suggests that about 36,738 man-days of police time are spent on this aspect of controls in one year.

TABLE 52   *Registration of firearms dealers—time spent on administration*

	New grant	Annual renewal	Refusal
Number of forces in sample	9	All	4
Average % of total registration	4·47	100	0·6
Est. national total	101	2,267*	14
Average time per process (hrs)	5	$3\frac{1}{2}$	8
Total time taken—M/hr	505	7,934	112

* The total number of dealers has been estimated by relating the numbers in 25 forces to the numbers of certificate holders and applying this figure to the national total of certificate holders. No appeals against refusal to register a dealer came to notice. Taking account only of the processes listed above, the total time spent on these operations in England and Wales is 8,551 man-hours.

TABLE 53   *Shotgun certificates—time spent on administration*

	New grant	Renewal	Refusal	Appeal
Number of forces in sample	20	n/a*	17	6
Average % of total cert.	8·54	23·3*	0·1	0·035
Est. national total	56,493	154,856	664	233
Average time per process (hrs)	1¼	1	3	22
Total time taken (hrs)	70,616	154,856	1992	5,126

* The requirement for shotgun certificates came into force on 1 May 1968, and whilst provision was made for the spread of renewals over a period, it is obvious that the system has not been in operation for a sufficient time for the full turnover of renewals to be revealed. The figure used is the annual renewal rate for firearm certificates.

It has been suggested in parliament from time to time (see Chapter 6) that shotguns should be subjected to the full firearm certificate procedures. Using the figures produced here, the amount of time involved for each firearm certificate in existence is 0·95 man-hours per year, whilst that spent for each shotgun certificate in existence is 0·34 man-hours. If shotguns were to be brought under Section 1 controls, the time spent on them would be multiplied by 2·8, giving an annual time on shotgun certificates alone of 651,252 man-hours against the 232,590 already spent. If the two types of weapon were combined in the one certificate, there would be a reduction of about 17 per cent of the shotgun certificates (see note to Table 49), giving a total annual time for Section 1 firearms and shotguns only, of 740,256 man-hours against the 432,307 man-hours now involved.

The work involved in connection with the issue of certificates does not represent the total commitment of the police on firearms controls. Enforcement of the Act involves substantial numbers of prosecutions, each of which takes up a considerable amount of time. Figures extracted from the Criminal Statistics for 1969 indicate a rise in the number of prosecutions under the Firearms Act (see Table 53).

The number of prosecutions has been rising steadily. Part of this rise can be attributed to new legislation, creating new offences, but some of the rise must be attributed to the attitudes of Chief Officers indicated in the quotations from the annual reports. The amount of

229

time taken for each prosecution is subject to many variables, but to err on the side of caution, it can be accepted that the court time established in Martin and Wilson's study[1] in relation to traffic offences, 3·2 hours per case, is a reasonable guide. Added to this must be the time taken on investigation and preparation, and an average time of two hours would not be unreasonable, accepting

TABLE 54   *Persons dealt with summarily for offences under the Firearms Act, 1950–69*

| Annual Average | | | | | | | |
1950–4	1955–9	1960–4	1965	1966	1967	1968	1969
1,146	949	1,905	2,812	3,970	4,073	3,946	4,416

the fact that some prosecutions arise from enquiries being made in connection with the administration of the Act. Such time, of course, would be covered by the previous tables. Thus, a figure of approximately five hours per prosecution may be a reasonable estimate, giving a total time for 1969 of 22,080 man-hours.

Not all cases reported result in a prosecution. A survey of cases involving possession of a firearm without the appropriate certificate, in one force area, showed that of 55 cases, 25 resulted in cautions and 30 were prosecuted. If this figure were a reasonable guide to the number of cautions, the 4,416 prosecutions in 1969 suggest that somewhere in the region of 3,678 cases resulted in cautions. Such cases still require the completion of enquiries and thus a further 7,356 man-hours can be added to the total. The number of cautions estimated in this way, however, is almost certainly a gross underestimation. The cases examined referred only to possession without a certificate, and a number of other offences, such as failure to notify changes of address, result in cautions far more frequently than do cases of possession without a certificate.

As a rough estimate, therefore, something of the order of 30,000 man-hours, or 3,750 man-days, are involved in the enforcement of the Act, and this work is almost entirely undertaken by police officers. The 40,488 man-days of police time accounted for by the administration and enforcement of the Act could be calculated to represent the full-time employment of 184 police officers of middle rank in addition to the civilian staff involved. Taking account of leave, sickness, etc., a police officer is only effective on about 220 days per year. However, this would be to oversimplify and misrepresent the problem. Some of the prosecutions involve conduct which would have been prosecuted under some other Act if the firearms controls were not in force. A person prosecuted for possessing a shotgun without a certificate might well have been found committing other offences which would result in prosecution, for example, poaching. Equally, many of the prosecutions refer to conduct which is plainly undesirable whether or not certificate procedures are in force. It has been shown that the provisions against persons under 17 carrying uncovered air weapons in public places has probably substantially reduced the number of injuries caused by air weapons and, although air weapons are not subject to certificate procedures, a substantial proportion of the summary prosecutions relate to offences concerning these weapons. Table 55 shows figures supplied by the Home Office indicating the numbers of prosecutions for various offences under the Act.

Even taking account of all the factors in Table 55, it is clear that the administration and enforcement of the controls which, if anything are underestimated here, represents a considerable burden on the police. This burden must be measured against the effectiveness of the controls in achieving their primary objective, which, according to the debate on the 1920 Act when controls were first established, is to 'ensure, as far as possible, that criminals, or weak minded persons, and those who should not have firearms may be prevented from having these dangerous and lethal weapons' (see Chapter 3).

A brief examination of the 55 summary cases mentioned previously might give some indication of the importance to be attached to the number of summary prosecutions and, perhaps, give further guidance on how controls have restricted the availability of firearms. Two of the prosecutions were in respect of young men recently released from borstal training who were found in possession of air weapons. The circumstances of the remaining cases are indicated in Table 56.

In the cases which resulted in prosecution, possession of the weapon came to light, in almost every case, when the offender was committing another offence such as poaching, or when some incident attracted the attention of the police. It is interesting to compare the source of these weapons with those used in the various categories of indictable offences mentioned in Chapters 9 and 10. Of considerable significance is the proportion of weapons recently 'bought' (by which

231

TABLE 55 *Principal summary prosecutions in 1969*

Offence	Number of prosecutions referring to:		
	S1 Firearm	*Shotgun*	*Air weapon*
Possession without certificate (S1)	551	717	—
Transfer to person not holding certificate (S3(2))	25	51	—
Trading when not a dealer (S3(1))	11	9	—
Possess or distribute prohibited weapons (S5(1))	28	—	—
Shortening a shotgun	—	21	—
Carrying in public place without excuse (S19)	53	137	607
Trespass in building (S20)	10	17	13
Trespass on land (S20)	113	478	461
Possession by person previously convicted of crime (S21(4))	46	46	51
Supply to prohibited person (S21(5))	—	2	6
Person under 17 acquiring (S22)	15	26	130
Selling to person under 17 (S22)	15	12	113
Supplying firearm to person under 14 (under 15 in case of shotguns) (S22)	11	3	67
Person under 14 (15 in case of shotguns) in possession of firearm (S22)	15	11	183
Person under 17 with uncovered air weapon in public place (S22)	—	—	437
Person under 14 making improper use of air weapon when under supervision (S22)	—	—	5
Supervisor of person under 14 who made improper use of air weapon (S22)	—	—	2

is included trading, etc) despite the controls. Of all the people who possessed a shotgun without a certificate, 13 brought the fact to notice themselves in applying for a certificate and the remaining three had been caught poaching. Had they not come to notice in this way, it is difficult to see how their possession of the weapons would have come to light.

It has been established that, on 31 December 1969, there were 209,946 firearm certificates in existence in England and Wales (see Table 49). Each firearm certificate does not, however, represent a single weapon. Many certificates may relate to just one firearm, but

TABLE 56   *Summary cases—Possession of firearms without certificate*

| Source | Section 1 firearm | | Shotgun | | |
	Prosecuted	Caution	Prosecuted	Caution	Totals
Recently 'bought' off certificate	7	1	6	—	14
Owned prior to restrictions	—	2*	3	13†	18
Borrowed from friend	3	2	4	2	11
Failed to renew certificate	2	2	—	—	4
'Wartime' weapons found	—	3	—	—	3
Stolen	1	—	—	—	1
Source not established	—	—	2	—	2
Totals	13	10	15	15	53

* One, a very old rifle and one a 23 in. barrel shotgun which became a Section 1 firearm by virtue of the 1965 Act.

† In all cases the possession of the shotgun came to light when the owner visited the police station to apply for a shotgun certificate and stated that he already owned a shotgun.

many others relate to two or more weapons of different types. No firm figure is available to show the total number of weapons legitimately in circulation at any one time, and, of course, the figure is constantly changing as weapons are bought and sold. To provide an estimate of the number of firearms involved, and a breakdown by types, reliance must again be placed on projections from the figures of a relatively small number of forces. Although every effort has been made to ensure that the projection is as accurate as possible, the resulting figure can only be regarded as an estimate.

Q

Because of the varying methods of keeping records, many forces are unable to establish precisely how many weapons are covered by firearm certificates issued by them. However, a number of Chief Officers have published such figures in their annual reports, and others have made the figures available for this study. Figures from eight forces, providing a representative sample, show that the average number of firearms per certificate varies from 1·04 to 1·72 and an average of the eight indicates that each certificate represents 1·34 firearms, or a total of 281,327 Section 1 firearms in England and Wales. A further examination of the breakdown of weapons in a number of forces provides information for the estimated numbers of each type of weapon in England and Wales shown in Table 57.

TABLE 57   *Numbers and types of firearms held on firearm certificates in England and Wales, 1969*

Weapon	Number of forces in sample	Average % of each weapon	Est. national total
Pistols	6	22·4	63,017
Rifles*	6	65·3	183,706
Section 1 shotguns†	3	1·0	2,813
Humane killer	4	4·25	11,956
Signalling instrument	4	1·37	3,854
Others	–	–	15,981
Total	–	–	281,327

* A further breakdown amongst 5 forces indicates that of the 183,706 rifles, 155,966 are smallbore (.22) rifles, and 27,704 are of larger calibre.

† Most of the Section 1 shotguns are combination weapons with both rifled and smoothbore barrels. A number have barrels just short of the 24 in. limit set by the Firearms Act.

The holder of a shotgun certificate is not required to give information about the number of weapons held, but during 1969, one Chief Constable asked holders of certificates to supply this information voluntarily. The results of the enquiry show that, so far as that police area is concerned, each certificate represents 1·23 shotguns. The force concerned covers an urban area and it is to be expected that the numbers of shotgun per certificate would be higher in rural areas. The figure of 1·23, therefore, almost certainly represents an underestimation when applied to the country as a whole, but it is the only figure available. Using this figure, the total number of shotguns owned by the holders of shotgun certificates in England and Wales is 817,483, but it would be more reasonable to think in terms of something nearer one million.

The total number of weapons held on certificate does not represent the total number of weapons in the country. The fairly heavy increase in the number of shotgun certificates between 1968 and 1969, coupled with the figures in Tables 55 and 56 of persons reported for possessing a shotgun without certificate, indicates that a substantial number of shotgun owners may not yet have obtained a certificate. It is extremely difficult to obtain any sort of an estimate of the numbers of weapons illegally held in this country, but some

TABLE 58   *Weapons surrendered in amnesties prior to the Second World War*

Weapon	1933	1935	1937	Total
Pistols	12,622	5,476	10,000*	28,098
Rifles	3,706 ⎫		n/a	n/a
Shotguns	— ⎬ 2,313		n/a	n/a
Others	81	681	n/a	n/a
Totals	16,409	8,469	14,000	38,878

* The breakdown of weapons for the 1937 amnesty is not available. The proportion of pistols has been estimated relative to the proportions in the two previous amnesties. Source: parliamentary replies.

indication can be obtained by the numbers which are surrendered to or confiscated by the police.

From time to time, the Home Office has arranged with Chief Officers of Police for amnesties in respect of illegally held weapons when, during specified periods of about six or eight weeks, such weapons can be handed in at a police station on a 'no questions asked' basis and without fear of prosecution. Three such amnesties were held prior to the Second World War (see Table 58).

The Second World War resulted in large numbers of illegally

owned weapons appearing in this country, many of them brought back as souvenirs by soldiers. The effects of the pre-war amnesties must have been largely nullified by this and so the figures are shown separately (see Table 59).

TABLE 59   *Weapons surrendered in amnesties in England and Wales since 1946*

Weapon	1946	1961	1965	1968	Total
Pistols	58,885	53,255	26,417	8,847	147,404
Rifles	13,509	9,101	6,575	4,340	33,525
Shotguns	308	450	2,761	9,488	13,007
Others*	3,298†	7,194	5,247	2,413	18,152
Totals	76,000	70,000	41,000	25,088	212,088

* Except in 1968, this figure appears to have been adjusted to produce a total in round figures.

† In 1946, this total includes no less than 1,580 machine guns and sub-machine guns (prohibited weapons).

Sources: parliamentary replies, confirmed by letter from the Home Office.

It must not be thought that the total of weapons surrendered in amnesties represents anything like the total number of weapons which have been illegally in circulation. In the first place, it would be naïve to think that criminals who hold weapons are likely to take advantage of an amnesty, and in the second, it is clear from further evidence that large numbers of people have not surrendered their weapons during the amnesties. Thousands of firearms are surrendered to police forces year by year. In his annual reports, the Commissioner of Police for the Metropolis has published figures for the weapons surrendered in his force area (see Table 60).

These figures represent all weapons surrendered and confiscated during the year and not all were illegally held. Pistols appear to be the prime cause for concern, and to represent by far the largest class of weapon. A study of the records for 1969 indicates that no less than 75 per cent of the pistols surrendered during that year had been illegally held. Thus, over the years since 1946, approximately 26,735 pistols which have never been the subject of a firearm certificate have been surrendered to this one force, excluding those

TABLE 60 *Firearms surrendered to the Metropolitan Police excluding amnesties—1946–69*

	1946	1947	1948	1949	1950	1951
All weapons	4,141	4,185	3,325	2,382	2,400	2,052
Pistols	2,300*	2,790*	2,714	1,610	1,613	1,285
	1952	1953	1954	1955	1956	1957
All weapons	2,198	2,415	2,183	2,017	2,091	2,201
Pistols	1,415	1,653	2,426	1,314	1,253	1,252
	1958	1959	1960	1961	1962	1963
All weapons	2,106	2,403	2,312	1,850	2,382	2,323
Pistols	1,236	1,498	1,382	1,233*	1,391	1,314
	1964	1965	1966	1967	1968	1969
All weapons	2,040	2,270	2,145	2,253	2,061	2,271
Pistols	1,098	1,513*	1,065	1,086	1,091	1,114

Total weapons surrendered 1946–69

All weapons	58,006
Pistols	35,646

* In the case of the figures marked, the breakdown showing pistols separately was not given and the figure was calculated on the relatively constant proportion of pistols in other years.

surrendered in amnesties. The surprising thing is that, from 1948, the figures remain relatively constant year by year, indicating that the source is by no means drying up. Very few of these firearms represent pistols taken from criminals. The vast majority are simply handed in by people who are, as far as one can tell from the information available, perfectly respectable citizens. In each case the person handing in the weapon is asked where it came from, but the answer given is normally accepted without question. By far the most popular account was that some relative had recently died and the weapon had been found amongst his effects. The value of those accounts as an indication of the real source of the weapons is minimal.

The Metropolitan Police have, of course, taken part in the various amnesties along with other forces, and the number of weapons surrendered to them, extracted from the Commissioner's Reports, is shown in Table 61. Whilst a very small number of the weapons surrendered in amnesties may be held on a firearm certificate, the vast majority are illegally held. There is now no way of separating the small proportion of legally held weapons, but, from the writer's experience, it is negligible.

TABLE 61 *Firearms surrendered to the Metropolitan Police in amnesties since 1946*

	1946	1961	1965	1968	Total
All firearms	18,567	11,313	6,178	2,145	38,203
Pistols	12,378*	9,435	4,392	1,167	27,372

* Estimated on the proportion of pistols in other years.

Thus, since 1946, no less than 96,209 firearms of all types have been surrendered to the Metropolitan Police alone. Of these 63,018 were pistols, and 54,106 of these were illegally held. The total number of pistols held subject to a firearm certificate in the Metropolitan Police District is not known, but if the figure runs close to the national average, the 14,663 firearm certificates represents 19,648 firearms (1·34 per certificate). If 22·4 per cent of these are pistols, there are an estimated 4,401 pistols held subject to a firearm certificate at the present time—less than one twelfth of the illegally held pistols which have been surrendered. Firearms which have been surrendered have, of course, left the illegal market, but how many remain? The yearly surrender figure remains relatively constant and in the three years, 1967, 1968 and 1969, the total of pistols surrendered is 4,458—more than the legally held total. It seems safe to suggest that the number of illegally held pistols in circulation far exceeds the number held on firearm certificates.

It could be argued that London is a special case, but a check on the figures for the remainder of the country shows that this is not so, and a similar position applies to the whole of England and Wales. Details of surrendered weapons for 1969 obtained from 15 forces (including the Metropolitan Police) were examined. The forces concerned represent 41 per cent of the population of England and

Wales and provide a representative sample. It was found that the total number of firearms surrendered in these 15 forces during 1969 was 5,208. Projected to the whole of England and Wales, this suggests a figure of 13,020 firearms surrendered. Thirty-six per cent (4,687) of the surrendered firearms were pistols and of these no less than 80 per cent had never been subject to a firearm certificate. If the trend in the Metropolitan Police District is representative, this figure will be just slightly less than that for previous years and it is safe to say that in the twenty-four years since 1946 some 312,480 firearms have been surrendered year by year, including 112,488 pistols of which 89,976 were illegally held. If this is added to the amnesty figure, it is found that the total number of firearms surrendered to the police in England and Wales during the period is a startling 524,568 of which 259,892 were pistols. Of the total number of pistols, some 237,380 had been illegally held. These figures confirm the suggestion that, at least as far as pistols are concerned, the illegal market is far from deprived of weapons, and may well exceed the total of 63,000 pistols held on certificate. And this despite fifty years of the most stringent controls.

16 Conclusions and Suggestions

A study of the development of firearms legislation through the years reveals a pattern which is repeated several times with slight variations. There is an absence of reliable research, and in every case, except perhaps the Bodkin Committee Report, such statistics as have been presented have been vague and unreliable and have lacked any point of comparison. Legislation has frequently been related to relatively isolated incidents and has often reached beyond the scope of the incident to affect people in no way concerned with that type of event. In almost every case, the sponsors of Bills have expressed limited aims for the legislation. Yet, as soon as the Bill received the Royal Assent, it has been criticised for failing to achieve aims not set for it.

It is extremely difficult to establish the logic behind much of the legislation. In the first place none of the various Acts clearly expresses its objects. The Pistols Act 1903, was, 'An Act to regulate the sale and use of pistols or other firearms'. The Firearms Act 1920 was, 'An Act to amend the law relating to firearms and other weapons and ammunition'. With one exception, the remaining Acts have stated in their preamble merely the purpose of consolidating or amending the law. The Firearms and Imitation Firearms (Criminal Use) Act, 1933, had the stated intention of, 'Imposing penalties for the use, attempted use and possession of firearms and imitation firearms in certain cases'. Only the 1903 Act comes anywhere near a statement of its intention, but 'to regulate the sale and use of pistols' is a statement of method and not a statement of objectives.

To find some statement of the object of controls, it is necessary to go back to the debate on the 1920 Act to find that the legislation was designed for two purposes. First, to enable the government to control overseas trade in arms and so fulfil their commitment to the Paris Arms Convention of 1919. The Firearms Act 1968 contains reserve powers, in Section 6, which permit the Home Secretary to make Orders prohibiting the removal of firearms and ammunition from one place to another, either within the United Kingdom or for export. These powers have been continued from the 1920 Act and an Order made in 1922 prohibits the removal of firearms to a ship for export unless an export licence has been issued by the Board of Trade. Under present import and export controls, this power more or less duplicates the powers held by the Board of Trade. The power to prohibit movement of firearms within Great Britain, or to Northern Ireland, represents a useful reserve, and the commitment to control traffic in arms appears to be fully met. The second object, according to the statement of the Home Secretary on the Second Reading of the Bill in the Commons, was 'To maintain greater control so that, as far as possible, criminals or weak-minded persons and those who should not have firearms may be prevented from having these dangerous and lethal firearms' (see Chapter 3). If this represents a statement of the objects of controls, they seem to have been lost to sight from time to time.

One of the most glaring defects to be found in any study of the developments of the legislation is an almost complete absence of proper research. The statistics produced to support Bills have invariably been inadequate and have lacked points of comparison. The Blackwell Committee had little statistical information before it, and such as it had pointed to a downward trend in the criminal use of firearms (see Chapter 2). They did not, as far as can been seen, research into the types of firearm involved in crime, nor the sources of the weapons, before concluding that controls on pistols and rifles were required. This lack of research led them to pin all their hopes on the firearm certificate system as a means of preventing the criminal use of firearms; so much so that they did not recommend any legislation concerning the actual use of firearms, and they excluded shotguns and air weapons from the definition of 'firearms' for all purposes. That these methods were inadequate is demonstrated by the introduction of the Firearms and Imitation Firearms (Criminal Use) Act 1933, to penalise the criminal use of all types of firearm.

The Bodkin Committee made considerable efforts to repair the defects of earlier legislation, but its terms of reference excluded any real appraisal of the controls as they existed. Within its terms of reference, this Committee produced excellent results and it is to be regretted that it was not charged with enquiring into the results, in practical terms, of the legislation which had been in force for a considerable time. Following the 1937 Act, which embodied most of Bodkin's recommendations, there was no further legislation until

241

the 1960s. The Airguns, Shotguns Etc. Act 1962, was a Private Member's Bill, but the debates show that its sponsors had done their homework reasonably well, and were addressing legislation to a specific problem in a manner likely to meet with some success. Events leading to the Acts of 1965, 1967 and 1968 are fully outlined in Chapters 5 and 6. The only statistics used were those for 'indictable offences in which a firearm was involved', and the merit of this figure as a basis for legislation is discussed in Chapter 8. Certainly, none of this legislation was based on sound research.

A further recurring factor in the passing of legislation is that, in most cases, the sponsors have claimed only limited objects for their Bill. In all cases, during the debates, it has been accepted that the legislation would have only limited effects. Yet, as soon as each Act has been passed, everyone appears to have been surprised that the problem to which it was addressed did not disappear overnight. The Acts have been very quickly criticised for failing to do what they were not designed to do, or for failing to be completely effective when everyone had accepted that they could not be so. The failure of a particular Act to have a marked effect on the problem has frequently simply led to further legislation and not to research to determine the reasons for the failure.

How effective have these controls been in bringing within their terms all the firearms in the country, and in preventing criminals from obtaining and using firearms? The evidence produced in Chapter 15 indicates that fifty years of very strict controls on pistols have left a vast pool of illegal weapons. Large numbers are surrendered to the police each year and it is difficult to avoid the conclusion that this is only the tip of the iceberg. If so many illegally held pistols come into the hands of the police, how many remain in circulation? If the number of weapons surrendered year by year does not diminish, how many are being imported by one means or another? Whilst the size of the pool of illegal pistols cannot be estimated with any accuracy, there can surely be no doubt that it is very large. If this statement is true in relation to pistols, it must be much more so in relation to shotguns. Strict controls on pistols since 1920 have failed to bring under control large numbers of these weapons. The less strict controls on shotguns have applied since 1968 and, on this evidence, it would seem that the numbers of illegally held shotguns will still be vast in the year 2000.

The effect which these controls might have had on the use of firearms in crime is not easy to state with precision. It could be argued that we do not know what would have happened if there had been no controls, although the fact that shotguns were only recently controlled might help to gauge this factor. One of the greatest difficulties lies in finding comparable statistics. It is just not possible to take statistics gathered at the turn of the century and compare then with figures for the 1960s. Many things have changed during the period, not least of which is police reporting procedures. Until relatively recently, the procedures for reporting even the more serious crimes were quite haphazard. The only way in which a valid comparison can be made is to take the statistics supplied for a given period and set them against the background of their time to draw a general conclusion. As a a matter of judgment, comparisons can then be made. One thing is certain. The statistics produced in parliament in support of the various Bills had the object of justifying legislation. The politicians concerned will have selected figures which were best suited to that purpose, and the figures therefore are those most likely to state the problem in its strongest terms.

The figures produced in 1887 and 1892 (Chapter 1) refer to 'burglars' and it can probably be accepted that this was the class of crime in which firearms were most used at the time. The latter return shows that for the whole of England and Wales, during the five years ending in 1892, an average of only 6 burglars a year were found in possession of firearms when arrested, and fewer than 4 per year used firearms to escape. The returns for the period 1915–17 (Chapter 2), concern the use of firearms in 'crime' in London. This shows that, on average, fewer than 16 people a year used firearms in connection with all classes of crime. Such figures cannot be compared directly with the figures for robbery in London since 1946, but as the earlier figures relate to all crime, the robbery figures for the period can be supposed to represent only a part of this.

No matter how one approaches the figures, one is forced to the rather startling conclusion that the use of firearms in crime was very much less when there were no controls of any sort and when anyone, convicted criminal or lunatic, could buy any type of firearm without restriction. Half a century of strict controls on pistols has ended, perversely, with a far greater use of this class of weapon in crime than ever before. We do not know how much worse this would have been if there had been no controls, but it is possible to get some indication by looking at the position in relation to shotguns. Despite the fact that they were unrestricted until 1968, shotguns were used in only a relatively low proportion of robberies in the periods immediately before and after the imposition of controls. Table 62 shows the numbers and proportions of different types of weapons used in robberies in England and Wales since 1966.

TABLE 62   *Type of firearms used in robberies in England and Wales, 1966–9*

Year	Shotguns No.	Shotguns %	Pistols No.	Pistols %	Sawn-off shotguns (S1 firearm) No.	Sawn-off shotguns (S1 firearm) %	Others No.	Others %	Total No.
1966	53	15·5	*		18	5·2	269	79·3	340
1967	59	21·3	126	45·6	11	3·9	80	29·2	276
1968	98	25·3	140	36·1	37	9·5	112	29·1	387
1969	100	20·6	173	35·7	30	10·3	161	33·4	464

* A separate figure for pistols is not available for 1966 and they are included under 'Others'.

In just one case, statistics over a period of time may be more or less comparable. In 1913 the use of firearms in attacks against the police was the subject of a return to parliament (see Chapter 2). Similar figures were sought in 1966 and published in a parliamentary reply on 17 November 1966. The figure published for 1966 was for nine months only, but this was later completed for the whole year by the Home Office. Table 63 shows the comparisons of these figures.

During the period 1908–12, shots were fired, on average, at 18·4 officers per year. During the period 1963–6, this figure was 19·5. In the first period the average of officers killed was 1·2 per year and in the second period, it was 1·0. The numbers injured are 4·8 and 3·2 respectively. During the first period, the only form of control in operation was the Pistols Act 1903, and for all practical purposes it can be said that firearms were universally available. Yet, it will be noted there were on average slightly fewer cases in which shots were fired at police officers, though deaths and injuries were very slightly higher; taken overall, there is no appreciable difference in the figures for the two periods. Comparable figures are not available for subsequent years but, according to the Home Office, during 1968 and 1969, no police officers were killed by shooting and the numbers wounded were 3 and 2 respectively.

Careful examination of all the evidence available suggests, therefore, that legislation has failed to bring under control substantial numbers of firearms, and it certainly cannot be claimed that strict controls have reduced the use of firearms in crime. On the basis of these facts is might be argued that firearms controls have had little effect and do not justify the amount of police time involved. Indeed, it is possible to build up a sound case for abolishing or substantially reducing controls. One important aspect not covered by the statistics is the psychological effects of controls. It might be claimed that a tradition of restricted ownership of firearms has been built

TABLE 63   *Use of firearms against the police in England and Wales, 1902–12 and 1963–6*

	1908	1909	1910	1911	1912	1963	1964	1965	1966
Number of cases	3	8	4	15	18	*	*	*	*
Total of officers shot at	3	29	14	21	25	6	15	31	26
Number killed	0	2	3	0	1	0	0	1	3
Number wounded	1	4	3	10	6	1	1	7	3
Number not injured	2	23	8	11	18	5	14	23	20
Number menaced only	*	*	*	*	*	37	61	65	99

* Figures not supplied.

up, and that controls have helped to establish a state of public opinion in which firearms are regarded as potentially dangerous items which should be restricted as far as possible to responsible people. Any such psychological effects will, clearly, have been more effective amongst the law-abiding section of the community than they will against the criminal elements. This is clearly an important aspect of the problem and one which it is impossible to quantify, yet it is well illustrated in many of the debates in parliament on the various Bills. Prior to the passing of the Pistols Act, Members spoke frequently of their habit of carrying pistols and of their willingness to use them in self-defence. The facts show that they were rarely used, but it is clear that many people felt the need of a pistol for

245

defence. In later debates, this point does not arise. There are claims for the right to use firearms for sporting purposes, but claims for the need of firearms for defence rapidly diminish. Many factors have contributed to this. It seems that the actual risk involved was less before controls than it is in the present day, yet the demand for firearms for protection almost disappears in the early twentieth century. There is no doubt that the Common Law right to keep arms, and the tradition of owning arms for protection, was built up during a period when there was no effective police, when the individual was compelled to see to his own protection. Radzinowicz, in his *History of the English Criminal Law*,[1] details the weaknesses, inefficiencies and corruptness of such police systems as existed in the eighteenth century, quoting at length from contemporary sources which show that it was essential to travel well armed. By the early nineteenth century, the situation had, if anything, deteriorated so far as the police were concerned[2] and it was not until late in the nineteenth century that 'the improved police gave greater security'.[3] By the turn of the century, the public was at last feeling confident in placing its defence to a greater extent in the hands of police forces which were proving themselves to be generally efficient and effective. It is suggested that this is probably the major factor in the diminishing demand for the citizen to keep arms to defend himself. There is little doubt, too, that public confidence in the system of courts which, despite complaints, held the respect of the vast majority of people, added to this feeling of security. Once there had been established a substantial degree of public confidence in the ability of the forces of law and order to provide adequate protection, the public anxiety about their right to keep firearms for their own defence ceased to be a major factor. Firearms controls introduced before this point could have had little effect. Firearms controls introduced, as they were, after the establishment of this confidence may well have helped to bring about the final stages of what is undoubtedly a very substantial change in attitudes.

How, then, should policy on firearms controls be affected by the facts produced? The system of registering all firearms to which Section 1 applies as well as licensing the individual takes up a large part of the police time involved and causes a great deal of trouble and inconvenience. The voluminous records so produced appear to serve no useful purpose. In none of the cases examined in this study was the existence of these records of any assistance in detecting a crime and no one questioned during the course of the study could offer any evidence to establish the value of the system of registering weapons.

The evidence indicates that a much simplified system of licensing the individual would produce no less effect than the system now imposed. The amount of police time involved in administering the controls would be reduced by something of the order of 33,000 man-hours per year by such a step. In the light of these facts, it should surely be for the proponents of the system of registration to establish its value. If they fail to do so, the system should be abandoned.

Within the framework of the present controls, the proposition that further restrictions on the holders of firearm or shotgun certificates will help solve the problem of armed crime just cannot be supported. It is evident that the firearms at present in the hands of legitimate users who hold certificates present virtually no problem to the community. The vast amount of police time and effort spent on these people could be substantially reduced without increasing the risk. The strict policies which have applied since 1967 have materially increased the amount of police time spent on individual applications, and have resulted in a small reduction in the numbers of weapons held on certificate. They have not affected the numbers of illegal weapons in circulation and, if the proposition raised in Chapter 8, that thefts of weapons is not a major source of weapons used in crime, is correct, then even the relatively low risk of the weapons concerned being stolen ceases to be significant. The policies may, indeed, have been counter-productive. Having regard to the large numbers of illegal weapons in circulation, otherwise respectable persons denied a firearm certificate might well be tempted to obtain a weapon illegally and thus support the black market.

The general tenor of the policy does little to reduce the numbers of illegally held weapons. Where weapons are illegally held for criminal purposes, there is no hope that they will be voluntarily handed in, or that the owner will apply for a firearm certificate. It is clear, however, that substantial numbers of firearms are illegally held by otherwise respectable people. Many of these are souvenirs and of some sentimental value and, indeed, their cash value may be quite high. With such a weapon hidden away in a drawer, the chances of detection are very small and the evidence indicates that many such people are not tempted by offers to relieve them of a valued and often valuable weapon by way of surrender to the police. As a result of the stricter policy, such people now realise that if they go to the police, the weapon will be confiscated and they are likely to be prosecuted. It may well be that a more effective control would be established with a more liberal policy, so that if such people could be persuaded to come forward with their firearms, they could, whenever possible, be issued with a certificate to retain the weapons. Where, for some good reason, it was not possible to issue a certificate, a temporary permit could be granted allowing the owner to realise the full cash value of the firearm by sale to a registered dealer. Once entered in the dealer's books, illegal dealings in the weapon become almost impossible if proper police checks are made. Under existing law, there is nothing to prevent a dealer acquiring such a firearm, but he is required to make a full entry in his register. This procedure could be simplified by accepting that, if the vendor declines to give his name and address, the dealer would be relieved of liability for failure to have the details recorded. The situation could then be publicised and it may well be that people unwilling to go to the police would willingly go to a registered dealer to dispose of illegally held weapons.

The very substantial increases in fees made in 1971 are detailed in Chapter 13 and commented upon in Chapter 6. These appear to be a part of the strict policies referred to. It seems that the present fees go beyond the cost of the police in respect of the majority of the run-of-the-mill applications, and it may well be that these high charges will also be counter-productive. They may well deter applications for the grant or variation of a certificate, but they do nothing towards achieving the objects of the controls and may sway some individuals towards illegally acquiring or retaining firearms rather than pay a high fee for the grant and variation of a certificate. The object of the legislation is to benefit the community as a whole and the issue of firearm certificates is intended to facilitate the achievement of these objects. Whatever the total cost to the police, the fees should be so fixed that they do not dissuade a person from making an application.

The imposition of unduly restrictive conditions on the grant of a certificate appears to be increasing. Each of these conditions should be examined to see whether or not it contributes towards achieving the object of the controls. If the condition makes no significant contribution towards this end, it cannot be justified, and it is likely to do no more than to antagonise and inconvenience the certificate holder for no purpose.

The amount of time spent on administering the controls could be substantially decreased in a number of ways without in any way losing such effectiveness as the controls may have. In the first instance, it is necessary to keep in mind the object of the controls, and it is to be regretted that these are not clearly stated in the legislation. If the object is, as has been suggested, 'To prevent, as far as possible, firearms falling into the hands of criminals and unsuitable persons', then this must be clearly borne in mind. It is apparent that a number of Chief Officers believe that they also have a duty, through firearms controls, to promote public safety. It is not easy to find a brief for this in the legislation, but it could quite properly be included as one of the objects of controls.

The overlap of shotgun and firearm certificate holders shown in Chapter 15 is clearly creating a good deal of unnecessary work for the police and unnecessary inconvenience and excuse for the individuals who hold both types of certificate. By an amendment to the Firearms Rules, it would be possible to combine the documents and allow of one application form, one process and one fee to cover both types of weapon. This would reduce the work on shotgun certificates by approximately 17 per cent—a saving of somewhere in the region of 40,000 man-hours to the police. It would not materially increase the amount of work in connection with firearm certificates.

Firearm and shotgun certificates are renewable every three years, but a good many certificate holders have demonstrated over the years that their possession of firearms presents no threat to the community. In particular, it can be shown that rifles are very rarely used in crime. The person who has held a certificate without complaint for a number of years, particularly where the certificate refers only to rifles, could be permitted to renew for longer periods. If a firearm certificate were granted for three years (or even less) in the first instance, and Chief Officers of Police were given discretion to extend subsequent periods of validity to six years, there would be a substantial saving in the time spent on renewals, without any increase in the risk involved.

Such a case can be even better made out for shotgun certificates where details of the weapons held are not recorded. Indeed, there would seem to be little reason why a shotgun certificate could not be valid for life unless revoked. This might, however, cause some problems. In cases where a certificate was lost, its permanent validity might be of considerable help to a dishonest finder, although the presence on the certificate of the signature of the holder would help reduce this risk. Changes in the circumstances of the holder could occur and fail to be noted if a certificate were valid for life.

R

Any convictions incurred should be brought to notice by the present system of checking convictions against certificate holders which operates in most forces, but changes in mental state or other grounds for unsuitability would not come to light so easily. Obviously, there will be few such changes, but when considered along with other factors such as the problem of keeping check on holders who have died, or moved from area to area, it might be thought that the most reasonable compromise would be to make a certificate relating to shotguns only valid for three years in the first instance, and then valid for six years for subsequent renewals. This would cut the work on renewals by something in the order of 40 per cent and would allow of a reappraisal of the holder after the first three year period.

In the case of firearm certificates, the holder may at any time apply for a variation. The lengthy procedures involved are set out in Chapter 14. There is clearly a case for examining the need for such applications, particularly where the holder is merely seeking to exchange one firearm for another of similar type. For example, the owner of a .22 target rifle may wish to sell that rifle and purchase another .22 target rifle, perhaps of better quality. The only change brought about by this is in the details of the weapon held. At present these are entered on the certificate and notified to the police by the vendor. In such cases the lengthy process of variation seems unnecessary. Time would also be saved if, in cases where a variation was thought necessary (for instance, where a completely different type of weapon was required), and the certificate has, say, less than one year to run, the Chief Officer had discretion to renew at the same time.

A fairly large number of free firearm certificates relate only to captive bolt humane killers. Implementation of the Bodkin Committee's suggestion that these should not be treated as Section 1 firearms would save a good deal of time and would have the added advantage of encouraging the use of captive bolt humane killers except where the free bullet type was absolutely essential. Details of the Bodkin Committee's recommendations are shown in Chapter 4 and it seems that captive bolt killers do not properly come within the definition of a firearm and, in any event, they are less liable to misuse than other implements at present held to be outside the scope of the controls.

The Dangerous Air Weapons Rules are discussed at length in Chapter 6, and it is shown that the weapons subject to certificate procedures are, in some cases, no more powerful than a catapult. There is no record of a case in which such weapons have been used in crime, and there is no evidence to show that the slightly greater power of these weapons has contributed to an accident. Whilst the reserve power to declare certain air weapons to be particularly dangerous might be useful, the evidence indicates that there is no justification for the present rules. The amount of work created by them is quite out of proportion to any benefit. In many cases it is necessary to have the individual weapon checked at a laboratory to establish whether or not it is within the terms of the definition. Although the numbers are small, the time spent on them is completely wasted. The rules should either be repealed, or should be amended to specify energies much higher than those at present imposed, or to specify individual models of weapons which achieve a very high energy output.

A number of certificates relate to shotguns with 23 in. barrels. The minimum barrel length at which a shotgun became a Section 1 firearm was changed in 1965 from 20 in. to 24 in. The object was to discourage the use of sawn-off shotguns, but such weapons used in crime are invariably cut down to a length much less than 20 in. The amendment bringing in this change was introduced at a late stage in the progress of the hurried Bill and it is clear that the problem was inadequately considered (see Chapter 5). The Bodkin Committee gave a good deal of thought to this problem before recommending the 20 in. length (see Chapter 4) and there is no evidence to show that this has ever caused any problems. Similarly, the complete prohibition on the shortening of barrels by registered dealers has achieved nothing and has caused anomalies. A return to the minimum length of 20 in. for shotgun barrels would eliminate the need for a small number of certificates (the number would undoubtedly be greater if all the 23 in. barrel shotguns were to be declared) and would cause no greater risk from the use of sawn-off shotguns.

Present legislation contains a number of anomalies, many of which are mentioned in this study. There are other restrictions which cause particular problems to certain classes of user and these may not be detailed here. Each of these should be examined in the light of the objects of the legislation. If, as is certainly the case in a number of instances they do nothing to promote the objects of the legislation, they should be scrapped. There is some evidence to suggest that certain restrictions are retained for the sake of bureaucratic tidiness and that controls are often seen as an end in themselves rather than as a means to an end.

For the future, it is essential that the whole problem of controls

251

and their relationship to armed crime should be the subject of objective review. If this is to be done, there must be available accurate and informative statistical data. It is suggested that the present Home Office figures for indictable offences involving a firearm are neither particularly accurate, especially when considered over a period of years, not do they shed much light on the problem. The question of the use of firearms in crime has to be seen in the context of the use of violence in crime and not in isolation. The use of firearms has to be related to the sources of those firearms before sensible efforts can be made to eliminate the sources. The most useful information published to date is to be extracted from the Reports of the Commissioner of Police for the Metropolis where information is supplied for all robberies, with a breakdown showing the types of weapon involved. However, this information is in itself insufficient to ensure a continuing objective study. The use of firearms is often involved with the use of other weapons. The use of firerearms in crime other than robbery is not covered in detail and, most important, no information is supplied about the sources of the weapons used. It is suggested that, if this problem which is a matter of considerable public concern is to be kept properly under review, the statistical information must provide:

1. *A sensible and acceptable definition of the criminal use of firearms in this context.* Whilst it is desirable to record the incidence of such offences as the assaults with air weapons discussed in Chapter 9, these and similar matters should not be confused with the more serious and dangerous crimes. In this connection, the evidence produced in Chapter 9 indicates the desirability of being able to separate domestic assaults from assaults by strangers. Thefts of weapons should be excluded from the figures as they are largely irrelevant. Where stolen firearms are used in crime, this can be indicated under item 5 below.

2. *The general incidence of violence in connection with the types of crime considered above.* It seems clearly established that the criminal use of firearms is directly related to the general incidence of violence used in the furtherance of crimes (though not necessarily with the incidence of crimes where violence is the object of the offence) and to consider the use of firearms in isolation is likely to be misleading.

3. *The use in connection with 'crime' of all types of weapon.* This information should provide details of all weapons used, including cases where more than one type of weapon was employed. It has been shown, for example, that in many robberies in which firearms

are used, blunt instruments are also employed and the latter are more likely to cause injury than the former. The simple breakdown employed in the Metropolitan Police figures, where the crime is classified according to the 'most serious' weapon involved, is not fully informative and tends to be misleading.

4. *A detailed breakdown of types of firearms used.* There is evidence to support a broad generalisation that crimes committeed with air weapons or imitation firearms tend to be the work of amateurs or adolescents. The risks to the public are less from this type of crime and they hardly fall into the same category as crimes committed with Section 1 firearms or shotguns. Moreover, evidence of the relative use of different types of weapons over a period can clearly help in assessing the value of controls.

5. *As much information as possible about the source of firearms used.* In the majority of cases, this will only be available if the crime is detected, but it is important to know what proportion of weapons have been stolen, and from what sources; what weapons apparently originate from the black market; and what weapons have been recently imported. Information about makers, dates of manufacture, proof marks and the like may be necessary to reach a reasonable conclusion and this may require expert interpretation. In many cases, it would not be possible for this to be done, but where a weapon used in crime has been recovered by the police, it is frequently submitted to a forensic science laboratory for examination. If such a requirement were made known, the relevant information could, in many cases, be supplied by the laboratory and recorded by the police.

Statistics gathered on such a basis would be likely to fulfil the criteria suggested by the Perks Committee[4] of 'providing society with information, both as a matter of public interest and as a basis for action'. Implementation of the recommendations of that Committee would go some way towards solving this problem, but the specialised information needed in this connection will require a more detailed approach to some aspects.

Relatively small variations from year to year may have little significance. For the information to have real value, a system o recording should contain information which could be directly compared to the present information concerning robberies which, as has been shown, provides a realistic index to the criminal use of firearms and represents the most significant part of the problem.

To continue with the process of attempting to deal with the

criminal use of firearms by placing more restrictions on legitimate users is not likely to achieve anything. But the great danger lies, not in the ineffectiveness of such restrictions, but in a belief that they will solve the problem. Whilst this mistaken belief persists, the real problem will not receive the attention and action which it clearly and urgently requires.

Appendix   A Personal View of the Relevance of Capital Punishment

The rise in the criminal use of firearms, as illustrated particularly by the number of robberies in London in which a firearm was used or carried (see Chapter 11) does not appear to have been influenced in any significant way by changes in the system of firearms controls. Why then this rise—a rise which is, in reality, an increase in the willingness to use violence of which the use of firearms is just a part? To attempt to isolate a single cause is clearly unwise, for very few such phenomena have a single cause. There must, however, be some major factor to account for trends which seem to be common to the problem no matter how it is examined. It has been illustrated at every stage of the examination of the problem that certain years mark distinct changes in the level of the use of weapons in robbery. There appear to be peaks around 1948 and in 1956. The period after 1957 marks a general rise in the level of the use of violence and 1964 marks a further steepening of virtually every graph in Chapter 11.

This research, which was directed at evaluating the effectiveness of firearms controls, cannot hope to explore every aspect of such a complicated problem, but it has produced what is submitted as evidence of a link between the increase in the use of a high degree of violence in robbery and the various stages of the abolition of the death penalty. In advancing this personal view of what may be a major factor in accounting for the rise in the use of firearms, and of weapons generally, by criminals, it is accepted that there may be, and probably are, other factors involved. Specific research into this aspect has not been undertaken as part of the study, and part of the view expressed may well be conjecture which in turn may be influenced by the writer's personal and professional attitudes. As such, it does not belong in the main text of the work. Yet, if a conclusion of this study has been that firearms controls have not been a major factor in the rise, and there is evidence which points towards some

255

other factor as having influenced the situation, it seems essential that this view should be expressed. For this reason the views are expressed in an appendix, not part of the main work though closely connected with it and, possibly, not substantiated in the way that the views expressed in the main body of the text have been substantiated.

If there is any relationship between the degree of violence used in robbery and the abolition of capital punishment, it will be necessary to trace the various stages along the road to complete abolition so that a comparison can be made. The movement towards abolition had its beginnings long before the period covered in this survey of robbery, but its effects only began to be felt during that period, and the effective part of the abolitionist campaign is covered in the twenty-four year period under review.

In 1947, the Parliamentary Penal Reform Group were particularly active on the death penalty issue and strong efforts were made to persuade the Home Secretary to include a clause to abolish capital punishment for a trial period of five years in the Criminal Justice Bill which was then being drafted. Despite this procedure, and a good deal of activity by the Group, when the Criminal Justice Bill was published, it contained no such clause. The pressures on the Home Secretary appear to have been substantial and, on the Second Reading of the Bill, in November 1947, he said that an amendment to abolish capital punishment could be admitted at the Report Stage when a free vote, unconnected with party politics, would be allowed.[1] During the intervening months, the well organised abolitionist group was extremely active and when, on 15 April 1948, the Amendment was proposed, it was accepted by 247 votes to 224. The Lords, however, rejected the amendment by a substantial majority on 2 June 1948. The Government then tried to compromise by proposing an amendment abolishing capital punishment for a five-year period for all except certain specific categories of murder (categories not dissimilar to those later introduced into the 1957 Act). This amendment was debated in the Commons on 15 July 1948 and passed by a narrow majority, but the Lords again rejected the clause and the Bill was once more returned to the Commons. Finally, the Commons accepted the Lords' amendment and the Criminal Justice Act 1948 became law on 30 July 1948, without abolishing the death penalty.

The debates had been the subject of tremendous press coverage, of numerous public opinion polls and public concern. No one in the country can have been unaware of the controversy. During the whole period covered by the debates, hanging was suspended. This fact, too, was well known and well publicised. The suspension of capital punishment was so much a fact that, in its report, a subsequent Royal Commission[2] added a footnote to the number of commuted sentences in 1948, 'This figure includes a number of cases where the sole reason for the decision to recommend commutation was the position resulting from the vote in the House of Commons on the Clause in the Criminal Justice Bill suspending capital punishment for 5 years'. When the Criminal Justice Act became law without the clause, executions were resumed.

One result of the efforts in parliament to secure abolition was the setting up in November 1948 of the Royal Commission on Capital Punishment. The Commission reported to parliament in September 1953, but the report was not debated in the Commons until 10 February 1955. On that occasion, a free vote was permitted on a Government resolution that the death penalty should be retained, but the law of murder amended. The motion was defeated and this was followed by the introduction of the Private Member's Bill which eventually passed through the Commons but was again rejected by the Lords. Finally, in November 1956, the Government introduced the Homicide Bill which eventually became law. Once again the debates on the subject were fully reported in the press and, again, no one in the country could have failed to be aware of the controversy. Whilst the problem was being debated, capital punishment was again suspended, and no executions took place between August 1955 and March 1957. The suspension of the death penalty, though unofficial, was a well known and fully established fact.

The Homicide Act 1957 retained the death penalty for certain specific types of murder (known as capital murders). One such case was a second murder done on a separate occasion (Section 6), but the principal types of murder for which the death penalty was retained were set out in Section 5(1):

(a) Murder done in the course or furtherance of theft.

(b) Murder by shooting or causing an explosion.

(c) Murder done in the course or for the purpose of resisting or avoiding or preventing a lawful arrest, or effecting or assisting an escape or rescue from legal custody.

(d) Murder of a police officer acting in the execution of his duty or of a person assisting a police officer so acting.

(e) In the case of a person who was a prisoner at the time when he did or was a party to the murder, any murder of a prison officer acting in the execution of his duty or of a person assisting a prison officer so acting.

There was nothing in these provisions which would affect a calculation on whether or not to carry firearms or other weapons in a robbery, for the death penalty would, apparently, still apply. However, sub-section (2) of Section 5 provided that in the case of any murder falling into one of the above categories, it was to be capital murder only against the person who 'by his own act caused the death of, or inflicted or attempted to inflict grievous bodily harm on, the person murdered, or who himself used force on that person in the course or furtherance of an attack upon him'. Further, Section 1 of the Act abolished the doctrine of 'constructive malice', 'Where a person kills another in the course or furtherance of some other offence, the killing shall not amount to murder unless done with the same malice aforethought (express or implied) as is required for a killing to amount to murder when not done in the course or furtherance of another offence.' The doctrine of 'constructive malice' had laid down that if a person caused death during the course of carrying out a felony which involved violence, the killing was murder even if the killer had not intended to cause death and the nature of his actions were such that an intention to cause death could not be implied. (For an elaboration on the effect of this Section, see R.v. Vickers (1957 2 AllER 741)).

The position prior to the passing of the 1957 Act was that, if four men were to take part in a robbery and one of them killed the victim, all four were likely to hang, even if the killing had been against the wishes of the remainder. With the passing of the 1957 Act, the liability to the death penalty was limited to the person who actually did the shooting, or struck the blows, and the abolition of 'constructive malice' reduced the probability of the other being convicted even of non-capital murder. Previously, each member of the gang had a vested interest in ensuring that the others did not kill, but with the passing of the Act, this interest diminished.

Complete abolition of the death penalty came when the Murder (Abolition of Death Penalty) Act 1965, was passed in November 1965. However, a *de facto* abolition had been in force for a considerable time before that. The last executions took place on 13 August 1964, when Peter Anthony Allen and Gwynne Owen Evans were hanged for the murder, in the course of theft, of John Alan West at Workington. The case is featured in Elwyn Jones's *The Last Two to Hang*,[3] who commented on the possibility of reprieve:

> Statistically, then, they stood a good chance of not being hanged. Indeed, I think that few people really believed they would hand. The police in the North of England did not; they felt, or at least a great many of them did, that in the 7 years since the last Act, the abolitionist case had gained considerable ground and that, in particular, if the Home Secretary had thought fit to reprieve a recent case of capital murder they thought more calculated and more brutal than the present one, he would certainly reprieve Allen and Evans.

The reprieved case referred to was that of Joseph William Masters, found guilty at Lancaster Assize on 1 May 1964 of capital murder. When his appeal failed, Masters was reprieved.

The Murder (Abolition of Death Penalty) Bill was introduced into parliament on 4 December 1964, and received a Second Reading on 21 December 1964. On 23 December, the Home Secretary, Sir Frank Soskice, was asked, in view of the decision of the House on the Second Reading of the Bill, what course he proposed to adopt in considering the cases of persons sentenced under existing law. He replied:

> My Right Honourable Friend the Secretary of State for Scotland and I have given careful consideration to this matter. It would be unconstitutional for us to abrogate capital punishment by administrative action in anticipation of the amendment of the law: it is out duty to apply our minds to the circumstances of each particular case. In doing so we shall have regard to all relevant considerations, *including the recent decision of the House*.

This was obviously as far as the Home Secretary could go, but it seems to have been perfectly clear to everyone that, in line with the practice followed in 1948 and 1956, he would reprieve all murderers condemned to death whilst the matter was the subject of discussion in parliament. Doubtless each case would be considered, but, un-constitutional or not, abolition became fact in mid-1964, long before it became law in November 1965.[4]

The progress can be summarised. There was a temporary suspension of capital punishment in 1947–48, after which it resumed its

259

previous position. Following a further suspension in 1956, capital punishment was restored with partial application, and then, in 1964, it was abolished completely. This progress can, for the sake of comparisons, be charted in the form of a graph (see Figure 7).

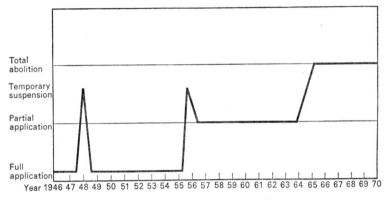

FIGURE 7 *Stages in the abolition of the death penalty*

Figures 1–6 in Chapter 11 express the incidence of the various aspects of robbery, robbery involving all types of weapons and robbery involving firearms, both numerically and as percentages. Comparison is invited between Figure 7 which shows the stages in the abolition of capital punishment and each of the graphs in Chapter 11. What is remarkable, it is suggested, is that virtually every graph, examining robbery from all aspects, appears to indicate a link with the progress towards the abolition of capital punishment. In all the graphs, changes can be seen around 1948 and 1956. The period from 1958 marks a rise in the levels, both numerically and percentage-wise, and 1964 marks the beginning of a steeper rise which is most clearly indicated in the graphs expressed numerically. It is suggested that the number of points of similarity is just too great to be coincidental.

The important point about these comparisons is that we are not here considering casual violence, or unintentional violence. The fact of carrying weapons in robbery indicates a willingness to accept violence, a willingness expressed at the planning stage of the robbery. The robber is a gambler, and it is in the planning stage that he weighs the odds. This weighing of the odds includes estimating his chances of detection and punishment. He knows, as he always has, that for a professional robbery, the chances of detection are low and the rewards high. The maximum penalty is life imprisonment and he knows that if proved guilty, he is likely to receive a substantial prison sentence. The odds against being caught may be something of the order of 7 or 10 to one in his favour, and he is obviously prepared to accept these odds against a long term of imprisonment. When the death penalty applied, he was not prepared to accept 7 or 10 to one odds on a chance of being hanged. He seems prepared to accept the risk now, when the most that the death of his victim can mean is an increased likelihood of detection and a rather longer sentence.

Simply, what is being said is that the figures supplied here have produced evidence to indicate that the death penalty was and is a substantial deterrent in one small sphere—indeed, that it is a unique deterrent in that sphere in so much as no other penalty has shown itself capable of being effective against criminals in the planning stage of their crimes. It is suggested that it was the presence of this deterrent, not anything to do with the availability of firearms or other weapons, which kept the use of violence by professional criminals down to a very low level. This research was not, in the first instance, directed in any way towards establishing the deterrent value of capital punishment in this context; but close examination of the evidence leads inevitably to this conclusion and forces at least a partial study. That the study is far from complete cannot be denied. The Royal Commission, in Paragraph 61 of its report thought, 'It is in the nature of the case that little could be adduced in the way of specific evidence that criminals have been deterred by the death penalty'. It is suggested that the specific evidence adduced here makes that statement less acceptable in relation to one category of crime.

Many responsible people have been worried by this aspect of abolition over the years and it may be that Sir Peter Rawlinson was being unwittingly prophetic when he said, on the Second Reading of the Murder (Abolition of Death Penalty) Bill:

We wondered in 1956 and 1957 whether this country's crime
and criminal activities would develop as they have overseas;
into the use of gangs and gangsters armed with guns. Would
there be an increased danger to the public and would the police
have to be armed? All these questions were in our minds
during these debates. It was inevitable that our minds should be
exercised in that way . . . Is there any evidence of an increase

of crime by the professional criminal? Is there, in this sense an increase, or is there evidence of an increase of crime by highly organised gangs? Can they advise positively or can they forecast whether a Bill such as this will, in their view, and in the view of the enforcement machinery, lead to any greater danger to the public? This is the sort of information which I hope we will receive from the Home Secretary.

The information in this appendix, and in the preceding chapters, up to the end of 1964, was available at that time to anyone who sought it, but Sir Frank Soskice's reply was:

But in answer to all the questions which he [Sir Peter Rawlinson] asked, the available evidence is that the death penalty makes no difference, or at least it cannot be shown that it makes any difference or has any real utility. That must be the answer to all the questions which he asked.

With the further experience since 1964, as illustrated here, could the same answer honestly be put forward now?

Bibliographical References

Introduction

1 Herbert Asbury, *The Gangs of New York*, Alfred A. Knopf, New York, 1928.
2 Hugh David Graham and Ted Robert Gurr, *Violence in America—Historical and Comparative Perspectives*, Staff Report to the National Commission on the Causes and Prevention of Violence, US Government Printing Office, Washington DC, 1969.

Chapter 1

1 For a fuller description of events summarised see, for example, T. A. Critchley, *The Conquest of Violence: Order and Liberty in Britain*, Constable, London, 1970.
2 George D. Newton and Franklin E. Zimring, *Firearms and Violence in American Life*, Staff Report to the National Commission on the Causes and Prevention of Violence, US Government Printing Office, Washington DC, 1969.
3 J. W. Cecil Turner, ed., *Russell on Crime*, Stevens & Sons, London, 12th edition, 1964, p. 265.
4 According to Samuel R. Mayrick in his paper, *Observations Upon the History of Hand Firearms*, 1829 (reprinted by The Richmond Publishing Co., Richmond, Surrey, 1970), 'Handgun' referred to a development of the earliest hand cannon, distinguished by a wider butt and a covered pan. The hagbutt was a further development in which the stock was bent to allow of taking a proper sight. A demyhake is described as 'A kind of long pistol, the butt of which is made to curve so as almost to become a semicircle.'
5 Geoffrey Cousins, *The Defenders—A History of the British Volunteer*, Frederick Muller, London, 1968—which also see for a fuller account of the development of the militia system.
6 W. W. Greener, *The Gun and Its Development*, Cassell, London, 1881.
7 Sir William Blackstone, *Commentaries on the Laws of England*, Clarendon Press, Oxford, 17th edition, 1966, vol. 1, ch. 1.
8 F. C. Mather, *Public Order in the Age of the Chartists*, Manchester University Press, Manchester, 1959, which also see for a fuller description of the disturbances in the Chartist period with a number of references to the use of firearms in these disturbances.
9 'Artifex and Opifex', *The Causes of Decay in a British Industry*, Longmans, Green, London, 1907.

Chapter 2

1 George D. Newton and Franklin E. Zimring, *Firearms and Violence in American Life*, Staff Report to the National Commission on the Causes and Prevention of Violence, US Government Printing Office, Washington DC, 1969, pp. 13, 14.
2 'Artifex and Opifex', *The Causes of Decay in a British Industry*, Longmans, Green, London, 1907, pp. 144–9.
3 'Report of the Committee on Control of Firearms', Chairman Sir Ernley Blackwell, KCB, unpublished Home Office Paper, presented 15 November 1918.
4 Official Reports of Parliamentary Debates (Hansard) for the dates quoted in the text.

Chapter 5

1 A. D. Weatherhead and B.M. Robinson, *Firearms in Crime*, Home Office Statistical Division, HMSO, London, 1970.

Chapter 7

1 Ian Brownlie and D. G. T. Williams, 'Judicial Legislation in Criminal Law', *Canadian Bar Review*, December 1964.

Chapter 8

1 A. D. Weatherhead and B. M. Robinson, *Firearms in Crime*, Home Office Statistical Division, HMSO, London, 1970.
2 Official Report of Parliamentary Debates (Hansard). Written Replies on the dates shown in the text.
3 Tom Tullett and Roger Todd, 'Gun Law in Britain', *Daily Mirror*, Thursday 27 July 1967.
4 See, for example, F. H. McClintock, *Crimes Against the Person*, Manchester Statistical Society, Manchester, 1963.

Chapter 9

1 A private communication from the Gun Trade Association indicates that in this country, there are about 120,000 air weapons sold each year, of which 40–50,000 are imported. Once in circulation, these weapons will last a long time and the factories report that they often receive weapons for repair which were made in 1918 or 1920.
2 A. D. Weatherhead and B. M. Robinson, *Firearms in Crime*, Home Office Statistical Division, HMSO, London, 1970.
3 F. H. McClintock, *Crimes of Violence*, Macmillan, London, 1963, p. 36.
4 Marvin E. Wolfgang, *Patterns in Criminal Homicide*, University of Pennsylvania Press, Philadelphia, 1958, p. 82.

5 Franklin E. Zimring, 'Is gun control likely to reduce violent killing?', *University of Chicago Law Review*, summer 1968, vol. 35, p. 721.
6 Mark K. Benenson, 'A controlled look at gun controls', *New York Law Forum*, winter 1968, vol. xiv, no. 4.

Chapter 11

1 F. H. McClintock and Evelyn Gibson, *Robbery in London*, Macmillan, London, 1961.
2 A. D. Weatherhead and B. M. Robinson, *Firearms in Crime*, Home Office Statistical Division, HMSO, London, 1970.

Chapter 14

1 'Use of computers for registration of firearms and registration of shotguns', study by the Local Authorities Management Service and Computer Committee, July 1969.

Chapter 15

1 J. P. Martin and Gail Wilson, *The Police: A Study in Manpower*, Heinemann Educational, London, 1969.

Chapter 16

1 Leon Radzinowicz, *A History of English Criminal Law and Its Administration from 1750*, Stevens & Sons, London, 4 vols, 1948–68. vol. I, pp. 28, 29.
2 Ibid., vol. II, p. 276 et seq.
3 Ibid., vol. IV, p. 340.
4 *Report of the Departmental Committee on Criminal Statistics* (Perks Committee), Cmd 3448, HMSO, London, 1967.

Appendix

1 See Official Reports of Parliamentary Debates (Hansard) for the dates quoted throughout this Appendix.
2 *Report of the Royal Commission on Capital Punishment*, 1949–54, Cmd 8932, HMSO, London, 1953.
3 Elwyn Jones, *The Last Two to Hang: G. O. Evans and P. A. Allen*, Macmillan, London, 1966.
4 Additional material on the political organisation and operations of the campaign to abolish capital punishment may be found in James B. Cristoph, *Capital Punishment and British Politics*, Allen & Unwin, London, 1962.

S

Index